COMMUNICATION and EDUCATION

_____ PEOPLE AND COMMUNICATION _____

Series Editors:
PETER CLARKE   *University of Southern California*
F. GERALD KLINE   *University of Minnesota*

Volumes in this series:

COMMUNICATION
and
EDUCATION
Social and Psychological Interactions

Gavriel Salomon

S SAGE PUBLICATIONS   Beverly Hills   London

For information address:

SAGE Publications, Inc.
275 South Beverly Drive
Beverly Hills, California 90212

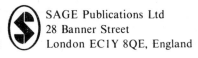

SAGE Publications Ltd
28 Banner Street
London EC1Y 8QE, England

Printed in the United States of America

Library of Congress Cataloging in Publication Data

Main entry under title:
Salomon, Gavriel.
  Communication and education.

  (People and communication ; v. 13)
  Bibliography: p.
  Includes index.
  1. Interaction analysis in education. 2. Communication in
education. 3. Interpersonal communication. I. Title. II. Series.
LB1033.S23   370.15   81-9309
ISBN 0-8039-1717-1   AACR2
ISBN 0-8039-1718-X (pbk.)

FIRST PRINTING

TABLE OF CONTENTS

to Wilbur Schramm

> *a great teacher who taught me important lessons about communication media and education*

and to my wife Varda

> *who taught me the real meaning of interpersonal relations*

Preface

Much of my past research has been devoted to exploring how media symbol systems cultivate children's mastery of mental skills. This kind of research fit well with the mainstream of work carried out by researchers in education, educational psychology, and communication. The basic assumption underlying it was that events, messages, instructional procedures, and media are all external to the individuals and exert influences on them, and these can be manipulated, observed, and measured. Such influences were considered to be mediated by internal psychological states, mental abilities, preferences, and the like.

Like many others, I had little reason to question this basic assumption. Still, even while completing my previous book (Salomon, 1979), I began to feel uneasy about it. Somehow I felt that the assumption of external events operating upon us, the innocent subjects, does not seem to encompass a number of phenomena.

Why, if external events so powerfully affect us, do we evade information, discredit unsettling new scientific contributions, dismiss our own experimental procedures when they fail but not our theories, and frequently find in other people's books the very proof we were looking for, but hardly ever disproof? And why do communicational solutions, well intended as they may be, often end up worsening the problems they were designed to solve (Watzlawick et al., 1974)? How, for example, do social-psychological findings that show how biased and erroneous some of our inferences are (Nisbett and Ross, 1980) affect us when they do not conform to our basic assumptions? Indeed, is it not often the case that people determine through

9

their a priori expectations, stored knowledge, assumptions, and pet theories what will be permitted to affect them, how it will affect them, and to what extent?

I gradually became intrigued by the possibility (which, due to the way I was brought up as a researcher, I failed to notice in the writings of others) that the commerce between people and their surrounding is *reciprocal* rather than unidirectional. Once drawn to this idea, I could not help but discover reciprocal influences all around me, in recent research, in scholarly writings, even in my own social interaction. How curious! Once you are guided by an idea, an assumption, an expectation, you start soliciting and finding confirmatory evidence for it.

The idea of reciprocal relations is not really new, but it needs closer examination. For the question is not whether it is correct, but rather how it applies to human behavior, what its implications are, and what new insights it can offer us.

There is no better domain for closely examining a reciprocal approach to human behavior than the one that combines communication and education. For whatever we apply to the world around us must have been learned, and much of what we have learned must have been communicated to us. The two— communication and education—seem to serve each other and (surprise!) to be reciprocally related: What we have learned influences our communicational interactions, which in turn influence what we learn.

Exploring such an argument further, one cannot avoid the conclusion that the existence of communication itself (not just specific meanings) is a function of the intentions people attribute to each other on the basis of their existing knowledge, culturally shared assumptions, immediate inclinations, and the like. Having the privilege of frequent visits to the United States, I can easily observe that my wearing a tie in American university classes is often taken as just a natural act (at best transmitting information about my taste in clothes); but it is taken as an intended message in my home country, Israel. Once my ties are seen as such, responses are addressed both to the communicational meaning found in them and to the intentions attributed to me (quite irrespective of my "real" communicational intentions).

Numerous implications follow from here, and I try to explore them throughout the book. The purpose of the book, then, is to offer the outlines of a reciprocal-interactionist views of communication and education, to show some of its applications and implications, and to stimulate new questions for exploration. This is no mean, simple, or modest task.

First of all, while there is a vast literature of research and numerous theories in the areas of interest here, there is hardly any systematic research and research methodology, let alone theory, that deal with reciprocal interdependencies in communication and education.

Second, the study of both communication and education is expanding with stunning speed and shows increasing complexity, differentiation, and fragmentation. Topics that are included in these two related fields of study range from media effects on children to discipline problems in schools, from questions of information processing to interpersonal relations, and from issues of aesthetics to social animosity, labeling, and self-fulfilling prophecies. Thus, while the time may be ripe to climb out of the rut of specifics and offer a new overall approach to the field, its vast complexity and diversity makes such an attempt extremely difficult.

I have attempted to take this complexity into account without being pulled back by it into the rut. Nor have I allowed the history of past problems with other reciprocal approaches to prevent me from trying anew one of my own. After all, the book is intended to stimulate, not to create premature closure.

Thus I first present the outlines of a reciprocal-interactionist approach in Chapter 1 and the outlines of an attributional conception of communication in Chapter 2. This is followed by a cyclical view of perception and communication (Chapter 3) and three chapters of application to education. In each of these chapters I try to apply basic conceptions and a number of their derivations to three selected areas of educational interest: exposure to the media, classroom learning, and interpersonal relations. It is not my intention to exhaust these areas, for each alone could fill numerous volumes, but only to exemplify my general thesis. I try to show, for example, how media and mental schemata exert reciprocal influences, how depth of processing is determined both by the message and the intention attributed to it, what difference it makes whether we perceive behavior in the context of personality or interaction, what television's pictoriality means, and more.

In Chapter 7 I review the many loops, cycles, and spirals dealt with in preceding chapters. I attempt to show, for example, when and how self-fulfilling prophecies take place, when "solutions" worsen "problems," and how attributions of communicational intents propel or slow down loops and spirals. Finally, I discuss the role of education both as victim or beneficiary of circular processes and as a base for creating and breaking out of them.

Many people have contributed, knowingly and unknowingly, to the writing of this book. Wilbur Schramm, to whom the book is dedicated, gave me the first conceptual tools to deal with communication and education while I was privileged to be his student at Stanford University in the late 1960s. Albert Bandura, also at Stanford, and Paul Watzlawick of the Palo Alto Mental Research Institute taught me (independently of each other) the first lessons in reciprocal, interdependent relations in psychological research.

Others with whom I have had enlightening conversations do not even know how much they have contributed to my work: Richard Snow and Don Roberts at Stanford; Percy Tannenbaum at the University of California at Berkeley; Camille Wortman and Bruce Watkins at the University of Michigan; Shalom Schwartz, Elihu Katz, Mordechai Nisan, and Ya'akov Kareev at my own university—The Hebrew University of Jerusalem, Israel; Richard Clark at the University of Southern California; and many others.

I also owe much to my students at Stanford University, the University of Michigan, the University of Southern California, and the Hebrew University, who allowed me to hear myself teach some of the ideas presented here, raised intriguing questions, served as critics, and provided new insights.

I completed the book while visiting as a Marsh Professor at the Department of Communication at the University of Michigan. The department's Howard R. Marsh Center provided assistance with the manuscript. I am especially grateful to my editor, Judy Timberg, without whose tireless efforts this book would have remained well intended but quite unintelligible.

Gavriel Salomon
Ann Arbor, Michigan
March, 1981

Chapter 1

ON THE NATURE OF INTERACTIONS

If men define situations as real, they
are real in their consequences.

(Thomas and Thomas, 1928;
 quoted by Bronfenbrenner, 1977)

The subtitle of this book promises an interactional approach to the discussion of communication and education. This may sound redundant; after all, who would question the existence of interactions among people or the fact that education itself is an interactional process? Why, then, emphasize interaction in the title, as if the approach taken here is different from that of most other people?

The major reason is that the term "interaction," while presently in vogue, means different things to different people. One's conception of what interaction means guides research and interpretation in particular ways, directing interest toward some processes and relations and away from others. For some people interaction is the equivalent of dialogue or conversation. For others the term means that two factors or variables combine with each other to produce a particular outcome that neither could have produced alone. One's mood plus the nature of a newspaper item, for example, produce together one's impression of the severity of economic events. A good mood mellows the effects of bad news, whereas a poor mood makes only moderately bad news look worse.

For still others, interaction means a statistical fact as discerned from analyses of variance. For example, Bowers (1973) shows that neither personalogical variables nor situational variables when taken alone account for as much behavior variance as they do together. Their interaction in work situations, for example, implies that trait A (much work experience) predicts performance better under condition X (stressful work relations), while trait B (high intelligence) predicts performance better under condition Y (nonstressful relations) (Fiedler et al., 1979).

Finally, there are those (such as Weick, 1979) who see interaction as a series of reciprocal relations or influences—A influences B who influences A who in turn influences B again. Here it is the interdependence among people or factors that is the focus of interest.

Although such diverse meanings are not incompatible with each other, they do lead to different kinds of questions and suggest different ways of interpreting data. For example, we might want to study what children learn from the media. Using an analysis-of-variance paradigm, we would probably examine the interactions between, say, children's abilities (or ages) and different media to see which combinations produce greater or smaller knowledge acquisition. Approaching the same question from the point of view of interaction as reciprocity, we would also ask how the differential acquisition of knowledge then affects children's abilities and how these abilities then affect the children's subsequent responses to the media.

In this book I wish to emphasize one meaning of the term interaction, a meaning that is not really new but is as yet rarely taken seriously. Its general assumptions and outlines appear in the writings of Dewey (1930), Watzlawick, Beavin, and Jackson (1967), McGuire (1973), Bowers (1973), Berlo (1977), Bandura (1978), Gibbs (1979), and others that preceded and followed them. The gist of the approach I take is the underlying assumption that people's behaviors, dispositions, and the environmental contexts, messages, and events with which they deal, mutually influence each other. Such an approach is based upon the perception of interaction as *reciprocal influences* or *interdependencies of influences* and emphasizes spiral rather than linear cause-and-effect relations.

INTERACTIONAL AND NONINTERACTIONAL APPROACHES

The reciprocal interaction approach shares a number of characteristics with other (nonreciprocal) interactional views. All interactional views assume some measure of interdependency and thus differ from noninteractional views, which ascribe most if not all causal responsibility for producing a behavior to one particular class of factors, most often either to people's traits (including dispositions and attitudes) or to situations.

A *trait* approach, with its stronghold in clinical and differential psychology, assumes human beings to behave quite consistently and perceives in such consistencies some underlying tendencies, abilities, or hidden drives and motives which determine overt behavior. Traditionally, traits have been perceived both as psychological realities of some tangible form and as causes of behavior (Allport, 1966; see critique by Mischel, 1968). A trait approach is not particularly concerned with situational differences that could affect behavior. Thus, if a trait such as external or internal locus of control is studied, one would expect it to correlate consistently with certain behaviors, such as susceptibility to persuasion, even when external conditions change. It would be an embarrassment to discover that the trait is unstable or situationally dependent.

A *situational* approach, with its stronghold in experimental, ecological, and social psychology, assumes that behavior is very much determined by external stimuli. Thus, when situational factors are manipulated (high threat vs. low threat messages) or when existing situations are compared (school versus summer camp), one expects the dependent variable, behavior, to change as a function of situational differences. Individual differences ("variance within") are sometimes an embarrassment and often constitute the "error" component in comparisons among experimental group means.

Most past research in communication (aside from some developmental studies) and much research in education was situation-oriented. "Situations" in the form of media, messages, educational treatments, and the like were studied as they affected people on the average. The laboratory or the "natural" experiment reigned. Typical cases in point are the many studies of the effects of violent television programs on children's aggressive behaviors, studies of how various attributes of messages affect attitude change, and research on classroom teaching and achievements. Such predominance of situation-oriented research is easily understood, considering the fact that both educators and communication researchers tend to regard behavior as a function of external, manipulable forces, including messages, media, contents, symbol systems, instructional strategies, and ecological contexts.

While trait or situation-oriented approaches examine human behavior as stemming from one dominant source (stable human properties or environmental conditions and stimuli), all interactional approaches, of which the reciprocal approach is one, assume that behavior is a result, or even an active determinant, of forces that interact with each other. In this view, aggression learned from television results from children's initial inclinations as well as the television fare to which they are exposed, and people's views of TV result from their initial beliefs about TV, as well as what is presented on the screen. The reciprocal interaction approach would suggest further that people's beliefs about the medium also affect what they seek out from the medium, and these beliefs are in turn influenced by what they find there. Neither dispositions nor situations are taken by interactional approaches to have any necessary precedence.

MEANINGS AND LEVELS OF INTERACTIONS

As the example above suggests, not all interactional approaches are alike. Common to lay and scientific meanings of the term interaction is the assumption that interacting entities influence each other in some way. Taking this idea a step further, one can distinguish two major kinds of influence in interaction: unidirectional and multidirectional (Olweus, 1977).

Unidirectional interactions pertain to the combination or multiplication of two or more factors to produce some observable outcome. For example, Campbell (1979) has found that office tidiness interacts with students' sex to produce stronger or weaker feelings of comfort and well-being. Tidier offices produce stronger feelings of comfort and untidy offices produce stronger feelings of discomfort, but the difference is more pronounced in females than in males. Behavior outcomes such as learning achievements, attitudes, or emotions are taken to be outcomes of other factors, often personal predispositions and external events, which combine or moderate each other. When personalogical variables (for example, initial knowledge) and situational variables (for example, the structure of a message) are studied as interactants that produce behavior, one assumes neither that behavior is a function of personal characteristics—$B = f(P)$—nor that it is a function of environment—$B = f(E)$—but rather that $B = f(P,E)$. Notice, however, that in unidirectional interaction, the behavior (B) is not assumed to have a reciprocal influence on either personality (P) or the environment (E). Personality and environment are taken to be independent variables which interact with each other and affect behavior; the behavior itself is outside the interaction.

Consider the study by Fiedler et al. (1979) mentioned earlier. They found a clear interaction between intelligence or experience (personalogical variables) and stressful or unstressful relations with superiors (environmental factors). Under stressful conditions experience predicts job performance best, while under relaxed conditions intelligence is the better predictor. The outcome, job performance, is outside the interaction, as it is not expected (within the context of that study) to influence reciprocally any of its determinants. Still, it would be reasonable to expect people's performance to have some influence on their relations with their superiors, so E would be in part a function of B as B is a function of E.

A case in point is the class of interactions called Aptitude-Treatment-Interaction (ATI) originally proposed by Cronbach (1957) and later developed by Snow and Salomon (1968),

Salomon (1971), Cronbach and Snow (1977), Snow (1977), and others. The ATI approach is based on a combination of correlational and experimental methods. For the correlational approach, individual differences (variance) are a necessity; for experiments in which the averages of experimental and control groups are compared, variance is "noise" to be reduced. Similarly, correlational methods focus on differences in behavior resulting from situations, whereas experimental methods tend to ignore individual differences.

The combination of the two approaches, as originally suggested by Cronbach, leads one to examine how personalogical variables (abilities, personality dispositions, prior knowledge, all labeled "aptitudes") interact with external events, situations, or treatments (all commonly labeled "treatments") to produce some outcome. According to Cronbach (1957: 681):

> Applied psychologists should deal with treatments and persons simultaneously. Treatments are characterized by many dimensions; so are persons. The two sets of dimensions together determine a payoff surface. . . . We should design treatments, not to fit the average person, but to fit groups of students with particular aptitude patterns. Conversely, we should seek out the aptitudes which correspond to (interact with) modifiable aspects of the treatment.

The following illustrate ATI studies. Hunt (1971) has found that students who are conceptually complex learn better in unstructured schools, while less conceptually complex students benefit more from structured schools. Domino (1974) found that high anxiety students learned more in traditional classrooms and low anxiety students learned more in open classrooms. An unpublished study carried out in 1967 by the Israel Institute of Applied Social Research during the tense days preceding the Six Day War found that the morale of better-educated people received a stronger boost from analytic commentary broadcast over the radio; the morale of less educated people was boosted more strongly by direct broadcasts from "where the boys were." Krull and Husson (1979) report that children ages 4 to 5 are little affected by program variables on

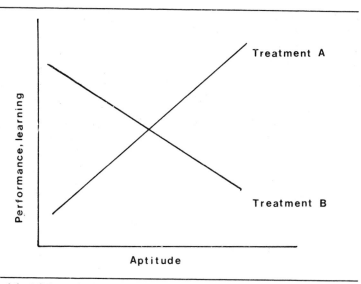

Figure 1.1   A Schematized Example of a Disordinal ATI

television; the major factor affecting their attention is prior attention, that is, whether they are already watching TV when a new program comes on. Older children, on the other hand, react to a variety of program variables and are far less affected by attention interdependence. Thus, age and the two "treatments"—prior attention and program variables—interact with each other to produce attention.

Aptitude and treatment—the "input" variables—can be *ordinal* (when one treatment works well for everybody and another only for some) or *disordinal* (when one treatment benefits only those with high aptitude but depresses performance of those with low aptitude, while a second treatment does the exact opposite). Figure 1.1 shows a graph of disordinal interaction.

A similar interaction was found by Salomon, King, and Yuen (1980) in their reanalyses of school data. Schools that were complex (an institutional "aptitude") produced higher student achievements when governed by informal means such as discussions with the principals and when teachers felt they were personally supported by their principals (the "treatment"). Such schools fared far less well when governed by formal procedures such as explicit policies and rule enforcement. On the other hand, noncomplex schools (more traditional ones) benefited from formal procedures far more than informal ones (this was called Structure-Governance-Interaction, or SGI).

The general paradigm underlying ATI and SGI studies guides most current research and thinking both in communication and education. It has become common practice to look at how people's dispositions, cognitions, or abilities interact with external events to produce behavior outcomes. But if the resultant behavior is not assumed to feed back and to influence the factors that produced it, then the postulated interaction is *unidirectional.* In unidirectionality, behavior is assumed to be only a product or output, but not a factor that affects its alleged determinants. It assumes human beings having certain dispositions, to be relatively reactive rather than active, responding only to external events that have an independent existence and a temporal priority to their internal or external reactions. As Collingwood argues (1970; quoted by Gibbs, 1979: 131), such assumptions underlie modern efforts to explain "all change and process by the action of material things already existing at the commencement of change."

Bronfenbrenner (1977) describes a series of studies based on this assumption carried out by investigators from the Department of Pediatrics at Case Western Reserve University. The results showed that when mothers were permitted to have their naked newborns with them for an hour after delivery and for several hours daily thereafter (contrary to common practice), they became more attentive, affectionate, and solicitous about their infants. Differences between experimental and control mothers were in evidence even two years after the study, and included the use of more questions, adjectives, and relational terms by the experimental mothers. As Bronfenbrenner (1977: 520) shows, these experiments, like so many other studies, accept reciprocal relations in principle but do not study them:

> The principle of reciprocity, of course, raises the question of whether the distinctive behavior of the mothers in the experimental

group might not have occurred, at least in part, as a response to a sequence of activities initiated by the developing infant and reciprocated by the mother in a progressively evolving pattern of social interaction. Regrettably, the possibility remains unexplored. In keeping with the classical experimental model, the focus of scientific attention in these studies was limited to the subjects of the research who, in this instance, were not the children but the mothers. The omission is all the more remarkable given the fact that the infants were always present in the research situation and, what is more, that all of the mothers' behavior being observed was directed toward them.

Unlike unidirectional interactionism, multidirectional interactionism assumes that events (behaviors, dispositions, environments) affect each other reciprocally. Thus, students' achievements, affected by a combination of their abilities and supportive classroom climate, are expected to affect that climate in turn; mothers' affectionate behaviors are assumed not only to affect their infants' behavior but to be influenced by it as well; and one person's counterarguments would be assumed not only to result from another's persuasions but (in real life) also to influence the other person reciprocally.

Such an approach disagrees with trait approaches, because it assumes that people are affected by the situations they are in. According to Bandura (1978: 345):

> To contend that mind creates reality fails to acknowledge that environmental influences partly determine what people attend to, perceive and think.

A reciprocal interactionist approach also disagrees with strict situational approaches because it assumes (to an extent, at least) that people's preferences, dispositions, and selections affect not only their behavior but also the situations they are in, and may even create these situations:

> The situation is a function of the person in the sense that the observer's cognitive schemas filter and organize the environment in a fashion that makes it impossible ever to completely separate the environment from the person observing it [Bowers, 1973: 328].

Finally, such an approach disagrees in principle with unidirectional interactionism because it assumes that whatever produces behavior is also affected by that behavior. Given environmental circumstances and people's cognitive or emotional dispositions, certain actions are produced. However,

> by their actions, people play a role in creating the social milieu and other circumstances that arise in their daily transactions. Thus . . . psychological functioning involves a continuous reciprocal interaction between *behavioral, cognitive* and *environmental* influences. [Bandura, 1978: 345; italics added].

An example of such a chain of events is a study by Dykman and Reis (1979). Children with poor self-concepts actively choose low-risk seats in their classrooms (back and margin seats), which then allow them to refrain from active classroom participation. It stands to reason that these children receive fewer communications, respond less frequently, learn less, and thus retain their poor self-concepts. Because of these self-concepts, such children perceive teacher-generated messages to them as coercive or demeaning, further reinforcing their withdrawal behavior, which in turn . . . and so on in vicious circles.

What this means, then, is that

$$B = f(P,E)$$
$$P = f(B,E), \text{ and}$$
$$E = f(B,P)$$

That behavior is a function of personalogical variables and environmental ones, or $B = f(P,E)$, has been shown already. That personalogical variables can be a function of behaviors and environmental factors, or $P = f(B,E)$, is evident when we observe how people's belief in their own ability is often influenced by the actions the environment demands of them. (For example, when students who believe they could never understand a journal article are required to read one, they often discover that they can understand it.) Finally, that the environment is a function of people's behaviors and personalogical tendencies, or $E = f(B,P)$, can be easily seen in the following: people *perceive* a situation in light of their desires (for example, readers see in these lines confirmation of their own thinking or notice most what fits their own experience); people *modify* their environment by their actions (a competitive person may turn every social situation into an opportunity for one-upmanship); and people *choose* situations to fit them (it is the reader's choice to skim this book or to read it closely).

Bandura (1978) labeled such multidirectional interactions *reciprocal determinism* and offered the following formal model to describe it:

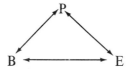

Personality, dispositions, abilities, self-concepts, tendencies, and the like (P) affect behaviors (B) and are affected by them, and environmental factors (E) affect and are affected by both P and B.

That behavior shapes, modifies, and interprets the environment is a common observation, as are the effects of the environment on behavior. It is also generally agreed that personality influences behavior. But how does behavior influence personality? A simple example is the observation that people's outlook on their surrounding world is gradually shaped by their choices of what television programs they watch. Another example is how people's unsuccessful attempts at mastering a new skill, say advanced statistics, modify their own self-concepts as statisticians.

Many examples suggest how the environment affects personality. But how does personality affect the environment reciprocally, apart from affecting one's behavior? First, people with different dispositions tend to choose different environments and by so doing affect their environments. Second, their physical characteristics and socially conferred attributes, statuses, and roles activate certain responses in their environments. These in turn reinforce, modify, and gradually shape people's self-concepts and even their physical properties (as when obesity becomes less accepted socially and obese people try to lose weight).

In sum, then, the conception of reciprocal interaction allows more freedom to individuals, assuming them to be influenced by their surroundings, and influencing those surroundings in return. The conception of reciprocal interaction builds upon that of unidirectional interaction. The latter addresses mainly the ways in which personality and environment affect behavior, that is:

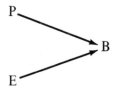

The reciprocal interaction approach addresses in addition the missing influences drawn below as dashed arrows:

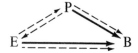

Seen in such a way, one can treat unidirectional interactions as Level I and reciprocal ones, which build upon that level, as Level II interactions. Given the methodological limitations we face when attempting to study Level II interactions, we often have no choice but to study Level I interaction in a sequence. That sequence, in which output variables of one study are examined as input variables in a subsequent one, can ultimately yield an outline of reciprocal influences.

Such a sequence is well illustrated by studies on teacher expectations. Numerous studies have shown how teacher expectations are communicated to their students, affect the students' behaviors, and thus turn the expectations into self-fulfilling prophecies, that is: P teachers ⟶ B teachers⟶ B students (see Braun, 1976; Jones, 1977; Cooper, 1979). Brophy and Good (1974) have even suggested that teachers' personalities moderate these effects in that some teachers are more strongly guided by their expectations than others. Other writers (such as Seaver, 1973) have shown how expectations result from teachers' natural experiences (E ⟶ P teachers ⟶ B teachers ⟶ B students ⟶ E). Still others have shown how students' behaviors influence teacher expectations: B students ⟶ P teachers ⟶ B teachers (such as Feldman and Prohaska, 1979; Rappaport and Rappaport, 1975). The overall picture is one of reciprocal influences: Teachers encounter students, and this yields certain expectations that guide teachers' behaviors; these in turn influence students' behaviors, which then perpetuate or modify teachers' expectations. Examined in this way, the question of where it all started is akin to the question of whether the egg preceded the chicken or vice versa.

Level II (reciprocal) interactions build upon Level I (unidirectional) interactions partly for methodological reasons that make the study of reciprocity so difficult.[1] Level II interactions usually deal with sequences of events over time, while Level I interactions are limited to single episodes. Thus, ATI or SGI studies punctuate, so to speak, a sequence of events to single out the determinants of, say, learning achievement. But learning achievement, changed attitude, or teachers' morale, could easily become one of the interacting independent variables (aptitude) of another study. Such a study would be designed to complement the preceding study so that a developing sequence could be investigated.

Snow and Salomon (1968) wrote of aptitudes (the independent variables) as interacting with media treatments to produce learning and also of changes in aptitudes as outcomes of ATIs. In past work I studied how better mental skill mastery could be brought about by interactions between initial skill mastery and specific television formats (Salomon, 1974). Had I been guided then by a reciprocal view (which I was not), I would have asked how the newly developed skill mastery (the outcome in that series of studies) comes to affect how television is handled subsequently. By failing to do so, I could not really show that the children whose skill mastery was improved came to treat TV any differently than before. Such reciprocal relations began to occur to me much later (Salomon, 1979).

WHY RECIPROCAL INTERACTIONISM?

Having presented the two major kinds of interactionism, I can now turn to the question of why one might prefer one approach over the other. The way one describes and comprehends how communication or education operate, or for that matter how human beings operate in general, is really a question of choice. If we agree with Nelson Goodman (1968, 1978) that the world is as many things as there are ways to describe it, then it is impossible to argue that one model is better than another in any absolute sense. But one model or approach can be conceptually more satisfying and empirically more warranted than another when it describes and explains more about the phenomena it is concerned with and is ecologically more valid.

Obviously these are not absolute criteria (Kuhn, 1970), but the very knowledge that they are not absolutes implies the kind of circularity I have been discussing: We cultivate criteria of validity, guide our research and observations accordingly, and erect a view of the world in accordance with our initial criteria.

Is a reciprocal paradigm more ecologically valid than other paradigms? It appears that it is (see, for example, Bowers, 1973; Bronfenbrenner, 1977; Nuttin, 1977; Raush, 1979; Bandura, 1978). According to Gibbs (1979: 135),

> The scientistic/objectivist strategy on the one hand and the personalistic/subjectivist strategy on the other have found impressive proponents because each is partly right, each is plausible as far as it goes; yet each approach is ultimately untenable because each fails to capture the full integrity of scientific or ordinary knowing. Ecologically oriented inquiry is a transaction. Theory, manipulation, and controls are essential to the enterprise but not more so than holistic data, exploration, and ecological validity.

A reciprocal view is ecologically more valid mainly because

> in the conditions of real life, the psychological "stimuli" that people encounter are neither questionnaire items, nor experimental instructions, nor inanimate events, but involve people and reciprocal relationships (e.g., with spouse, with boss, with children). We continuously influence the "situation" of our lives as well as being affected by them in a mutual organic interaction [Mischel, 1977: 248].

And as Dewey (1930: 412) wrote,

> Behavior is serial, not mere succession. It can be resolved—it must be—into discrete acts, but no act can be understood apart from the series to which it belongs. . . . Even instances in which abrupt succession is most marked, i.e., jumping at noise when engaged in deep study, have to be treated as limiting cases of the serial principle and not as typical cases from which to derive the standard notion of behavior acts.

All this does not mean that each and every event, percept, message, or action always relates to other events reciprocally. Everything is not necessarily interdependent: All people, regardless of disposition, will rush out of a burning theater; devoted chess players will start playing wherever they can regardless of situation; and agoraphobics will shun most outdoor places regardless of how nice and accommodating these places are. But such unidirectional influences are the exceptions rather than the rule, for people *usually* interact reciprocally with each other and with their close surroundings. Only research, for which the control of "extraneous" factors has become so sacred, disregards reciprocity or interdependencies. What was supposed to be merely a practical necessity in research (that is, studying linear chains of cause and effect) has become a dominant paradigm which has gradually moved research away from the ecology it was initially designed to study (see McGuire, 1973; Bronfenbrenner, 1977).

Contrary to that trend, I feel (it is a question of choice!) that a reciprocal outlook allows us to view issues of communication and education through a wider lens and offers us more interesting interpretations.

Consider by way of illustration the early onset of smoking among teenagers and the effectiveness of smoking prevention campaigns. Much research has examined which personalogical variables predict the onset of smoking. Rebelliousness (see Stewart and Livson, 1966), deviancy (Palmer, 1970), and "desire to be older" (Newman, 1970), are among the more frequently identified predictors. Much research has also gone into the effects of external forces such as peer pressure (for example, Hill, 1971) and parents' modeling of smoking behavior (Borland and Rudolph, 1975).

Such findings have led to the conclusion that youngsters do not know enough about the health hazards involved in smoking; therefore they give in to social pressure to smoke and believe smoking to signify maturity and independence. Smoking prevention programs that followed from these assumptions were designed to correct this basic deficiency by imparting relevant knowledge to youngsters about the long-range dangers of smoking (see Edson, 1973). However, as a number of researchers have observed, such direct-communication, knowledge-based programs have been generally ineffective (see Evans et al., 1979) and have even increased smoking behavior (see Tennants, Weaver, and Lewis, 1973).

Such results should come as no surprise for two reasons. First, lack of knowledge about the health hazards and long-term dangers of smoking does not cause the onset of smoking (Palmer, 1970). Thus, addressing an illusionary cause could not be very effective. Second, even if lack of knowledge were the original cause, other factors such as heavy peer group pressure, inability to resist pressure, and a pro-smoking norm advocated by a "deviant" and "daring" subculture would still become interdependent and reinforce each other. The stronger the pro-smoking social pressure, the more it affects youngsters who are poorly equipped to resist pressure; and the more they submit to the pressure, the more they reinforce the pro-smoking norm of the deviant group. In this situation, an educational program, with the threats and pleas it entails, becomes interdependent with the behaviors it wants to prevent. The more such a program condemns smoking and advocates a restrained and mature approach, the more it singles out and legitimizes the "deviancy" of the "daring," "adventurous," and "rebellious." It thus *cannot* be effective.

A reciprocal approach would start out with quite a different set of assumptions. Let me illustrate this with reference to the reciprocal approach developed at the Palo Alto Mental Research Institute (MRI) and presented by Watzlawick and his associates (1967, 1974, 1978), among others. Their assumptions are as follows. (1) No behavior can be understood outside the context in which it takes place. If examined outside its context, that behavior would be attributed to the people's *nature,* as indeed trait psychology would examine it. Seen in context, the focus of interest shifts from the people's "personality," or in the case of disturbance, from their "madness, badness, or stupidity," to the relationship between parts of the social system. (2) Thus follows an emphasis on the present, relinquishing the search for a linear "cause" for behavior in one's past and psyche; rather, one needs to ask how the system that a person inhabits maintains itself, often circularly (Jackson, 1977; Palazzoli et al., 1978), and how attempted changes of one's behavior come to maintain it (Watzlawick et al., 1974).

Equipped with such assumptions, one would analyze the reactions of the people in young smokers' environments to their smoking (notice: smoking is considered temporarily as a "stimulus") and how these reactions (for example, designating smokers as "deviants," "heroes," "nonconformists") come to stimulate and maintain smoking behavior. Such an analysis would suggest that direct, informative anti-smoking campaigns could become reinforcers and escalators of the very behavior they intend to stop. If anything is to be done about early smoking, it must be designed to break, not reinforce, vicious circles.

So, let my bias be explicit from the outset. I have made the choice to examine communication and education from an interactional, *reciprocal* standpoint. While building upon research findings, most of which are of the Level I type, the theoretical approach I take is of the Level II type. I hope I can convince the reader that this is more useful and powerful a way to examine how communication applies to education. After all, the traditional way of studying behavior as the result of environmental and internal forces is but a convention, not a natural necessity.

I am quite aware that such an approach, as adopted here, raises a host of new difficulties. First, the very choice I have made, ecologically valid and practical as it may be, can easily make me "fit" the issues to be handled in subsequent chapters into my chosen perspective. But then, a reciprocal interactionist approach is no more susceptible to such biases than its alternatives. The question then remains whether such an approach offers us new insights into communication and education.

Second, since our research methodologies and in fact the ways we usually tend to think about social affairs are linear rather than circular (Bowers, 1973), we may be able only to speculate about reciprocal relations without being able to demonstrate them. Indeed, very little research in communication or education has been deliberately designed and appropriately carried out to demonstrate empirically how reciprocity operates.

Guided by the awareness of such dangers, I approach the world of communication and education as interdependent, reciprocally related processes (others call such a view *transactional*). Two kinds of reciprocity are mentioned in subsequent chapters. One is mainly *perceptual*: "The subject's interpretation and evaluation of the object . . . is a product of the mutual play of commerce between the subject's anticipations and the external properties of the object" (Gibbs, 1979: 134). The second deals with longer sequences of events whereby people bring into existence or shape the behaviors of others, which then partly influence the behavior of the former. This may be called social reciprocity.

Perceptual reciprocity often underlies social reciprocity. If I hold the belief that candidates for a new job who present professionally prepared vitae have little to show and much to obscure, I may interview such people in ways that could easily make them conform to expectations. But the candidates may *have* something to show for past achievements, and so my expectations may change somewhat, and the nature of the interaction during the interview could change. Perceptual and social reciprocities become intertwined. For this reason I do not continue to consider systematically the distinction between the two kinds of reciprocity.

NOTE

1. A whole recent volume edited by Kahle (1979) is addressed to the methodologies for the study of person-situation interactions.

Chapter 2

COMMUNICATION IN RECIPROCAL INTERACTIONS

*While it is true that conceptions govern
behavior, the conceptions themselves are
partly fashioned from direct or mediated
transactions with the environment.*

(Bandura, 1978)

COMMUNICATION AND EDUCATION

Reciprocal relations exist not only among individuals or between individuals and their environment, but also between fields of human activity. Such is the relationship between communication and education. One could hardly argue with the assertion that education depends on acts of communication. A book never written (or if written never published), a comment intended but not expressed, a lecture never given, and justice made but not seen, cannot serve in any educational capacity, as they have not been communicated. Thus no educational goal can be achieved in the absence of communication.

But this is only half the story. Could communication exist without education? Not really, for there can be no act of communication without the sharing of some codes, symbols, expectations, or meanings. Creating these is an educational undertaking in its wider sense. Indeed, laying the foundations of a shared culture and, to an extent, perpetuating it is one of the most important and time-honored aspects of what is called education. How could any act of communication take place in a Tower of Babel where people do not even share the convention that, say, a frown is supposed to communicate something but a sneeze is not?

Thus we face the first case of reciprocity: Communication must occur for education to take place, and education must occur for communication to take place. Given such relations, the question of which precedes and which follows is totally beside the point, as each makes possible and maintains the other. More specifically, the way we comprehend a message, or for that matter any event, is very much a function of what we bring to bear on it, as Goodman (1978: 14-15) observes:

> That we find what we are prepared to find (what we look for or what forcefully affronts our expectations), and that we are likely to be blind to what neither helps nor hinders our pursuits, are commonplaces of everyday life and amply attested in the psychological laboratory. . . . In the painful experience of proofreading and the more pleasurable one of watching a skilled magician, we incurably miss something that is there and see something that is not there. Memory edits more ruthlessly; a person with equal command of two languages may remember a learned list of items while forgetting in which language they were listed. And even within what we do perceive and remember, we dismiss as illusory or negligible what cannot be fitted into the architecture of the world we are building.

The "architecture of the world" that we build might be called an educational achievement. It is what we learn, copy, and become socialized into, and it serves, in turn, as the groundwork for new communications. Thus, for example, the meanings of the present lines will quite likely be different for readers who have been "educated" by the preceding chapter than for those who skipped it. The meanings cannot be detached from the groundwork. Furthermore, the groundwork itself develops through communication. As MacNamara (1977) shows, only a very few nonverbal (let alone verbal) signals are known and understood by a newborn. Even pointing at objects to teach a child to look at them is an early educational effort based on communication.

At this point it might be desirable to distinguish between education as process and education as outcome. As process, education is a communicational activity. It is considered "educational" because its outcome is considered to be socially desirable. For example, "sex education" is a communicational process with a particular content the outcomes of which are deemed to have a desirable effect on youngsters' upbringing; thus, to be "educational." Notice, however, that while the process itself is communicational, its "educational" quality is judged by its outcomes. Sex instruction is presently "educational," but table manners no longer are; free expression of feelings is gradually becoming "educational," but gentlemanly self-restraint is not.

If communication is the process whose outcomes can be considered educational by some cultural criteria, and if the process and its outcomes are reciprocally related, then two implications seem to follow. First, the image of communication as processes that continuously "pump" knowledge into a person whose educational achievements continue to grow is a misleading image, which fails to take into account the fact that not only does communication add to one's knowledge; changes in knowledge also affect communication.

Consider the following example. Garbarino (1975) studied the effects of external rewards on the way older children teach younger ones a symbol substitution game and on the quality of the resultant learning. As expected, Garbarino found that when external rewards were offered for carrying out the teaching task (versus a no reward condition), "teachers" were more negative, more demanding, and less patient with their "tutees." The learning of the younger children shows corresponding differences: those who were taught by the rewarded "teachers" showed poorer task ability and made more errors. An examination of the ongoing interaction suggests that as the "tutees" committed an error, frustrating attempts of the "teachers" at quickly receiving their rewards, the "teachers" began to devaluate the "tutees," which seems to have led to an even more impatient and demanding style of instruction. Not only did the initial teaching under reward conditions lead to relatively poor learning, the poor learning also had an effect on the subsequent processes of teaching.

Cognitive learning itself, regardless of teaching style, is a reciprocal experience. Olson (1978: 10) argues that newly acquired language concepts map upon and summarize already available knowledge and experience, but at the same time they also "lead us to see nature in a new way," to investigate the world differently, guided by the newly acquired concepts. Again, something communicated has educational consequences which then change subsequent communication with others or with oneself.

A second and related implication is that the very nature of communication is not objectively determined by virtue of some of its intrinsic qualities. Rather, *the nature of communication is subjectively determined by the characteristics that people—on the basis of their prior education and experience—attribute to it.* In other words, the reciprocity between education and communication applies not only to the *meanings* people learn to ascribe to messages (De Fleur and Ball-Rokeach, 1975) but also to the *very nature* of communication. Certain body movements would be considered communications by people who have learned something about body language. But the same movements would be considered just movements and no more by people who are "uneducated" in this field because they have not learned to attribute to people an intention to communicate through body movements.

Communication, then, is a matter of personal or commonly shared attributions; an event becomes a communication only when people have learned to regard it as a communication.

COMMUNICATION AS ATTRIBUTION

Communication in its wider sense is a process whereby people convey knowledge, influence each other, and create and maintain a basis of shared notions (a "social reality") which they then use as a personal and shared guide.

This, of course, is no definition of communication. As with education, one can easily get lost among the many suggested definitions (95, as counted by Dance in 1970, and many more since then). By trying to define the term, one is likely to find oneself in the situation so well described by Berkeley: We first raise the dust and then claim that we cannot see. I intend only to point out some necessary and sufficient conditions for communication and then some of its major properties.

Traditionally, communication has been perceived as the process through which one mind affects another (Shannon and Weaver, 1949), as a source transmitting a message to a receiver with the intent of influencing the latter's behavior (Miller, 1966), or as one person producing symbolic content with the anticipation that it will be consumed by another who uses the same code (Dance and Larson, 1976). Unlike earlier definitions, more current ones include the concepts of intent and anticipation. But in spite of obvious differences among these and numerous other definitions, two elements are common to most of them: (1) communication is perceived as having two "ends" to it—a sender or source and a receiver or destination—and (2) communication includes a real message transmitted between the two. Mortensen (1972: 14), whose definition differs somewhat from the ones above, defines communication as occurring "whenever persons attribute significance to message-related behavior." Even in this definition there is an "objective" entity (a message), and only its significance is a question of attribution. Is there anything wrong with such conceptions and definitions? Does not communication require the actual existence of a sender, a receiver, and a real message? The answer is a qualified yes, but the qualification makes a substantial difference.

To begin, one needs to establish some criteria according to which events can be judged as communicational. But given the point of view I have sketched out in Chapter 1, the question is not whether events *are* communicational but rather whether they are *perceived* as such and responded to accordingly. Thus, it appears that whenever a person (or group) feels inclined to respond (even if the response is a withdrawal) to what is perceived to be a communicational message, then communication has taken place for that person. To paraphrase the opening quote of Chapter 1: If people perceive an event to be communicational, it *is* communicational in its consequences for them.

Note that the emphasis here shifts to the pragmatic aspect of communication. The question is not what communication is but rather under what conditions it takes place.

Consider the behavior of a somewhat supersititious person who anticipates trouble on Friday the 13th. On this day (never on others?) that person misses the bus, is late to work, fails to find the keys, forgets an important book, yells at a colleague, and so on. When to all this a missed appointment is added, he raises his eyes (half jokingly?) and whispers something like, "You, up there, I think I got your message!" He then decides that Friday the 13th is indeed no lucky day for him and goes home earlier than usual. Did he enter into a communication? Apparently he did; whether there was a sender "up there" and whether there really was a transmitted message is not for us to determine. Nor is it necessary to determine it, as for all practical purposes and as seen from that person's vantage point, communication took place.

Consider now two other examples. Many towns have their persons who are considered "crazy" and who stand at street corners giving long speeches to which nobody listens. It appears that in spite of the obvious existence of sender and message, communication somehow does not take place. Or consider what is happening when a man winks at a woman only to be regarded as having a tick in his eye. Common to both examples is the existence of senders and messages which are overlooked by potential receivers; thus no communication is taking place.

Indeed, the question is not really whether sender or message exist, because (1) senders can be imagined or inferred, as can the act of sending, and (2) any event, behavior, even object, can be perceived as carrying a message, as is the case with the "cruel sea," the "evil eye," a fortune-teller's crystal ball, table corners that toddlers try to appease, and mysterious bank computers that haunt us. The real question is whether a person attributes an intent to communicate to some source (who may or may not have such an intent) and whether the person perceives the source's acts as messages. For example, a person's (perhaps innocent) slip of the tongue is perceived by some clinicians as a "sign" of an inner self communicating. For those who do not attribute communicational intents to inner selves, the slip of the tongue is simply a mistake with no message value.

If we are to judge such cases against the criterion I have offered, then we can accept the idea that (1) communication can take place without a real sender or event that "objectively" qualifies as a message; (2) communication can take place in the absence of a "real" intent; and (3) communication cannot take place where no intent is attributed by a so-called receiver. Some people see a message in Mona Lisa's smile; whether Leonardo Da Vinci intended it or not, they think she is communicating something. A *Peanuts* cartoon by Charles Schultz exemplifies the same point. Lucy is sent by her teacher to the principal and can hardly reach the doorknob of the principal's office. She then says to herself: "I think they purposely put the door knob up high to make you feel inferior." There is a sender, a message, and an intent for all that Lucy knows, but it is in her perception. And as she perceives the situation to be communicational, she proceeds to react accordingly.

Here is the crux of the matter: Communication exists to the extent that one attributes a communicational intent to another. Put in a different way, communication exists whenever one assumes that an event is intended to convey a message. If no such intent is perceived, one can see the event as neutrally informative but not as communicational.[1] Footprints in the sand may be informative to the extent that one infers from them some meaning beyond themselves (for example, "somebody with flat feet walked here a while ago"), but that is not the same as the inference that "somebody left footprints to show me the way." For the latter, but not the former, assumes the existence of a communicational intent.

What does the "attribution of communicational intent" mean? First, it means that one attributes meaning to or explains somebody else's acts (Weiner, 1979). Such explanations are often rapid and automatic, and one can infer their existence only from the behaviors that follow. If the failure of a student in school is attributed to an inability to learn, punishment would usually not follow. But if the failure is explained as a result of too little effort invested in studying, then attempts to increase the student's motivation or to reduce freedom of choice are more likely to follow.

Second, the attribution of communicational intent is only one of several possible explanations of an action. These could include personality traits, or reactions to situational factors. The attribution of communicational intent implies perceiving a deliberate attempt at self-expression by another person with the purpose of influencing someone else. Communication is thus considered a deliberate act (even when other people are unaware of their own intentions because it is the "inner psyche" that intends to express itself). When no deliberate intention to communicate is attributed, not even to the other person's subconscious, then that person's act is explained in terms of character, traits, physiognomy, and the like. (One can attribute the act of spilling a glass of milk to a child's desire to communicate defiance, or to simple clumsiness.)

The attribution of intent usually also implies some degree of freedom (Fishbein and Ajzen, 1975). The response "ouch" to the touch of a burning cigarette is usually considered involuntary, and while it can be perceived as expressive (and hence informative), it will not be considered communicational unless one attributes some intent to influence, say, the cigarette smoker.

Does it follow, then, that people behave differently when they attribute to somebody a communicational intent than when they make no such attribution? The answer is positive. A doorknob is just that unless Lucy perceives it as a message attributed to somebody (or some undefined source like "they"). Only in the latter case does it have a message value with some meaning beyond itself. Now the doorknob "invites" Lucy to respond to the meaning she sees in it as well as to its attributed intent. That meaning literally puts her down. She is now inclined to respond to the principal, or whoever is the "sender" in her eyes, accordingly.

If Lucy did not attribute any communicational intent to the doorknob, it would be only a doorknob to her, to be turned open. Similarly, the person who sees me shrug and interprets the shrug as intended to communicate indifference (even if the intent is attributed to my "hidden self") is likely to respond to the message of indifference, not just to the shrug per se. It is possible to generalize the case and argue that whenever communicational intent is attributed, (1) there is an increased tendency to respond by communicating, (2) the response is to the meaning one attributes to the perceived message, and (3) the response is addressed also to the intent to communicate that one attributes to the source.

This third principle, perhaps the hardest one to picture, is illustrated by Hovland, Janis, and Kelley (1953: 23) in the following hypothesis:

> One of the most general hypotheses is that when a person is perceived as having a definite intention to persuade others, the likelihood is increased that he will be perceived as having something to gain and, hence, as less worthy of trust.

A number of studies were carried out to test this hypothesis and its implications. In two such studies by Walster and Festinger (1962) students either "overheard" a discussion concerning smoking or heard it knowing that the discussants knew they were listening. It makes sense to assume that the "over-hearers" regarded the conversation as information but not as communication intended for them. And indeed, as expected, the "overhearers" changed their opinions regarding smoking significantly more than the others. Interestingly enough, the discussion was pro-smoking (the year was 1962!), but even this did not change the opinions of smokers in the "intended message" group. Thus, the mere attribution of an intent to influence is enough to make an event less influential.

Brehm (1966: 94) developed a theory about *reactance,* arguing that

> there is a crucial distinction between the communicator's offering information and arguments which may help the individual to decide upon his own position, and the communicator's attempting to get the individual to adopt a particular position. Information and arguments can be quite helpful to the individual and may result in positive influence, but the perception that the communicator is attempting to influence will tend to be seen as a threat to one's freedom to decide for oneself.

Thus, Brehm (1966: 104-105) claims,

> Whatever factors promote the perception that the communicator is attempting influence may also arouse reactance and a consequent tendency to disagree with the advocated position. For example, the perception that the communicator has something to gain by having his audience accept a certain position, the perception that the communicator is purposely leaving out crucial facts or arguments, the perception that the communicator is trying "too hard" to make his case, etc., would tend to give rise to the perception of intent to influence.

Does this then mean that one is inclined to reject or show reactance to every event that is perceived as a message with communicational intent? In practice, no. The perceived threat of a communicational event should be reduced and come closer to that of a neutral informative event when the issue under consideration is subjectively unimportant or uninvolving. Reactance develops to messages if they are perceived to limit one's freedom of thought or choice (Brehm, 1966). But when the information in events is perceived as neutral or as intended only to impart knowledge ("the capital of Venezuela is . . ."), less threat should be felt.

If you ask me for the time and I answer as expected, neither the request nor the response is threatening to either one of us. Thus we can distinguish between different kinds of communicational events according to their perceived intent: to persuade, to educate, to inform, to entertain, or to share. Notice that these intents fall into three general categories: intent to *entertain* or please, intent to *convey,* and intent to *change.* Attributing to another the intent to entertain or to convey (for example to inform or to share) should be far less threatening than attributing an intent to change (to persuade, to win over, to educate). It appears that the hypothesis of Hovland, Janis, and Kelley (1953) and the findings of Brehm (1966) pertain to communication with an intent to change rather than an intent to convey.

Recently my students and I conducted a study with grade school pupils to test the difference between informative and communicational events. The pupils were played an audiotape of a woman advocating vegetarianism. One group listened to the tape under the pretext that "one can learn how people convince themselves about something they are unsure of" (informative event); a second group heard the same tape under the pretext that "there's something to be learned about vegetarianism" (a communicational intent to convey); a third group listened to the tape under the pretext that "we want you to consider the merits of becoming vegetarians" (a communicational intent to persuade). While the three groups learned the same amount from the tape, the "persuasion" group claimed to have invested the most amount of effort in understanding it (21 percent), the "conveying" group came second, (9 percent), and the "just information" group was last (4 percent). The two communicational groups had more participants who expressed a desire to interact with the taped woman (52 percent), and the "just information" group had fewer such participants (41 percent). The "persuasion" group also showed the greatest negative change in attitudes toward vegetarianism (38 percent negative change), the "conveying" group came second (25 percent), and the "informative" group came last (8 percent). The results suggest that when an event is perceived as communicational, particularly when perceived as intended to change, more mental effort is invested in it (generation of counterarguments?), it invites more interaction, and often (as shown also in other studies) it is countereffective. Events that are perceived as communication with the intent only to convey, but not to change, are more effective.

Two implications immediately follow. First, a behavior which is not perceived as intended to communicate is not a communication, even if its "source" did intend it to be communicational. It is rather aggravating to express your anger when the person you are angry at "analyzes" your expression as a piece of information about your "dispositions" or "traits." The second implication is more complex: Some behaviors, events, or objects may be defined as simply that (or as neutrally informative), while others may be defined as communicational. In this respect I differ with Watzlawick, Beavin, and Jackson (1967: 48-49), who argue that (1) there is nothing that is a nonbehavior, since "behavior has no opposite" and "one cannot *not* behave"; (2) "all behavior in an interactional situation has message value, i.e., is communication"; thus (3) regardless of one's effort, one cannot *not* communicate.

The difficulty with such a conception is that it is much too wide. If all behavior is communication, then a valuable differentiation is lost. There are behaviors (for example, a sneeze or hiccups) which are not necessarily communicational, even if they are informative (for instance, frequent sneezes might tell me that you have a cold), and that applies even if these behaviors affect other people in an interaction. A teacher may send for a child's parents who, in spite of repeated invitations, fail to show up. If the teacher interprets this behavior as indifference (a *trait* attributed to the parents) or as their being overworked, she may consider this behavior as informative and try to arouse the parents' interest or schedule a meeting on a weekend. Her response in this case is to a behavior, not to a message. She may, however, interpret the parents' behavior as an intended *message* of indifference (not a trait!) or perhaps of expressed superiority and scorn. In that case her response will be to the attributed meaning and to the attributed intent, not just to the behavior.

Likewise, McLuhan (1965) alerted us to the message value in sunglasses. I had never before perceived the wearing of sunglasses as communicating anything, and so I had never responded to that behavior as a message intended for me. Only since I have been "educated" to see such behavior as communication have I started to search for its meanings and respond to the intentions of the wearer. It thus seems to be the case that not all behaviors and events are perceived as communicational. It also follows that not everything that exerts an influence on people's behaviors is necessarily communicational. Indeed, objects influence our behavior (as in lifting a quarter from the ground) but only some (doorknobs sometimes included) are perceived by us as messages.

The reader has probably noticed that two issues are involved here: the attribution of communicational intent and the attribution of meaning to the message. Thus, an uttered word is just a string of sounds unless one sees it as symbolizing something beyond the sounds. Similarly, a houseplant is just a houseplant unless one sees in it a symbol of beauty, nature, nature loving, or the like.

The attribution of symbolic meaning is an essential feature of communication; in fact, everything that is considered to be communicational is also perceived as symbolic. If you consider an antique oak desk as communicating something, you also read into it symbolic meanings, for example, that the intent of past carpenters was to leave behind a sample of their work that expresses their devotion to fine woodwork. Similarly, if you read into my frown a communicational intent (and not that I am blinded by the sun) then you also assign it meaning, perhaps as an expression of dissatisfaction. However, it does not work the other way around: everything that is considered symbolic is not necessarily perceived as communication. The oak desk may be perceived as representing the fine woodwork of yesteryear and my frown as representing my worrisome nature. But reading such symbolic meanings into the desk or frown does not make them communications, because no intent (conscious or not) to convey a message was attributed. Endless things that are symbolic, such as figures on pocket calculators, phone dials, and watches, are not considered communicational.

Perceiving an event as symbolic or meaningful, then, is a necessary but not sufficient condition to qualify it as a communication. On the other hand, perceiving in it an intent to communicate presumes that it is meaningful and a message and is therefore both a necessary and sufficient condition to qualify the event as communication. Again, perceiving intent to communicate is the central issue for defining an event as communication.

By suggesting the necessary and sufficient conditions for communication to occur, I narrow the scope of communicational events. For one thing, it follows that machines do not communicate with each other except in a metaphoric sense, although they affect each other. For another, not every stimulus that evokes a behavior, nor even every behavior that leads to another behavior, is communication. Behaviors by machines do not meet either the necessary or sufficient conditions for communication; human behaviors may meet them, but only when other people attribute to their source an intent to communicate.

The two conditions I have described also widen the range of events to include certain cases which are not often considered communications. One such class of cases occurs whenever people, children in particular, attribute communicational intents to real or imaginary sources that communicate through what others might consider "natural events," such as desk corners that intentionally get in our way. Another class pertains to relations between people and machines, whenever the latter are perceived (and then responded to) as if they can intend to communicate. For example, when we attribute to the bank's computer the intent to harrass us, communication can be said to have taken place.

THE NATURE OF COMMUNICATION

If an event qualifies as a communication whenever one attributes a relevant intent to its source, then a heavy responsibility is assigned to attributors. They do not just respond to events that have objective qualities of messages; they have to draw from their own mental resources to make such attributions. Thus, the act of communication does not begin with the onset of a "stimulus." Preceding it is one's anticipation, one's mental schema or storehouse of knowledge and beliefs, which directs the exploratory behavior that brings one into contact with an event (see Berlo, 1977). Once encountered, events that are perceived as communications are assigned meanings. These meanings, generally speaking, are a mixture of what one sees in the event and what the event entails. Barring occasions where the nature of the event is totally disregarded, as when an ideological preconception completely blinds the person, the result of this encounter is a change in one's mental schemata. Hence comes Barlund's (1975) thesis that communication is unrepeatable (see also Dance, 1970; Mortensen, 1972), as no mental schema remains the same upon encountering an event a second time.

Where, then, does the communication end? It certainly does not end with the last word said in a conversation nor with the words "The End" in a movie. Since the movement is a spiral one, from anticipatory schemata to event and back to the schemata, one cannot really punctuate the process to isolate the communication event and single it out of the process (see also Dance, 1970; Dance and Larson, 1976). It is, as has often been postulated, a continuous process. What this implies is that interdependence develops between one's way of handling events to which one attributes communicational intent and meaning, and the events themselves. In other words, people anticipate certain events (as when readers "know" that these lines will not deal with cheese making but with communication) and assign them meanings in light of their schemata (these lines will be read in one way by communicators, in a different way by psychologists, and in still another way by educators). But the assignment of meanings is not totally independent of what an event entails. People learn new things and add them to their schemata. As Mischel (1979: 748) put it: "Perceivers certainly go beyond the information they are given, but it seems unlikely that they regularly invent the information itself." This, then, is a continuous relationship of interdependence between people's schemata and external events.

Indeed, communication is interdependence of relations, regardless of whether we speak of how one person's communicational behavior affects and is affected by another's or whether we speak of one's study of an artist's work in solitude. In both cases, the spirality I have briefly described above takes place. This interdependence can be more easily observed when human beings interact. The behavior of one is influenced by that of another and influences it reciprocally. This observation has led to the conclusion that one should not search for internal, hypothetical causes for a person's behavior, but rather examine that behavior "in terms of the context of [inter] relationships he creates and inhabits" (Haley, 1977: 33). But the same is also the case outside the contexts of interpersonal relations: I believe what I see, and I also see what I believe.

Consider the following example. A teacher complains that a particular student of hers has become impossible to handle, is undisciplined, uncooperative, and disruptive, and that she sees in this behavior clear messages of rebellion. Observing the student, one would indeed conclude that all the teacher said was true. Something must be wrong with him, and if nothing else works one would be well advised to send him to the school counselor or psychologist. But then you talk with the student only to find out that he feels that the teacher picks on him, overcontrols him, and constantly communicates to him that he is being watched and guarded against. It does not really matter whether the teacher actually communicates coercive supervision of his behavior. What does matter is that this is the way the two communicants interpret the behavior of each other.

More to the point, it is easy to observe how the behavior of the teacher and her communicational attributions are contingent upon those of the student, and how his depend on those of the teacher. The pattern that emerges is one of communicational interdependence, to which the question of who started it or what "madness, badness, or stupidity" initiated it are quite irrelevant. By now the two are interlocked in a circle of inter-dependent communications, each serving as "stimulus" as well as "response" to the other. Intervention, therefore, would need to focus on the relationship, not the teacher's or student's psyche. Once we examine such events from the standpoint of communication as continuity and interdependence, we may find that there is nothing necessarily wrong with either the teacher or the student. The problem lies in a communicational vicious circle of interdependence. And it is this circle, not anybody's psyche, that needs a change (see Chapter 6).

Thus, we may say that whether we speak of a single individual perceiving an event as an intended message and treating it accordingly or whether we speak of different individuals interacting with each other, interdependence is involved. All this leads to the examination of communication from two complementary aspects: the psychological and the social. The psychological aspect pertains to the attributions of intent and meaning that people make; the social aspect pertains to the interdependence that characterizes human communication. Clearly the two aspects are related. The intent and meaning one attributes to a communication influence the way one behaves, which in turn determines (in interaction with the attributions of the other) the nature of the interdependence between the two people. Thus we may say that communication is an interdependence of relations conditional upon the attributions of communicational intent and meanings.

CONCLUSION

I began this chapter with the assertion that communication (the process) and education (the socially desired outcome) are reciprocally related. I also developed the argument that communication is not an "objective" entity (that is, the transfer of messages as if they are buckets of water), but rather, first and foremost, a matter of attributing an intent to communicate. This, then, leads to a distinction between events that represent only themselves; events that represent something beyond themselves (that is, are "informative"); and events that, in addition, are perceived as communicational messages, that is, their "sources" are perceived to have intended them to communicate something. Thus, the necessary condition for communication is attributing meaning to an event (the smile that expresses one's mood); the necessary and sufficient condition for communication is attributing to the alleged source an intent to influence (the smile is a voluntary act, not a reflex, and is designed to introduce a more relaxed atmosphere).

The distinctions between simple events, informative events, and communicational events have behavioral consequences. We respond to each differently and are differentially susceptible to each one's influence. Responses to events that are perceived as only informative (such as being given a road map) are addressed to the meanings we get out of the event (what turn should we take?). Responses to events that are perceived as communicational are addressed in addition to the alleged intent of the perceived source (why did they give me the map?). This intent can be of three general kinds: an intent to entertain, or to convey information, or an intent to change. When the latter intent is attributed, it is often suspected of being biased and self-serving and thus may arouse reactance. Hence "informative" events can be more influential than "communicational" ones. The latter also invite more communicational interaction than the former.

These conceptions lead to the description of communication as a continuous and interdependent process. It is continuous in the sense that the process does not begin with the first word of a conversation or with the teacher's opening remarks, as its nature is very much influenced by the a priori mental makeup ("schemata") that one brings to bear on it and with which one gives it meaning, even seeks it out. The same applies to the "end" of the process, which does not really end with the last words of a conversation. The words change one's mental makeup and thus prepare it for another cycle.

Communication is interdependent in the sense that one's mental schemata influence what is and is not perceived as a message and what meaning it has, and the schemata are influenced, in turn, by the encountered event. Similarly, interdependence exists among people who communicate, each of whom influences the other and is in turn influenced.

Educationally speaking, no "instructional message" is what it is intended to be unless the receiver perceives it and attributes to it communicational intentions. On the other hand, not everything that is perceived as a "message" is necessarily an act really intended to influence others. But since acts that are perceived as communicationally intended are responded to accordingly (responses are addressed to the meaning and to the attributed intent), many an error is committed.

Certain misbehaviors of students are perceived as "messages" sent by their "inner psyches" (are we all not mind readers?) and are treated as messages rather than just behaviors. Moreover, the responses of others are addressed to the "inner psyches" of the students ("to make her less insecure"), which are the alleged sources of the misbehaviors. Now the students' "inner psyches" are being "treated." The students, for their part, either submit to the treatment or resist it. But whatever they do constitutes "proof" for the initial assumption that their misbehaviors are "messages." Furthermore, the students' responses to the treatment come to depend on what the treatment has taught them. At the same time, however, their responses influence the way the treatment is conducted. Communication and education have become interdependent.

NOTE

1. A similar distinction, based on somewhat different assumptions, has been offered by Galloway (1972: 13) with respect to nonverbal communication: "Nonverbal information is always available in some form, but information is not always communication."

Chapter 3
THE ROLE OF MENTAL SCHEMATA

What a preferred method does not
readily see can become less and less
important to our conceptualization
of the phenomena; what a method sees
easily sometimes becomes the sole
basis of our understanding.

(Bowers, 1973: 317)

A SIMPLE MODEL AND A COMPLEX DILEMMA

People are influenced by communications, particularly under specific favorable conditions. For example, children learn more material when provided with clear objectives (Duell, 1974), and adults are more strongly persuaded when the source of a message is credible (see for review Cronkhite and Liska, 1980). It would seem that we could describe the "effects of communication" in a relatively simple way: Messages with particular objective qualities are processed by a person's perceptual and cognitive apparatus and then result in certain outcomes. The perceptual and cognitive mechanisms are thus assigned an important *moderating* or *mediating* role between the preceding external message and the subsequent response.

Calder, Insko, and Yandell (1974) have shown, for example, that persuasion in a trial-like setting is a function of the number of pro-defense arguments, thus pointing to the role of the objective qualities of a message. Other studies highlight the role of cognitive mediation. For example, Petty (1977) has shown in a persuasion experiment that subjects recalled more of their own thoughts evoked by a message than the message itself, and that own-thought recall was the better predictor of subjects' later opinions. In other fields, studies investigate how violent

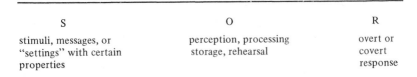

S	O	R
stimuli, messages, or "settings" with certain properties	perception, processing storage, rehearsal	overt or covert response

Figure 3.1 The S-O-R Model for Communication, Perception, and Effects of the Environment

content on television affects children's aggression through the mediation of their cognitions (Comstock et al., 1978) and how organizational characteristics affect communicational patterns, which in turn affect behavior (Rogers and Agarwala-Rogers, 1976).

The overall paradigm that underlies all these studies is, in effect, an extension of earlier S-R (Stimulus-Response) paradigms, converted to an S-O-R pattern. The O generally stands for some kind of mediation—cognitive activity for individuals or social activity for groups and organizations. The paradigm, as traditionally applied to communication, can be described as shown in Figure 3.1.

This paradigm is so basic and so widely employed that research and argumentation focus mainly (even exclusively) on matching S properties with those of O and O properties with those of R. Thus, Perloff and Brock (1980) argue forcibly that a cognitive response approach is the best way to describe mediating responses to persuasion messages. Brophy (1979) similarly calls for a closer examination of classroom processes that mediate between instruction and learning. He shows that teacher praise correlates positively with achievements if the praise occurs during teacher-initiated interactions and negatively if it occurs when students initiate interactions.

Two assumptions (often overlooked) underlie this paradigm, as I have pointed out in Chapter 1. First, the outcome, R, is hardly ever considered to affect the input, S, or the mediators, O, although it is quite clear, for example, that student-initiated interactions, teacher praise, and achievements affect each other reciprocally. Second, the S-O-R paradigm gives precedence to S, while Os are considered only as responses (Bowers, 1973).

So-called mediators are somehow not supposed to seek out stimuli, structure them, or give them a priori meaning. But cognitions are not only responses to messages; cognitions also affect the perceived nature of the messages from the outset.

These two assumptions of the S-O-R model are disturbing, first because philosophically speaking they assign only a reactive role to people. Second, a paradigm based on these assumptions fails to account for a number of daily observations and research findings. How does such a paradigm account for the fact that different people anticipate and observe different events in a given context, differ with respect to what they consider to be communications, assign different meanings to the same events, and distort available information, assimilating it into preexisting "templates"? Gombrich (1960) tells us how an anonymous sixteenth-century German artist drew a locust that looked like a horse while informing us that it was (no less!) an "exact counterfeit." Interestingly enough, the German name for locust is *Heupferd* (hay horse), suggesting that the a priori label affected the way locusts were perceived. Gombrich (1960: 63) offers numerous other examples of how a priori expectations, and knowledge which he calls *schemata*, affect what is perceived and how it is interpreted. Thus, he concludes:

> The individual visual information . . . [is] entered, as it were, upon a preexisting blank or formulary. And as it often happens with blanks, if they have no provisions for certain kinds of information we consider essential, it is just too bad for the information.

Recent history provides us with other illustrations. At least twice in this century military men have had all the necessary information to sense a threat (Pearl Harbor in 1941, Israel in early October 1973) and yet failed to perceive it accurately in time. Preexisting "conceptions," more than the intrinsic qualities of the intelligence information, determined the quality of the information. Similarly, while conducting a series of studies about the cognitive effects of *Sesame Street*'s forms of presentation on Israeli children's mastery of cognitive skills, we found that only 4 percent of the children even mentioned the fact that one of the program's popular figures was black. Many of his other characteristics were mentioned, but children who have hardly seen a black person before somehow failed to notice that property. The same would surely not happen with American children.

Watzlawick (1977) describes a study by Bavelas in which some subjects had to make certain visual discriminations while receiving, in fact, random feedback. Subject generated complex explanations to account for their discriminations, which of course had little validity. Yet their conjectures became so "self-sealing" that no new information to the contrary succeeded in refuting them (see Ross, 1977, for a similar study). Rothbart and Maccoby (1966) have shown that when parents listened to a prerecorded voice of a child labeled in advance as "boy" or as "girl," fathers expressed more permissiveness toward the voices of the "girls" while mothers expressed the same towards the voices of the "boys." In both cases, attitude depended on the parents' a priori mental set.

The common denominator of all these examples is that people's beliefs, prior knowledge, expectations, and the like are not just responses to stimuli; they determine what will or will not be an effective stimulus and how it will be interpreted. People do not enter communicational situations as blank slates. They enter them with some expectations, hoping to satisfy certain a priori needs and obtain specific gratifications. Moreover, they often define through their attributions what will be perceived as communication and what meanings it will have. It appears that the model presented above, according to which cognitions only mediate between stimuli and responses, is conceptually unsatisfying and empirically limited in scope. People's beliefs, knowledge, world view, and expectations often precede the onset of events (even seek them out) and affect them. Cognitions are not just mediators.

However, while this may indeed be the case, it is not the whole case. After all, people are also affected by stimulus properties for which they are *not* prepared. They also often respond to messages in rather uniform ways that are easily accounted for by stimulus properties rather than by mental anticipations. Moreover, people acquire new knowledge, change their opinions, and in general take externally presented events into account. Children respond to the external demands of a physical education class by engaging in athletics, while they respond differently to other events, such as a history class or parents' moralizing speeches. Thus we face a dilemma: Is the information in the message or is it in "the head" and attributed to events which are perceived and mentally constructed by one's mental sets? Is information extracted from messages or is it construed and constructed? But then, could it be that both possibilities coexist?

ANOTHER MODEL AND ANOTHER DILEMMA

Neisser (1976: 22) tried to resolve this dilemma within the context of human perception. He proposed a theory based on the premise that mental anticipatory schemata serve as the medium through which "information already acquired determines what will be picked up next," and this information, in turn, modifies the original schemata.

More specifically, a mental schema is a more or less organized body of already acquired knowledge plus the skilled operations for processing it. A schema is like a storehouse for a category of knowledge, and also like a collection of computer routines. Schemata can be more specific (think of all you know about and associate with the concept of, say, "steam") or more general (think of all your plans and knowledge about achieving goals in life). Extensive or more general schemata embed simpler and narrower ones within them in a hierarchical structure. In addition, schemata are connected to other schemata in complex ways. Thus, for example, while we may associate different thoughts with "steam" and with "vapor," it may take us just a short while to associate the two schemata and combine them directly or through another superordinate schema (such as states of matter).

The idea of such a mental apparatus overlaps, roughly, with similar notions such as *cognitive maps* (Downs and Stea, 1973), *mental plans* (Miller, Galanter, and Pribram, 1960), *organized settings* (Bartlett, 1932), or *schema* (Sotland and Canon, 1972). The latter (1972: 67) argued that

> persons generate relatively abstract and generalizable rules, called schemas, regarding certain regularities in the relationships among events. Once established they serve as a guide to behavior and as a framework which influences the manner in which relevant new information will be assimilated.

Indeed, one's mental schemata operate in a guiding or anticipatory capacity. They direct exploration and information pickup; that is, "schemata prepare the perceiver to accept certain kinds of information rather than others" (Neisser, 1976: 20). Schemata also influence how that information is sampled, structured, and meaningfully construed. Thus, for example, Anderson et al. (1977) showed how people's personal history, knowledge, and beliefs influence their interpretations of a prose passage. They found that physical education and music education students not only interpreted prose passages in line with their respective professional inclinations but also introduced intrusions that were more strongly associated with their respective schemata than with the available passage. In short, directed by their schemata, people become attentive to certain events (even make them up) and sample, structure, and give them meaning in light of their anticipations.

If this were the end of the process then one could agree without reservation with the paradoxical maxim: "I'll see it when I believe it." Yet, as Neisser (1976: 43) points out,

> Perception does not merely serve to confirm preexisting assumptions, but to provide organisms with new information. Although this is true, it is also true that without some preexisting structure, no information could be acquired at all. There is a dialectical contradiction between these two requirements: we cannot perceive unless we anticipate, but we must not see only what we anticipate.

In other words, "The outcome of the 'schema directed' explorations—the information pick-up—modifies the original schema.
Thus modified, it directs further exploration and becomes ready
for more information" (Neisser, 1976: 21). To use Piaget's
terms, schemata assimilate information as anticipated by them,
but while doing so they also accommodate to the information
so encountered. Thus perception (and, as I see it, communication in general) as described by Neisser is a cyclical process.

A relevant example is the study by Meichenbaum, Bowers,
and Ross (1969). The researchers arbitrarily singled out six of
fourteen females in a training school for juvenile offenders as
"late bloomers." Three of the six were initially not expected by
their teachers to succeed well in the school. But once the
teachers' schemata (expectations) were changed (when the
researchers' "predictions" were made known to them), the
teachers started to notice the "promising potential" these girls
seemed to display. Meichenbaum et al. (1969: 308-309)
reported:

> Initially, the teachers expressed some surprise about the inclusion of
> the three girls for whom they had prior low expectancy. Then, very
> quickly, one of the group reported some relatively insignificant
> observations she had made of a low-expectancy girl which indicated
> that she had potential. The other teachers who had been talking
> about the girls as having limited potential followed the lead and
> started to describe other situations which justified the fact that these
> girls were intellectual bloomers.

Moreover, observers noticed that the *actual behavior* of the girls
improved significantly as well.

Figure 3.2, adopted from Neisser (1976) and slightly modified (that is, assimilated into *my* schemata) diagrams the cycle I
have been describing.

The dilemma presented earlier seems to disappear with this
model. People selectively attend to events, attribute intentions,
and construe meanings in light of their anticipatory schemata.
But these schemata also accommodate to the events and what

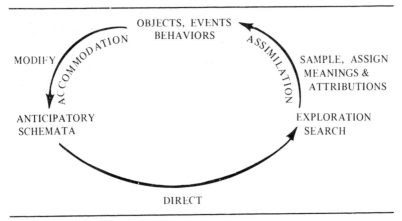

Figure 3.2 The Communicational Cycle

NOTE: Adapted from Neisser (1976).

they entail. In sum, both processes take place in a cyclical manner.

But this model raises a new dilemma which may not have a simple or a single answer. The question is which of the two determinants of the process—anticipatory schemata or external events—plays the more influential role? That is, under what conditions are people's schemata more influential in determining the selection of events and attribution of meaning to them (thus sometimes distorting or evading events to fit schemata), and when do the events have the upper hand? When do people perceive events as they desire to see them, distort messages, project their own feeling onto others, and so on, and when do they accept, so to speak, what the messages "really" tell them? This question pertains to the balance between assimilation and accommodation or between a *closed-circuit cycle* and an *open spiral.*

To answer the question, we will have to begin with an assumption. Whatever we perceive, select, give meaning to, and are possibly later affected by is picked up by schemata. That is, the first (but not the only) determinant of the perceptual-communicational cycle is schemata. The effects of stimuli are subsequent to the influence of schemata. Our prior knowledge, beliefs, and expectations determine whether we interpret an event as a message and whether we see it as clear, ambiguous, paradoxical, a command, an expression of feeling, a threat, or something different from all of these. Accommodation of schemata to the events comes subsequently.

Consider, for example, Berlyne's research (1965) on stimuli that arouse uncertainty and lead people to be curious and seek information. Such stimuli are ambiguous, confusing, irregular, or entail conflict (for example, the observation of a Rodin sculpture in the city dump or a lecturer who brushes his teeth while on the podium). These stimuli either contradict an existing expectation (the lecturer brushing his teeth) or call upon mutually exclusive schemata (the sculpture in the city dump). In either case, the unsettling and uncertainty-arousing properties of the stimuli are perceived, if at all, in light of one's preexisting schemata, not independently of them.

We find that generally people evade, distort, or ignore extremely discrepant information, discredit the alleged source, or generate a separate schema for it. Aronson, Turner, and Carlsmith (1963), and numerous other researchers since then, have shown that as the felt discrepancy between message and schemata increases, schemata accommodate themselves up to a point. When the discrepancy exceeds that point, accommodation ceases, and rejection, evasion, and the like set in. Assimilation takes over. Indeed, when stimuli are too novel, ambiguous, confusing, or unclear relative to one's schemata, then meaning is ascribed by the schemata with little subsequent influence of the stimuli; assimilation dominates. This principle underlies the use of TAT and other projective test techniques which are employed to reveal the hidden layers of people's schemata. As Anderson et al. (1977: 377) state in their study mentioned earlier, intrusions and schemata-dominated distortions appear when

> [a] text is incompletely specified, and the reader fills the gap . . . when the set of relations expected on the basis of a schema is deliberately distorted by the author . . . when the schemata employed by the reader are incongruent with the schemata of the author; or finally when the text is capable of being assimilated to more than one high-level schemata.

This leads Anderson et al. (1977: 378) to conclude that "from the perspective of schema theory, the principal determinant of the knowledge a person can acquire . . . is the knowledge s/he already possesses."

It becomes clear, then, that one important condition for more or less assimilation is the size of the perceived incongruity, mismatch, or conflict between schemata and stimuli. When the perceived incongruity is large, it is unlikely that the stimulus will modify schemata. For this reason, people are more likely to become favorable toward an idea to which they are positively inclined from the outset; more likely to increase their negative attitude toward it when they initially oppose it (see Roloff and Miller, 1980); or more likely to evade it altogether.

Another variable that affects the balance of assimilation and accommodation is *importance* or *centrality* of the relevant schemata. The amount of uncertainty aroused by the choice between two morning newspapers and that aroused by the choice of two careers would be the same if importance were not considered (Sieber and Lanzetta, 1964). Petty and Cacioppo (1977) have shown that resistance to persuasion is greater when subjects are highly involved in the issue and smaller when they are less involved. Under high involvement conditions subjects also become more favorable to an issue when presented with a message in favor of it. When schemata are central or important to people, the cognitive price for allowing them to become modified by discrepant messages may be much too high. Thus, the combination of large discrepancies and centrality of relevant schemata reduces the chance for accommodation.

A third factor enters the balance between assimilation and accommodation: *relative strength* of a schema. A strong schema is more salient, is more easily applied to stimuli, stands closer to the fore of one's store of applicable schemata, and, as Kahneman and Tversky (1973) have argued, is more readily available. Readers may remember that for a few days after buying a bicycle they "suddenly" noticed how many bike riders were around. The reason is that a mental schema, stored way back in their cognitive storehouse, temporarily became more salient.

Research on persuasion bears this out. When people are either forewarned about forthcoming arguments with which they disagree (McGuire and Papageorgis, 1963) or are asked to list their thoughts about such messages (Petty and Cacioppo, 1977), they are less likely to be persuaded by the arguments. Forewarning or listing one's own thoughts about a message bring one's relevant attitudinal schemata to the fore, help in the formulation of counterarguments, and thus make salient the incongruity between the message and the person's expectations or opinions. Related research suggests that when persuasion attempts to change highly salient schemata, it increases experienced threat and creates more reactance (Brehm, 1966). For similar reasons, "sidetracking" subjects' schemata increases the chance of persuasion as irrelevant schemata are brought to the fore (Roberts and Maccoby, 1973).

Messaris and Gross (1977) showed a sequence of photos to children. The series depicts a physician leaving his clinic, walking out, and seeing an accident and an injured person. The physician then passes the injured by and goes on to share a drink with a lady. Although the children identified each picture correctly, 65 percent of the second graders and 35 percent of the fifth graders described the sequence as if the physician attended to the injured. Clearly, younger children entertain mainly one schema, that of "the good doctor." Older children have other schemata, including concepts of staged behavior, of less-than-probable events, and the like. For the older, but not for the younger, the "good doctor" schema is relatively weaker as it competes with alternative schemata.

My students and I have recently replicated the study by Messaris and Gross with a different kind of material (the division of labor between the sexes). Subjects were sixth and eighth graders. Unlike Messaris and Gross, we manipulated the salience of the students' schemata directly, lecturing half the subjects on the "importance of the time-honored idea of division of labor and roles in society." The other half heard a lecture on an irrelevant topic. Subjects were then given a message describing a family's day in which the women played "liberated" roles. As expected, the group in which the relevant schema was strengthened and made salient showed less attitude change in the "liberated" direction than the group for whom the relevant schema was not salient. The former group also tended to interpret the message in a far more "traditional" way. The group in which the relevant schema was not salient showed far fewer distortions in its interpretations.

Finally, a fourth factor that can affect the balance between assimilation and accommodation is the attribution of intent to communicate a message, to entertain, or to convey neutral information. As pointed out in Chapter 2, when one sees an event as a message that is intended to change one's behavior, one is likely to resist. That is, one is likely to assimilate the message into one's preexisting mental schemata rather than accommodate the schemata to any new information in the message. The resistance is likely to be less strong if one perceives an event as intended only to convey information or to entertain. Therefore, we should expect schemata to accommodate more to information if it is seen as "true" or "objective" than if it is seen as "contrived," "biased," or otherwise intended to persuade. The latter is more likely to be discredited, evaded, or distorted to conform to one's existing knowledge and beliefs.

Underlying the four factors I have discussed above—perceived discrepancy, relative centrality of schemata, relative strength of schemata, and attribution of intent—is a common guiding principle of *cognitive consistency* (of which dissonance is but one case). Large accommodations of important and salient schemata may upset one's cognitive structure. After all, having well-connected, hierarchically ordered, and consistent schemata is an important, even crucial, cognitive structure; without it we could hardly manage our commerce with the world (see Insko, 1967). Upsetting such a structure may be extremely painful. No wonder people evade information (recall the classic "Mr. Biggott" studies), single out a case so it will not affect a class stereotype ("some of my best friends are . . . but . . ."), and take great pains in other ways to maintain consistency.

When, then, does accommodation of schemata to stimuli take place? The answer follows from the preceding discussion: when the needed adjustment of a schema to a novel stimulus is relatively small, when it pertains to a schema that is not very central, when the schema is weak, and when an event is perceived as neutral information rather than an effort to cause change, more change will take place. These conditions were apparently *not* met for the Lenin Prize winner Sergey Mikhalkov, thus leading him to claim that "no convinced communist can turn anti-communist. Solzhenitsyn never was a communist" (quoted by Watzlawick, 1977). On the other hand, von Schirach, the leader of the Third Reich's Hitler Jugend, intuited the powers of assimilation when he declared that if given a "good communist" he could easily turn him into a "good national socialist" over a fortnight.

At this point, two qualifications need to be introduced, lest one get the impression that change of schemata is more difficult to come by than it sometimes is (a conclusion that could be very discouraging to an educator). First, as Ross (1977: 210) points out, "new evidence that is strongly and consistently contrary to one's impressions or theories can, and frequently does, produce change, albeit at a slower rate than would result from an unbiased or dispassionate view of the evidence." In other words, even important and salient schemata can change in the face of discrepant information if the latter is frequently enough presented in a way that allows its gradual assimilation. The term "gradual" implies that each encounter with the information is carried out by means of schemata that have been somewhat changed by preceding encounters. Demands for immediate changes would, however, fail.

Second, and of greater interest, are the dramatic, near total changes that take place when one undergoes a religious or ideological conversion. As Ross (1977: 211) argues, "These conversions seem to be the product not of new data nor attacks on old beliefs but, rather, involve assaults on whole belief systems." These are changes of a higher order (Watzlawick,

Weakland, and Fisch, 1974), not of a single schema nor of the content of a few schemata; they touch upon a whole part of a cognitive system to which the new information pertains. Thus, for example, in one of Ross's experiments (Ross, Lepper, and Hubbard, 1975) subjects persevered in constructing erroneous explanations for their successes and failures in a task, even after they were debriefed about the way the experimenters had manipulated feedback messages, and deceived them ("outcome debriefing"). But far less perseverance took place when subjects were told about the perseverance phenomenon itself and the mechanisms that led them to retain inappropriate self-percep-tions ("process debriefing"). The "process debriefing" in effect moved up a notch in the hierarchy of schemata and offered the subjects a way to view a whole part of their belief system in relation to this experience "from the outside," that is, from a *meta* level. It did not offer discrepant information within the same system—a change of the first order (Watzlawick et al., 1974). Rather, it proposed totally different terms for under-standing the experience and allowed the subjects to step outside the limits set by their original schemata and reconcile the problems felt between the schemata and the evidence of their experience (a change of the second order). This is very much like the difference between attempts to persuade people that they are wrong by increasingly insisting on how right we are, on the one hand, and reframing the disagreement in entirely new terms that show how all of us become entrenched.

Consider another illustration. For many researchers who have sought evidence to show that teaching with TV is superior on the average to face-to-face teaching, the accumulation of find-ings that TV made no significant difference has not changed the belief that TV *must* be superior. Discrepant information within the same system was resisted, and no improved research methodologies or better achievement measures (changes of the first order) could affect the belief. What *did* change it was the introduction of the aptitude-treatment-interaction (ATI) idea; it reframed the original question of "what is superior to what, on the average" to become "what benefits whom more." This was a schemata change of the second order, as it did not assault the prevailing belief with more evidence of the same kind (first-order change) but introduced a new superordinate schema (treatments and aptitudes interact). The new schema rendered the belief in TV's overall superiority and the inconsistent evidence perfectly reconcilable as seen from the new, meta perspective.

It thus appears possible that large-scale schemata changes are not likely to take place when specific schemata are directly attacked by means of new, discrepant information that threatens to introduce incompatibility between these and other schemata. Large-scale changes can take place, however, when the relations between schemata are redefined or reframed by means of a superordinate schema (more on this in Chapter 7).

SCHEMATA AND COMMUNICATION

The schemata model presented above was originally developed to account for processes of perception, but it appears to account for almost all human encounters with objects, events, and behaviors. Does it carry any specific and unique import for communication?

Communication, I have claimed, takes place when events are assigned symbolic meanings and when an intent to communicate is attributed to their perceived source. This implies that no communication can take place if one's schemata do not make the two attributions. We may ask, then, why it is so common to attribute communicational and meaning intents to verbal utterances, TV shows, and election buttons but (usually) not to sneezes, hiccups, or fossils.

To some extent, our decision about when to assign communicational intent is based on shared attributions embedded in our schemata. For example, a clinical psychologist socialized into the trade within a psychodynamic tradition is more likely to attribute unconscious communicational intents to a patient's behavior than is a psychosocially or behaviorally oriented psychologist (Shoham-Salomon, 1981).

But shared conceptions do not prescribe *all* symbolic meanings, nor do they prescribe all the contingencies for the attribution of communicational intent. Whether my wink is perceived as an intended message, whether somebody's style of speaking is seen as putting others down, or whether a specific political act is perceived as communicating a new governmental spirit are not culturally shared conceptions. Evidently, within given cultural constraints we have to decide on such issues on our own through an *epistemic process.* That is, we acquire information about ourselves and our surroundings so that we can choose among mutually exclusive propositions, thoughts, feelings, meanings, and beliefs (Kruglanski, 1980). Whenever prior education has not equipped us with clear anticipations, attributions, and meanings, we have to gather new information to make choices among alternatives. For example, we may want to find out if another person is in a friendly mood so we can approach him with a sensitive issue. Since little is culturally prescribed in such a situation, we have to engage in an epistemic process to decide if that person communicates anything and if so, what meanings we should read into it.

All encounters with the surrounding world involve some measure of epistemic behavior, but gathering information does not necessarily imply that the choice arrived at will be an unbiased one. In effect, since this information is part of what might be called social reality, it inevitably *is* biased. It is inferential knowledge "based on incomplete arrays of evidence with no objective basis for feeling certain about the truth of any . . . propositions" (Kruglanski and Jaffe, 1981: 4). Thus, for example, there is no objective certainty that the drawing of a cat on a mat is indeed a drawing of a cat and not of a mammal or a symbol of relaxation, or a drawing of myself-as-cat in a reflective mood (Gombrich, 1974). Furthermore, the choice arrived at is a "subjectively-based preference for a given conclusion over alternative conclusions . . . as any amount of evidence is compatible with a vast (in fact, an infinite) number of alternative interpretations or conclusions" (Kruglanski and Jaffe, 1981: 4).

Anticipatory schemata, which are partly based on social reality, bias from the outset the epistemic process and the choices ultimately made. Schemata bias, *the choice of alternatives.* Ideas that are (even momentarily) more easily available and come more readily to one's mind (Kahneman and Tversky, 1973), having been brought to the fore by experience (Anderson et al., 1977), instruction (Pichert and Anderson, 1977), or motivation bias the range of considered alternatives from the outset. And schemata also bias the weight, credibility, and validity of the gathered information. They lead, for example, to the common "basic attributional error" (Ross, 1977) of giving more weight to evidence that helps explain behavior in terms of disposition rather than situation. A superordinate schema apparently sees to it that cognitive consistency is maintained.

One class of biases particularly pertinent to issues of communication has been studied by Snyder and his associates (forthcoming). They have found that people tend to formulate hypotheses about the nature of other people and then set out to test these in rather biased ways. Specifically, people tend to set out to gather confirming rather than disconfirming evidence. Thus, when told that somebody else is, say, a possible extravert (or introvert), people formulate their hypotheses and generate questions that confirm their initial hypothesis. They neither formulate nor seek disconfirming evidence. And as extraversion or introversion are rather loose categories (as are the categories of "normal," "lazy," "capable," "culturally disadvantaged," or "lovable"), no wonder they succeed in marshaling confirming evidence. People do this regardless of the source's credibility, knowledge of base rates, or number of competing possibilities; they even do it when given disconfirming attributes of the person they are considering. In short, as long as people have some hypotheses to test, they test them in biased ways.

Snyder's most important finding, from the present perspective, is the observation that while soliciting the confirmatory evidence, hypothesis testers shape the other person's behavior such that responses provide actual behavioral confirmation for the hypothesis being tested. Indeed, naive bystanders who listen to a tape recording of the respondent's answers (and only those answers) come to conclude that the subject *is* what the hypothesis tester hypothesized from the outset. Thus, hypothesis testers not only preferentially solicit from their "targets" evidence that tends to confirm their hypotheses, they also shape the behaviors of their targets in a way that makes a naive judge reach the same conclusions. The same is found in educational settings (Feldman and Prohaska, 1979; Meichenbaum et al., 1969).

Herein lies the major and unique place of schemata-guided behavior in communication. All our epistemic behavior (guided by idiosyncratic or culturally shared schemata) is biased, but these biases do not necessarily affect the world of objects; they do, however, affect human beings in social interaction. As Snyder (forthcoming) points out, "Objects, and accordingly the truth value of propositions about them, exist independently of our transactions with them. . . . However . . . the behavior of other people is very much a product of our own actions toward them. How others present themselves to us is, in large measure, a product of how we first treat them." In other words, being guided in our transactions with the surrounding world by our anticipatory schemata, we tend to bias what we are looking for and how we interpret it. But these biases also shape and modify that world when the transactions involve human communication (a clear case of perceptual and social interdependence). This, as Snyder argues, is what is so inherently social about *social* reality. Indeed, my schemata-guided biases may lead me to interpret certain objects as pleasant, aggravating, disturbing, or, say, breakable. But by interpreting them as such I do not necessarily make them have such attributes. On the other hand, interpreting another person's behavior as an intended message of friendliness leads me to react accordingly, with a fair chance of shaping that person's behavior to become more friendly toward me.

Consider a more complex interaction. A teacher entertains certain hypotheses concerning some of her students. These hypotheses are, in part, professionally shared (that is, "institutional"), for example, that minority children are less than well prepared for school, create disciplinary problems, think more concretely, and so forth. Now the teacher engages in an epistemic process, but *contrary* to her expectations, she cannot ignore the high achievements and the perfectly docile behavior of one of these students. Consequently, her expectations become somewhat modified to accommodate what she may come to consider unanticipated yet pleasant information, and she interprets the behavior of that student as that of an over-achiever, which makes him (relative to his category) an "exceptional student." Equipped with the now modified schemata, she communicates to the student acceptance, support, and rein-forcement, further molding the student in line with her modified expectations.

CONCLUSION

While it can be shown that different kinds of external "inputs," mediated by internal cognitive processes, affect "output" behavior, this view is deficient. Using Neisser's (1976) model of perceptual cycles, I have argued that our previously cultivated schemata—hierarchically ordered stores of knowledge and skill—guide us in our information search and perception and direct our communicational interactions. But schemata are also influenced by external events which have attributes of their own: We may expect TV to entertain us, but alas, some of its contents are not entertaining at all and may force us to change our expectations.

Schemata do not change easily. The more central, general, and important ones change more slowly, if at all. Direct attacks on them with contradictory information often lead to entrench-ment. Apparently, contradictory information changes schemata up to a point beyond which the information is rejected, evaded, or assimilated into the preexisting schemata in other ways.

While schemata change slowly and with difficulty, two kinds of large-scale changes have been noted. One kind pertains to gradual, hardly noticed changes which after a while turn out to be profound. This kind of change is of particular relevance to the impact of heavy and continuous exposure to the media (see Chapter 4). The second kind is more dramatic and pertains not to content changes *within* specific schemata (first-order change), but a change of relations *among* schemata. That is, large-scale changes can take place when an issue is examined from a meta level (second-order change), thereby causing a change in the relationships among schemata (see Chapter 7).

All this is of particular interest here for two reasons. First, if communication is a matter of "educated" attributions made by one's mental schemata, then the circularity between what schemata anticipate and attribute and what is entailed in encountered events becomes crucial. Second, as recent research tends to show (for example, Snyder, forthcoming), people's a priori expectations of each other bias the information solicited from the other (it is often confirmatory information); moreover, the behavior of the other is shaped to come into line with initial expectations.

The educational ramifications of schemata theory as presented here are discussed in the next chapter.

Chapter 4
SCHEMATA AND EDUCATIONAL ISSUES

*To study a subject best, understand it
thoroughly before you start.*
Finagle's rule

Thus far we have seen that people's anticipatory schemata develop through prior maturation, learning, and experience. These cognitive structures influence the kind of information gathered from surroundings and affect interpretation and reactions to information. We have also seen that within limits and bound by specific conditions (such as compatibility), anticipatory schemata accommodate to the nature of the encountered events. Such a spiral process implies that change (including educationally desirable change) is a function of external events and people's anticipatory schemata. These schemata not only influence one's interpretations of events but—at least in interpersonal contact—can actually shape the events. This chapter addresses *how schemata theory applies to educational issues and what implications follow from such an application.*

SCHEMATA AND MEDIA:
WHICH IS HORSE AND WHICH IS CART?

For many years, in fact for centuries, the communications media have been accused of having educationally undesirable effects as well as carrying great potential for educational outcomes. In the middle ages writing was not allowed to be taught in the schools; about a century ago juvenile fiction was accused of creating "thoughtless dreamers" (Bean, 1879, quoted by Morgan and Gross, 1980); and in our times TV is accused of facilitating violence and of serving as a new narcotic drug (Winn,

1977). In the late 1960s, S. I. Hayakawa, then a university president, blamed TV for making the young generation uncommunicative, and Gerbner and Gross (1976) argued that TV has replaced the tribal myth-teller in cultivating a new social reality. At the same time, great hopes for the "technological revolution" in education were also raised. An important government commission stated in 1970 that technology can make education far more productive, individual, and powerful. One way or another, the communications media have been charged with great, even magical powers.

Schemata theory suggests that the affects of the media are determined by people's schemata, and that these schemata in turn can be and probably are partly cultivated by the media. This approach differs from both situational and trait theories. A situational (environmental) theory would focus on how schemata accommodate to external inputs (in this case how people's perceptions are affected by the media). For example, Gerbner and Gross (1976: 9) suggest that television affects people's perceptions of the world. Specifically, heavy exposure to TV crime dramas is claimed to create a heightened sense of fear and mistrust, which "is manifested in their typically more apprehensive responses to questions about their own personal safety, about crime and law enforcement, and about trust in people." The implication from such a unidirectional, situational interpretation is that TV should show less crime.

But the same data could be interpreted from a "trait" position as Zillmann (1980) does, observing how schemata assimilate TV stimuli; for example, people with high levels of anxiety may seek out crime dramas with "just" endings so that their anxieties will be relieved. And Fenigstein (1979) showed that the expression of aggressive fantasies and aggressive behaviors increased subjects' preference for violence in films. The implications could be that anxious people should watch more crime dramas in which the "good guys" are victorious, and that aggressive people should watch less violent TV.

Schemata theory would approach such an issue differently. It would suggest first that people's anxieties stem from many sources, including television. Indeed, exposure to TV accounted for only 9 percent of the anxiety variance in the Gerbner and Gross work; Doob and MacDonald (1979) showed that the relationship between TV exposure and fear of victimization held only for people in high crime neighborhoods. The possible implication is that certain personality tendencies or experiences in a high crime area sensitize people to TV crime dramas, perhaps leading them to give such programs more weight. Exposure to crime programs, so perceived, sensitizes people in turn to dangers in their neighborhood. It is really unimportant (even arbitrary) to decide which comes first, sensitive schemata that seek out crime drama or crime drama that arouses fears.

Second, schemata theory would suggest that people with heightened anxiety turn to TV crime dramas for a variety of reasons—some to relieve anxieties temporarily (as Zillmann claims), others to reinforce and confirm their bleak outlook. Indeed, Bryant, Carveth, and Brown (1981) experimentally contrasted and tested the two seemingly contradicting hypotheses and found stronger support for the Gerbner and Gross (1976) unidirectional hypothesis that TV affects people's perceptions. Yet they also found that already highly anxious subjects became *less* anxious as a result of exposure to drama programs that depicted justice. Subjects in that study were experimentally exposed to drama and were not allowed the usual freedom of choice one has with regard to media. Nevertheless the mixed findings suggest that while exposure to drama may increase fears, it is also possible that some anxiety prone subjects will turn to the media to seek relief.

It then follows that the effects of exposure to crime drama depend to a large extent on what people anticipate. And if we follow Snyder's findings (forthcoming), we could argue that people turn to TV in an effort to solicit schemata-confirming evidence. Thus, people whose outlooks are bleak yet perceived by them to be socially reinforced (Hornik, 1974) tend to seek confirmation of such views. On the other hand, people who believe in the "just-world" theory (that is, people get what they deserve and deserve what they get) and perceive their social world to support such a view tend to seek confirmation in TV crime dramas for that view (or do not expose themselves to crime dramas at all).

Two general issues are raised when schemata theory is applied to the understanding of media effects. One concerns the ways in which specific schemata affect what is being learned from the media. The other concerns the ways in which the media affect the development of schemata. To word the questions in educational terms, we might ask first how prior education affects subsequent ways of responding to the media and second how responses to the media affect subsequent learning.

To begin, let us examine some recent experimental evidence. Lord, Ross, and Lepper (1979) presented undergraduate students, some of whom were proponents and others opponents of capital punishment, with a set of pro and con articles on the subject. The results provided strong and consistent support for the *attitude polarization* hypothesis: "The net effect of exposing proponents and opponents of capital punishment to identical evidence . . . was to increase further the gap between their views" (Lord et al., 1979: 2105). The subjects were ready to forego any search for flaws in the written evidence they were given and rely on previously processed evidence to make their hypotheses unfalsifiable.

Other studies have shown that prior tendencies (not just strong convictions) influence text interpretation (Anderson et al., 1977), and experimentally induced schemata demonstrate the same point (Pichert and Anderson, 1977). By assessing prior knowledge or inclinations, one can predict rather well what people will pick up from a text, what they will consider important, and how they will interpret it.

These experiments usually study print messages under experimental conditions. Do their findings apply also to exposure to the media under natural conditions? A number of studies carried out on selective perception of *All in the Family* point to a positive answer. Vidmar and Rokeach (1974) showed that racial prejudices of American (but not Canadian) adolescents became reinforced rather than changed by exposure to the program.

Wilhoit and de Bock (1976) found that authoritarian and conservative Dutch people were less likely to say that Archie Bunker was usually responsible for trouble in his family and more likely to say that he usually had the situation under control. Brigham and Giesbrecht (1976) found that liking for and identification with Archie was strongly related (up to r = .67) to racial attitudes in their white sample but not in their black sample. And Surlin and Tate (1976) discovered that authoritarian males and nonauthoritarian females thought the program was particularly funny. (It is conceivable that males and females attribute funniness to the program for quite different reasons.)[1]

While these findings clearly support the experimental ones, they also add an important variable. Under natural conditions people's schemata not only influence interpretation and perceptions of messages, they also influence whether people expose themselves at all to particular messages. One of the findings in the Wilhoit and de Bock (1976: 80) study carried out in Holland is that authoritarian viewers, who usually watch more television, chose to watch *All in the Family* significantly less than nonauthoritarian people:

> Whether these persons are avoiding the show because it holds up a mirror to themselves is not clear, but reasons given for not watching suggest that substantive rather than *de facto* reasons for not watching are dominant.

If fear of schemata change keeps such people away from the screen (something that cannot be detected in controlled experiments), then such behavior may be at odds with the desire to be entertained by TV. Thus, it is likely that for many, the choice of not watching a particular program may not be the best choice, in spite of the threat to their beliefs. Alternatively, they can watch and misperceive the program's message or watch the program in a way that is shallow enough to evade its message altogether. This way of protecting one's schemata, again something that cannot be easily seen in experiments, has not yet received sufficient attention. But as I will try to show in Chapter 5, the depth of processing is one of the choices communication offers and hence a way one can choose to avoid being affected by incompatible messages.

The previous argument assumes that people approach media messages in ways that test their own preexisting hypotheses rather than using TV messages to build up hypotheses. But what about children, who are less likely to have well-established, rich, hierarchically ordered schemata to bring to media messages? While children may be somewhat more susceptible to media effects, they nevertheless seem to use whatever schemata they have in responding to media messages. Lorch, Anderson, and Levin (1979: 4) studied young children's attention to and comprehension of *Sesame Street*. Their findings suggested that

> children's comprehension of a TV program is not simply subject to the whims of factors that affect attention. Rather, it appears that children are in control of their own attention, following the rule 'pay attention when the program is understandable, and do something else when it is not'.

As it turns out, children are attentive to aspects of programs they understand (dialogue, for example) and inattentive to those they cannot understand (as shown by their inability to recall the arrangement of sections within *Sesame Street* segments). In other words, even smaller children actively pick up the information that they can meaningfully assimilate into their schemata.

In my own research on the cognitive effects of *Sesame Street* in Israel (Salomon, 1976), I found that program formats affected children's cognitive skills quite differentially. Lower-class children who started out with poor mastery of analysis and synthesis skills showed improvement on the former but not on the latter. Further analysis showed that mastery of analytic skills must precede the mastery of synthesis. Thus, it became evident that children actively addressed themselves to those format elements that were only slightly removed from the ones they could already handle. More demanding formats were ignored. Middle-class children, who started out with better mastery of analytic skills, showed subsequent improvement of skills of synthesis, apparently because they addressed format elements that required such skills for the extraction of overall meaning. Research by Collins (1979) showed that preschool children were not sensitive to relations among program segments, the overall structure of a televised story, or relations between motives and outcomes. Not yet having acquired the necessary skills, these younger children picked up other information that was more salient for them (Huston-Stein and Wright, 1977) and in chunks that were small enough to be assimilated into their developing schemata.

Exposure to the media is influenced not only by what children *can* assimilate, but also by what they perceived to be appropriate, valid, informative, entertaining, or useful in light of their prior experience and anticipations. That is, given that numerous TV programs, books, and movies can be understood, children choose from among them according to schemata-guided preferences. This is particularly the case with media exposure, unlike exposure to school material (where less choice is usually available). Thus, Himmelweit (1977) reported that the introduction of a second commercial TV channel in England altered neither the amount of TV exposure nor the choice of preferred fare. Himmelweit (1977: 14) concluded:

> These data suggest that *choice reduces exposure to the novel* simply because risk of turning to an untried program becomes greater where known attractive alternatives exist than where there is no choice. . . . This fact explains the paradox that greater choice of channels often leads to greater sameness of diet.

Indeed, as Himmelweit's longitudinal study shows, tastes and usage in adolescence are good predictors of adult media consumption, particularly regarding "highbrow," highly stimulating (such as adventure), and sports contents. This seems to suggest further how important schemata are in determining patterns of media use.

Does this then mean that the media play no role in schemata change and development? While it is clear by now that neither all segments of the population nor all ages are equally susceptible to media effects, some people must surely learn something from the media. Moreover, schemata that adults and children bring to media messages come from somewhere. Would it not be reasonable to expect the media—so strongly affected by schemata—also to partake in schemata development? Schemata theory clearly implies such a possibility.

We have an idea of the general conditions under which schemata accommodate to external events, as described in Chapter 3. We are now ready to examine the ways that schemata specifically accommodate to the media. And these are far from being clear. Consider, for example, Olson and Bruner's (1974: 142) argument pertaining to verbal instruction:

> If the information intended by the speaker falls outside the listener's "competence", the listener will interpret that sentence in terms of the knowledge he already possesses. It follows that instruction through language is limited to rearranging, ordering and differentiating knowledge or information that the listener already has available from other sources.

If this is possible with *instruction,* a process that entails far less freedom of choice than exposure to the media, how could media (voluntarily chosen) be expected to have much of an effect? And how does such a possibility square with the many claims about media's strong effects?

Exposure to the media is like other kinds of communication in that it has incremental effects on knowledge and opinions when the material the media present is compatible with and can be easily assimilated into preexisting schemata. Indeed, there is good reason now to believe that aggression on TV may particularly affect children with inadequate peer relations, initial violent tendencies, and tense home relations (see for example McCarthy et al., 1975; Atkin et al., 1979). But are there any other media effects beyond the incremental changes of easily assimilated material?

Research suggests that media-induced changes seem to take place in three ways. These are not mutually exclusive; rather, they generally operate concurrently, reinforcing each other. Their presentation as discrete influences serves expository purposes only. First, media can change schemata when the schemata are weak, poorly integrated, isolated, not salient, not important, or not readily available (these may be called "naive changes"). Second, media can change schemata even when the schemata are central, salient, important, and well integrated if they are also insufficiently developed to handle certain novel events, thus setting off epistemic (information-seeking) processes. As epistemic processes are goal-oriented (carried out in order to find an answer, make a decision, take a stand), every information source of perceived validity, including the media, will serve to bring the epistemic processes to fruition ("epistemic changes"). Third, the media can change schemata— regardless of their centrality, salience, or development—by systematically, continuously, and consistently exposing them to easily assimilated messages ("drip effect changes").

Naive Change. The case of naive change pertains mainly to younger children. Wright, Watkins, and Huston-Stein (forthcoming) have proposed a developmental sequence from *exploration* to *search*. Exploration is typical of smaller children: it is guided by stimulus salience (sudden noises, changes on the screen from program to commercials, flashes of light) and gives way gradually, to search. Search is guided by more controlled hypothesis testing and considerations of relevance and informativeness. It appears that younger children's schemata, which are less developed, differentiated, and connected than those of older children, are more strongly dominated by stimulus properties and thus more open to accommodation. Processing is mainly of the "bottom-up" type, beginning with the stimuli and progressing through a number of interpretative levels until the child is satisfied with the meaning obtained.

Processing by older children is more like a "top-down" activity and is more strongly guided by the child's expectations, hypotheses, and guesses, or what Wright et al. (forthcoming) have termed *search*. Calfee and Drum (1978) suggest that the two processes affect reading in a developmental sequence, beginning with "bottom up" processes and developing into more search-like, "top-down" processes. It seems that the same is the case with learning from the media, as work by Wright and Huston-Stein (1979) suggests. Furthermore, younger children do not focus their attention on what *our* schemata would claim to be essential; they pick up central and peripheral events alike as a function of the events' saliency, not informativeness (see Collins, 1975; Hagen and Hale, 1973). It thus appears that as cognitions develop, children become more schemata-guided in their exposure to the media. Hence, they become less susceptible to naive changes induced by media.

On the other hand, when older children first encounter a subject through the media rather than through their own experience, they may be more than usually susceptible to naive changes. Himmelweit (1977) reported that children who were asked to draw a living room of a rich family "drew on the emblems of wealth traditionally displayed in television drama." The same occurred when they were asked to describe how a French or German person looks. However, when asked to draw a "typical" living room they based their images more on their own personal experiences. Caron (1979) studied the effects of Eskimo children's first encounters with TV and found that exposure to a series showing different cultures affected the children's images and evaluations of other cultures. This could easily lead us to the conclusion that the more "naive" children are about something, the more they are unselectively influenced by external media stimuli. Such a conclusion would be in line with Piaget's observations of early-age dependence on perceptual properties and with numerous other observations, such as the unquestioned faith that younger children put in TV (see Leifer et al., 1974). It would thus seem that the naive changes caused by TV are mainly schemata shaping, as Himmelweit writes (1977: 16):

> In the absence of contrary information, persistent labeling by the media will create attitudes about people and events, which, once

formed, will become part of the individual's value orientation and then may be as difficult to dislodge as those values acquired through personal experience.

But more must surely be involved here. Naive changes cannot be solely the result of impoverished schemata being bombarded by novel, well-articulated media presentations. After all, children are heavily exposed to TV, yet their learning is slow, gradual, and selective. And even naive changes can take place only when the information is actively picked up and understood, implying at least a modicum of schemata influence. In addition, and of greater importance here, naive changes have a better chance of occurring when, in addition to the weakness of schemata, the material is treated more as informative than communicationally intended. But children's "naiveté" is manifested in, among other things, their difficulty in attributing intentions to events and in distinguishing between fact and fiction on TV (see for example Roberts, 1979; Dorr et al., 1980). I wish to argue that younger children treat TV events more as real life and less as deliberately intended communications, and thus are more strongly affected by them. Even when smaller children perceive a televised event to be communicationally intended, they are more likely to perceive it as intended to convey knowledge than as intended to persuade.

Events, as I have argued in Chapter 2, can be perceived just as events and no more, as symbolic (hence informative), or as a result of somebody's communicational intent to entertain, convey, or change. In the latter cases we tend to address ourselves not only to the meaning of the event but also to the nature of the attributed intent. Should we decided that an intent to change, educate, or persuade us is involved, then we would become aware of a possible bias in the message (see Eagly, Wood, and Chaiken, 1978). This awareness, in turn, may make us somewhat less susceptible to the message's influence. On the other hand, we "allow" ourselves to be influenced by what we perceive as "natural," "unintended," as entertainment or informatively intended events, because (so we think) nobody's intentions have biased or structured the events to influence or control us. For this reason, self-observation on videotape has a stronger impact than other forms of feedback, as videotapes are "truthful" events, while other people's feedback is considered to be more biased messages (see Stroller, 1967; Salomon and McDonald, 1970). Likewise, children's reactions to TV advertisements change as the children grow older, apparently because they begin to see the commercial intent behind the ads (Roberts, 1979). While it is still unclear whether the understanding of the commercial intent eliminates influence (Roberts and Bachen, forthcoming), it is reasonable to expect it to make children less susceptible to persuasion.

It follows from the above that younger children, lacking well-differentiated and rich schemata, are more strongly influenced by media presentations, particularly when they perceive them as "mere entertainment," as "real" events (and thus informative) or at best as communications intended to convey information but not to change or influence. Ward and Wackman (1973) found that the majority of their five-year-old subjects were able to distinguish TV programs from ads on the basis of the way they look, but only 9-to-12-year-olds mentioned functional differences, pointing to the selling intention underlying ads. Wackman, Wartella, and Ward (1979) found that only 10 percent of kindergarten children could identify the persuasive intent of ads. Roberts (1979) has argued that only when children master role-taking skills are they able to comprehend the intended commercial (rather than informative) nature of ads and thus perhaps become less susceptible to their effects. In sum, smaller children are more susceptible to media-induced schemata developments and changes when their schemata are still underdeveloped and when they perceive media presentations as neutrally informative or as communications intended to convey or share rather than to change.

Similar processes may also occur among adults. First, schemata changes may take place when adults encounter media events that are novel, yet still understood, but to which no well-developed schemata can be applied. Second, naive changes may happen when the events encountered in the media are perceived as informative rather than intended to influence the audience. Cantril (1947) illustrates this point with the effectiveness of Orson Welles's Halloween *War of the Worlds* program among people who assumed it was informational as opposed to those who knew or found out it was staged.

Epistemic Changes. Unlike the naive change, epistemic changes pertain to cases where schemata are already relatively well developed but are insufficient to deal with novel events and contingencies. Hornik, Gonzalez, and Gould (1980) present a strong case to show that a guided search for information unobtainable from one's immediate environment results in a greater susceptibility to learning from the media. One is more likely to learn from the media about distant environments than about immediate ones, since one can learn about the latter more easily from firsthand experience. Furthermore, one learns from the media about distant places only to the extent that such information answers the particular questions of the epistemic search.

This type of process is set off when one experiences a mismatch between different schemata or between an undeveloped schema and a choice that cannot be made without more information. As Hornik et al. (1980) have pointed out, media will have an effect when one has to make a decision about a distant environment and thereby turns to various sources of information for guidance. For example, one might ask, "What clothes shall I take with me on my trip to Los Angeles? What is the weather like there in January?" Or "What might the consequences be if I choose to become a ranger?" To the extent that no other sources, or only less valid ones, offer the needed information, the media will be used to acquire the information.

Consider the following illustration. TV usually shows few older people (at least a smaller proportion than occurs in the population). If a young person had a reason to seek out contact with older people but knew none personally, the lack of older people on TV would probably cause an underestimation of the number of older people in the population. But the correlation between exposure to TV and underestimating the proportion of old people in the population should be lower among people who already have contact with older people or among young people who do not plan any contact with older people. For the former, old people are not outside their immediate experience and so they need not turn to the media in an epistemic search for information. For the latter, there is no epistemic drive to learn from TV about old people. These predictions were upheld in a national survey conducted by Gonzalez (reported in Hornik et al., 1980).

Additional evidence of a similar kind is found in studies on the knowledge gap. Initially it was hypothesized that there is a knowledge gap between members of groups of different socio-economic status because those with higher status show faster acquisition of knowledge from the media (better-developed anticipatory schemata?) than those with lower status (Tichenor et al., 1970). But more recently it has been found that under certain conditions the gap narrows. The most important condition turns out to be people's epistemic motivation. When the information presented concerns local affairs about which there is some conflict, more information is acquired (and more interpersonal debate goes on), thus narrowing the gap (Donohue et al., 1975).

I have labeled this kind of change *epistemic* because, unlike the naive change, it is guided by a goal-oriented information search (not stimulus-controlled exploration) directed by at least two kinds of schemata. One kind is the specific set of schemata that fails to provide the needed information (for example, my schemata would be ill equipped to tell me what clothes to take with me to Los Angeles in January if I had not learned about the California climate from TV programs). The other kind of schemata is the superordinate type that controls the information pick-up (Is TV to be trusted?), weighs the gathered information, and maintains consistency between new and previously stored information. As Hornik et al. (1980) suggest, when the novel information obtained from the media disagrees with existing experience-based knowledge, the former is more likely to be rejected. But this will depend on how central and salient the stored knowledge is and on the size of the discrepancy (see Chapter 3).

An important implication is that brief exposure to the media by people, even youngsters, will not have much of an effect on them in areas of knowledge or opinion that are served by well-developed schemata providing satisfactory guidance. To make a youngster learn from a televised presentation would require that the information to be learned pertains to a distant environment about which the learner has insufficient knowledge and on which the learner has to act.

Consider the following case. When *Sesame Street* was introduced to Israeli children in 1971, it was met by a relatively TV-naive young audience whose experience with the medium was short and limited to "old-fashioned" programs (*Lassie, Flipper,* and the like). The mosaic-like, fast-moving, and non-narrative structure of *Sesame Street* must have been quite novel for Israeli children. We studied the skill-cultivating effects of *Sesame Street* on Israeli children (Salomon, 1976, 1979) and confirmed that the program's formats were a newly encountered environment for which already mastered mental skills were partly inadequate. We anticipated that the children would attempt to acquire information from the program and that in the process they would become more skilled in handling its formats.

The overall findings supported our hypotheses, but the wisdom of hindsight directs us now to reexamine some of these findings. We observed a far stronger "net" effect on the ability to order pictures in a storylike sequence among middle-class children than among lower-class ones (exposure accounted for 9.8 versus 4.8 percent of the posttest variance, respectively, after all other predictors, including pretest ability, were partialled out). How can we explain this difference, assuming that the program's mosaic structure was an equally new environment for both groups? Claiming that middle-class children had better developed schemata, and were thus better prepared fails to account for the cases where the *lower-class* children showed greater improvement (for example in English letter matching, for which they were less well prepared).

We found that the middle-class children were guided more than the lower-class children by a desire to understand (mentally act upon) the *overall* story of the "environment" of *Sesame Street.* Indeed, our interviews with the children revealed that middle-class more than lower-class children sought to explain the discrete segments of the program as part of the general story, as past experience with TV would lead them to expect. Thus, the middle-class children in our sample were more strongly affected in their story-structuring skill because the overall story structure of the program was for them an "environment" on which they desired to act. Lower-class children turned their attention to other parts of that "environment" and thus were more affected by them.

In sum, exposure to the media may have relatively strong effects on schemata when their messages pertain to some distant environment for which not enough local cues are given and on which one has to act. I called this an epistemic change, as it is determined by one's goal-directed information search rather than by one's impoverished schemata.

Drip Effect Changes. Himmelweit (1977) lists four conditions for *maximum* media impact to occur. Paraphrased, these conditions are: (1) the existence of appropriate anticipatory schemata, (2) naiveté, (3) repeated exposure, and (4) social reinforcement. The first and last conditions seem to be generally necessary (the second condition was discussed earlier); but the third condition appears to constitute a distinctive way through which media have an impact, as does the epistemic change (which Himmelweit did not discuss in detail).

The drip effect differs from the other two kinds of media effects as it neither implies naiveté nor any epistemic drive. It takes place merely by repeated exposure to generally understood yet somewhat novel messages, leading to effects "unnoticeable at first until at a given time cognitive and attitudinal restructuring occurred" (Feather, 1971, quoted by Himmelweit, 1977).

The drip effect is not a case of subliminal or other (speculative) hidden influence. Information needs to be picked up and processed by existing schemata for *any* effect to take place (Roberts, 1979). Thus, cognitive activity is involved. However, information gathering need not be guided by any specific epistemic motives. After all, TV is watched mainly for entertainment purposes, and many a book is read for the same purpose. Perceived as entertainment, such exposure to the media may not strike the viewers as constraining or demanding much mental effort (see Chapter 5). Yet whatever is watched, assuming it is not totally redundant (which would turn viewers away), can leave a modest residue of acquired knowledge.

It is possible to postulate that repeated (even "shallow") exposure to mentally undemanding contents, once they are assimilated, makes them part of one's anticipatory schemata (they become familiar). This, in turn, guides one to be further exposed to similar contents, thereby allowing continued absorption of the same fare. *The Waltons, Mister Rogers' Neighborhood,* Kermit, or J.R. of *Dallas* become part of one's familiar world and thus lead to the accumulation of additional knowledge about them and their activities. Indeed, as Atkin (1978) shows, the more children are exposed to news on TV, the more political knowledge they acquire. This relationship seems to begin with a politically interested home which brings the child into early, relatively unguided contact with the news media, which in turn causes subsequent increases in political knowledge (see Chaffee et al., 1977).

Empirically, it is rather difficult to separate the drip effect from naive or epistemic changes. What may begin as a drip effect can easily arouse one's curiosity and lead to epistemic changes. Furthermore, drip effects accumulate to a measurable extent only over a relatively long period of time, so it is not easy to prove their existence. Nevertheless, several research findings lend support (albeit indirect) to the drip effect hypothesis. For example, in our series of *Sesame Street* studies (Salomon, 1976, 1979) we found that children who were experimentally exposed to the program over eight consecutive days showed a 26 percent decline in their tendency to persevere with an unrewarding task when compared with an adventure-film control group. Similar effects have been observed and complained about by kindergarten teachers (Winn, 1977) and seem to illustrate the drip effect.

What makes the drip effect possible? Moreland and Zajonc (1977) have shown a renewed interest in the *mere exposure* phenomenon, that is, positive changes in attitudes arising from repeated stimulus exposure. Earlier accounts of such a phenomenon usually postulated, as I just did, the mediating effects of stimulus recognition and familiarity. It was assumed that reactions to a stimulus become more positive as a function of more frequent exposure to it, because the stimulus gradually becomes better recognized and more familiar.[2] However, Moreland and Zajonc, in a series of experiments, showed that while stimulus recognition may be a sufficient condition for more positive attitudes to develop, it is not a necessary one. They found the frequency of exposure to have a significant and independent influence on one's positive reaction to the stimulus. Moreland and Zajonc (1977: 199) concluded that "it may thus be possible for an individual to have some affective reactions toward a stimulus either prior to or in the absence of any processing of information regarding its content."

Mita, Dermer, and Knight (1977) tested the same hypothesis in a different context. Subjects saw pictures of either themselves, a lover, or a friend. The pictures were of two kinds: seen from the perspective of one looking into a mirror and from the perspective of one looking at another person. (For example, one subject would see two pictures of himself: one taken as he looks at himself in a mirror and one taken as he looks at another person. Or he might see two pictures of a friend from the same two perspectives.) The researchers found that the subjects preferred their own picture more when it was a mirror-image of themselves (an image they see more frequently) while the lover or friend liked more the true-image picture of the same person (an image *they* see more frequently). The important point is that neither the subjects nor their lovers or friends were aware of the difference between mirror and true-image pictures. This lends support to the mere exposure hypothesis, since the subjects preferred images they had been exposed to more frequently.

Other evidence, however, suggests that while mere exposure may influence emotional affect even without conscious processes, it cannot affect higher order learning. Deregowski (1968) found that Zambian domestic servants did not show any greater facility in comprehending perspective in drawings than mine workers, in spite of their far more frequent exposure to European drawings. Passive exposure to drawings (while dusting, for example) did not lead to improved skill mastery.

Taking these two lines of research together, it seems that mere exposure to media presentations may first render them more likable, which then leads to familiarity (Moreland and Zajonc, 1979), and this can subsequently facilitate the acquisition of new information. But when schemata do not include the necessary rudimentary skills, little improvement in skill mastery can be expected from mere exposure. The drip effect can thus be initiated by mere repeated exposure that makes one like certain media fare and then become more familiar with it. Once it is recognized as familiar, curiosity may be aroused (who murdered J.R. after all?), and acquisition of knowledge takes place.

Given that the media can affect schemata through naive, epistemic, and drip effect changes, we can add that the extent of schemata change—or resistance to it—is strongly affected by social reinforcement. Change is facilitated when it is reinforced by social surroundings. For instance, increases in educational aspirations resulting from TV exposure in El Salvador were observed only in youngsters who were already in school, who knew that schooling provided access to more schooling and better jobs, and whose families reinforced such aspirations (Hornik, 1974).

Social reinforcement sets the agenda for change by pointing to what is socially more (or by implication, less) desirable. It also reduces the threat of change, for it suggests ways in which consistency among schemata can be maintained. For example, Hornik (1974) found that purchase of a TV set in an El Salvador sample *reduced* youngsters' aspirations to move to a city. This suggests that the social environment of these youngsters reinforced TV viewing, with all the excitement it arouses, but did not reinforce emigration to the city, instead assigning to TV a replacement or cathartic role. Thus, rather than allowing TV to introduce dissonant social notes, the social milieu reinforced exposure to TV as a substitute for socially dislocating action.

The most important implication of schemata theory to issues of media exposure is the circularity of influences that it suggests. Learning from the media (learning a new social reality, increasing sensitivities, gaining new perceptions of social agendas) becomes part of one's anticipatory schemata, which are then used for the assimilation of other media contents and possibly also nonmedia events. Thus, Hartman and Husband (1974) observed that British children who had no previous contact with racially different people were most likely to describe such people in terms they had learned from the media. In other words, schemata cultivated by the media "may color both interactive behavior and perception of that behavior—and thus cause the immediate environment to resemble the media-taught expected environment" (Hornik et al., 1980).

In a longitudinal study, Morgan (1980) found that early TV viewing positively predicted later amounts of reading: The more a youngster viewed TV at an early age and continued to do so later on, the *more* was read later on, while the less a youngster started out televiewing (and remained a light viewer), the less was read subsequently. But then an interesting finding surfaced: Heavy televiewers who became heavier readers appeared to prefer reading material reflecting the common TV fare. Apparently, TV cultivated schemata transferred to a nontelevision domain.

I would go as far as hypothesizing that in this respect at least, naive changes are the most powerful ones, as they tend to cultivate schemata rather than modify already well-developed schemata. Epistemic changes, on the other hand, are apparently the weakest, as they modify already established schemata and apply to specific information needs; the acquired epistemic information is more likely to be weighed and compared with information already stored. But then, size of media effects will also depend on what is being changed—a general outlook, an opinion, or specific bits of knowledge or skills.

At the same time, while information learned from the media comes to serve as part of one's schemata, acquisition of this information itself is determined by preceding schemata that may derive not from the media but from personal experience. For example, Greenberg (1972) found that black people seen on TV were rated as "real to life" by white children who had had previous contact with black children more often than by those who lacked such contact.

It appears that anticipatory schemata influence media effects (more so in the case of epistemic changes and less so in the cases of naive and drip effect changes) and are at the same time subject to these effects.

SCHOOL LEARNING:
THE NEED FOR SCHEMATA AND ITS PARADOX

Learning from the mass media is different from learning in school in at least one important way: The freedom one has in selecting, interpreting, and assmilating materials from the media in everyday life would seem to exceed by far the freedom one has when learning in school. After all, schools and other educational institutions (as in the army or industry) are designed, among other things, to impart particular kinds of knowledge and to cultivate specific classes of skills.[3] But while schools want to change specific schemata and gradually cultivate them, schemata theory suggests that such changes are anchored in the kinds of schemata that students can, choose to, or are instructed to apply. When such anchoring does not take place, learning (changes in the knowledge that schemata store or in the operations they apply) is badly handicapped.

The problems of teaching something that cannot be assimilated into the learners' schemata is well illustrated in the following study. Sinclair de Zwart (1967) attempted to teach nonconserving children how to conserve by means of words that denoted the principles of conservation, as picked up from already conserving children. The attempt was only partly successful. However, when the same was done with regard to seriation, significant learning outcomes were observed. It appears that the mental schemata of nonconservers could assimilate principles of seriation but (not yet) those of conservation.

The problems of teaching something when learners fail to choose the appropriate schema are illustrated in a study in which Hodgkinson (1967) tried to teach proper spelling by means of a basketball-like writing game and found that the children learned the rules of the game well but still did not learn how to spell. Evidently, they chose to apply an irrelevant schema to the exercise.

Finally, the importance of teaching learners which mental schema to employ is demonstrated in a study by Pichert and Anderson (1977). They asked students to read a passage concerning two children who skip school and go to one of their homes. A third of the subjects were instructed to read the passage from the point of view of burglars, a third from the point of view of potential house buyers, and a third were given no instructions. As schemata theory would predict, the subjects in the three groups remembered different story elements and gave different weights to the same elements, as if, indeed, they were reading different passages. The uninstructed group recalled less material than the two instructed groups. Pichert and Anderson (1977: 314) concluded that

> people learn more of the important than the unimportant ideas in stories. . . . The importance of an idea unit depends upon perspective: *It was an idea's significance in terms of a given perspective* that influenced whether it was learned.

Notice two issues that are highlighted by these studies. First, learners' perspectives, abilities, and inclinations determine how they treat the information they are given, how the information is assimilated, and how it is stored. This was also borne out in the study by Anderson et al. (1977) concerning the different ways in which the same material was learned by music and physical education students. Second, learners' schemata are susceptible to guidance that can cause specific schemata to be preferred over others and applied to the material. (The manipulation of contexts, as we shall see in Chapter 6, often serves precisely this purpose.)

This is a major issue when purposeful learning is desired: What schemata do the learners choose to apply to the information at hand? How does one influence the anticipatory schemata that influence students' epistemic behavior? And what does schemata theory tell us about how people interpret speech and conduct that seem to contradict each other? (Why should a student in a physical education class learn from the body movements of the demonstrating teacher but not from that teacher's verbal instructions? Why does a youngster pick up on a father's conduct more than on his moralizing speech? And how do professors see to it that students will attribute a communicational intent to what they *say* in class but not to the much too short a time they can allot each student after class?)

To maximize learning, educators need to help students apply a specific kind of schema to the material to be learned. This is precisely what Pichert and Anderson (1977) did when they told students what perspective they should use in reading a story. Such instructions are a specific example of a wider category conceptualized and studied by Ausubel (1968, 1978) and called "advanced organizers." Advanced organizers are "appropriately relevant and inclusive introductory materials . . . introduced in advance of learning . . . and presented at a higher level of abstraction, generality, and inclusiveness." Their function is to provide "ideational scaffolding for the stable incorporations and retention of the more detailed and differentiated material that follows" (Ausubel, 1968: 148).

As recent research suggests (see Ausubel, 1978; Mayer, 1979 for reviews), the use of advanced organizers significantly improves learning, particularly when the material to be learned is potentially meaningful and when learners are not likely to apply relevant past experience on their own. The improvement in learning does not manifest itself so much in amount of retention as in the transfer of the learned material to new material (Mayer, 1979).

Such improvement, and the conditions under which it takes place, follows logically from the nature of advanced organizers. If the material is not potentially meaningful, it cannot be assimilated into any schema, whether made salient or not; it will be learned in a rote manner. But if advanced organizers make a specific higher order schema salient so that the new, more specific material is assimilated into it, then the advanced organizers should (and do) mainly facilitate transfer to other equally specific material. The repeated finding that transfer to new material takes place as a consequence of using advanced organizers (Mayer, 1975, 1976) suggests that an important outcome of the material's assimilation is a change in the relevant schema. New material (for example a new computer language) is assimilated into a wider cognitive schema that is brought to the fore by an advanced organizer (for example a general model of computers), thereby changing the content of the assimilating schema. This, then, results in the schema's applicability to new materials.

Advanced organizers can be found in various forms such as book titles, headlines, and brief abstracts that precede journal articles. But while they may make salient specific mental schemata that could aid in the assimilation of subsequent material, there is no assurance that such indeed will be the case. Other schemata that are either higher up on one's schemata hierarchy or simply more dominant, may prevent an advanced organizer from accomplishing its function. Consider the following case. Jones and Harris (1967) have shown that people are often likely to attribute a person's remarks (pro-Castro statements in this experiment) to disposition, even though they have heard that person state contradictory opinions and witnessed the person being ordered by the experimenter to state remarks giving an opposite view.

I have informally replicated Jones and Harris's procedure in numerous classes I have taught, asking a female student with explicit pro-abortion opinions to give a ten-sentence speech against abortions. About 60 percent of the students in all the classes attribute the cause of the student's speech to her "inner" or "hidden" dispositions, although they always (1) hear her initial pro-abortion opinions, (2) see me coerce her into expressing anti-abortion claims, and (3) are aware that the class meeting deals with the "basic attributional error." It is reasonable to assume that these three "advanced organizers" should prevent the attributional error from occurring. Nevertheless, the tendency to attribute the causes of behavior to a disposition rather than a coercive situation appears to dominate.

On the other hand, we find that an advanced organizer (in the form of authentic clinical case histories) can serve as such a powerful superordinate schema, that it assimilates new hypothetical information as if the information were factual. Ross et al. (1976) gave subjects clinical case histories of patients and then described specific events in the patients' lives (for example, a hit-and-run accident or an altruistic deed) which the subjects had to explain. These events were presented to some subjects as hypothetical events after subjects offered their explanations, while other subjects were told in advance that these events were hypothetical. Regardless of whether subjects were told that the events were hypothetical, and regardless of when they were so told, they over- or underestimated the likelihood of the events' occurrence in accordance with their case history explanations. Once subjects identified case history antecedents that seemed to explain an event (the anticipatory schema), they increased or decreased their estimates of the event's likelihood.

On the one hand, then, we find that certain advanced organizers are ineffective, while on the other that they are much too effective. What does this teach us about learning? It becomes evident that while it is possible to invoke specific superordinate schemata in learners, the actual application of such schemata to new material is not easily controllable. The learner is free, even in controlled classroom instruction or in controlled experiments, to utilize the anticipatory schemata preferred. Thus, the relevant question to ask here is not just whether learners have the necessary prerequisite knowledge, skill, or aptitude that advanced organizers could potentially elicit (Mayer, 1979). One needs to ask in addition whether learners are likely actually to apply that knowledge, and under what conditions they are more or less likely to do so.

A related issue pertinent to questions of teaching and learning is that impressions, opinions, and bodies of knowledge that have been acquired as a result of instruction and serve as anticipatory schemata for new material are not easily replaceable by alternative schemata. And it seems that the more general (superordinate) and powerful the schemata are in assimilating new material, the less replaceable they are. Thus, the superordinate schema that "knows" that people are dispositionally driven rather than influenced by situational forces, the schema that "knows" that events are always linearly arranged in cause-and-effect chains, or the one that "knows well" the decimal base of mathematics, does not easily give way to instructors' attempts to bring alternative schemata to the fore.

Herein lies the danger of forming through instruction certain *general* schemata which cannot easily be modified. In particular it can be hypothesized that instruction that systematically emphasizes the *one* right answer, the *one* correct way of learning, or the *one* proper way to evaluate a student cultivates a superordinate schema that henceforth anticipates events to be of precisely such a nature. This is, perhaps, where the spiral relationship between schemata and application becomes most crucial. Specifically, students acquire an overall schema which guides them to seek out the one correct answer, the one correct interpretation, or the one correct way to study. This schema they then apply to numerous instances to the exclusion of alternative schemata.

A concrete example is provided by Lowenfeld and Brittain (1966). They quote an earlier study by Russell and Waugaman (1952) in which children were observed to draw birds in rather varied ways. However, after exposure to mathematical workbooks in which standard animals were to be colored, 63 percent of the children freely drew birds in the same standardized way. They seemed to have acquired a relatively general schema which they then applied even where it was inappropriate.

More general examples can be found in such areas as test-wiseness and extrinsic rewards. Test-wiseness has been defined as "a subject's capacity to utilize the characteristics and formats of the test and/or the test-taking situation to receive a high score." Test-wiseness is independent of the test taker's knowledge of the subject matter which the items supposedly measure (Millman, Bishop, and Ebel, 1965, quoted by Sarnacki, 1979: 253). Test-wiseness has been shown to be learned and to give the student an advantage over less test-wise peers. It qualifies as a rather general operational schema which can be applied to numerous tests and other materials. However, its application, while improving test scores, seems to come at the expense of deductive reasoning, which is what tests are designed to measure.

The frequent use of extrinsic rewards, whether in formal ways (as in token economies) or in informal face-to-face interactions, seems to cultivate a similar superordinate schema. Learners learn to anticipate extrinsic rewards and thereby fail to develop intrinsic reward systems. This leads Bates (1979: 573), who reviews the pertinent literature, to generalize that "in cases where task performance is already closely associated with extrinsic rewards, the absence of appropriate reinforcers would appear to be more damaging to intrinsic motivation than their presence."

It is reasonable to speculate that though cultivating a superordinate schema may be a desirable educational outcome at first, the schema may later be applied in less desirable ways, and its modification may become difficult. Most important, although a learned overall schema subsumes much new information easily and therefore aids education, it also restricts epistemic search and the testing of alternative ways of handling the information. Herein lies a paradox: education cannot avoid cultivating superordinate schemata, and yet these can limit future educational achievements. The way out of this paradox follows from the distinction between the two levels of change (Watzlawick et al., 1974) mentioned in Chapter 3. Instruction could, of course, strengthen certain superordinate schemata or equalize their mastery. Thus, Sarnacki (1979) proposes to make test-wiseness part of each junior high school program, thereby making all students equally test-wise. While this is perhaps attainable, the danger of accomplishing it at the expense of deductive reasoning is not eliminated. Nor could that danger be eliminated if tests were so smartly designed that test-wiseness would become (temporarily) useless, for then students could simply cultivate even more sophisticated test-wiseness. Similarly, neither increasing students' ability to produce the "one correct answer" nor refining extrinsic reinforcers would drastically alter the ways in which students view schools. Such changes of the first order modify, at best, the relative strength or centrality of one or another schema, but not its content or relationships to other schemata.

Another way out of the paradox is the cultivation of alternative schemata and the training of their exchangeable applicability to the same material. This is done in creativity training, where the same material is viewed from alternative viewpoints. Thus, students would learn that an answer is the correct one from one perspective, but another answer is equally correct from another perspective. Similarly, students would learn that there are alternative or even mutually exclusive ways to evaluate and grade them, or, for example, that there are different, equally valid ways to understand the causes for the American revolution. Students who encounter such alternatives may acquire a superordinate schema that directs them to apply alternative subordinate schemata to new materials. Thus, they may become more capable of changes of the second order.

INTERPERSONAL CONTACTS: BIAS AND ACCOMMODATION

As we have seen, interpersonal perception and communication are strongly affected by the contents of the participants' anticipatory schemata. It can be said that no interpersonal contact is free of schemata anticipations, as indeed there is no "naked eye" nor "naive perception" (Goodman, 1968). Even first interpersonal encounters, which one might expect to be free of a priori anticipations, are not free of them at all. The teacher who meets new kindergarteners on the first days of school has already encountered "such" students (ones who are tall, blond, bashful, neat, and so on) and thus has developed some idea of what to expect of the students, how to interpret their behaviors, and how to relate to them. On the basis of such guesses, the teacher may then assign children to "academic" and "nonacademic" tables, the latter being farther away from her (Rist, 1970). Military sergeants, similarly, are far from naive upon encountering black recruits (Hart, 1978), and so are interviewers (Tucker and Rowe, 1979).

Anticipatory schemata that affect interpersonal contacts can be of varying kinds. One of our more dominant schemata tends to tell us to underestimate situational factors in attributing causes to somebody else's behavior (but not to our own) and to overestimate dispositional ones. Social roles, a special case of situational forces, are often disregarded in favor of generalized traits that are attributed to the person performing a role. Thus, for example, when subjects were asked to generate ten hard-to-answer questions and address them to another person, that person as well as outside observers rated the questioners as more knowledgeable than others who were not told to generate questions, even though they knew that the questioners were set up by the situation (not by their particular traits) to display their personal store of knowledge (Ross, Amabile, and Steinmetz, 1977). Other schemata that serve in interpersonal contacts are sex stereotypes (Ickes and Barnes, 1978), trait prototypes (Cantor and Mischel, 1977), and consensual labels (Langer and Benevento, 1978), as well as more specific experience-based schemata.

Common to all kinds of such interpersonal schemata is the way they operate. First, schemata sample out, bracket, or punctuate the behaviors of others in accordance with initial cognitions. Once bracketed or sampled out, the behaviors are submitted to interpretation, or what Weick (1979) calls sense making. Such interpretations attribute causes to the behaviors and establish what can be expected from that person on the basis of such attributions. Teachers apparently expect poor readers to improve if their slow reading is explained in terms of too little effort (an internal, unstable, and partly controllable cause) but to fail to improve if the attributed cause is poor ability or poor upbringing (Bar-Tal, 1978; Weiner, 1979). Moreover, such expectations may be generalized: "poor readers" will be expected to be different in a variety of respects from "good readers." Their slow reading thus becomes a mark of deficiency in many academic activities (Stulac, 1975), leading back to the sampling of additional behavioral data that, once interpreted, further "justify" the initial label or diagnosis (see reviews by Jones, 1977; Cooper, 1979; Weick, 1979).

Rosenhan (1973) had students pretend to "hear voices" and admit themselves to mental wards. Once admitted, they behaved as "normally" as possible under the circumstances, only to be diagnosed as "schizophrenics in remission." Rosenhan (1973: 253) concluded,

> Once a person is designated abnormal, all of his other behaviors and characteristics are colored by that label. . . . One psychiatrist pointed to a group of patients who were sitting outside the cafeteria entrance half an hour before lunchtime. To a group of young residents he indicated that such behavior was characteristic of the oral-acquisitive nature of the syndrome.

Jones (1977: 103) added to this that "it apparently never occurred to the psychiatrist that life in a mental ward is incredibly dull and that there is not much to look forward to other than mealtime." Examining the psychiatrists' behavior in terms of processes, we can say that prior expectations and attributions led them to select certain observable behaviors rather than others, to attribute certain causes to them in light of these expectations, and to arrive at expectations concerning the future inability of the patients to recover. Generalizing, we can say that schemata-determined expectations (perceptions, cognitive appraisals) are enacted in the form of specific behaviors addressed at others. Thus for example, Willis (1970) found that teachers tended to ignore comments made by students who were expected to have "low efficacy" but actively responded to "high efficacy" students. Chaiken, Sigler, and Derlega (1974) found that teachers leaned forward, smiled, kept eye contact, and nodded their heads to "bright" students more than to "slow" ones. And Rosenthal (1973) observed that teachers called more upon students for whom they had high expectations, gave them more time to answer, and prompted them more toward the correct answer than they did with students for whom they had low expectations.

It should be noted, however, that only part of the many studies in which teachers' and others' anticipatory schemata (expectations) were manipulated showed the expected effects on either teachers' or students' behaviors. Rosenthal and Rubin (1978) reviewed 345 expectancy studies and found significant effects in about 30 to 40 percent of them, depending on the specific situations, expectations, and measures employed. What is clear is that experimentally induced expectancy effects can be found in some teachers whose expectations affect some students under some conditions.

One such condition involves how much a teacher (or any experimental subject) trusts information designed to change expectations (Pippert, 1969). Babad (1979) differentiated between *suggestibility* (that is, the extent to which one is likely to allow new information to modify existing schemata), and *communicability* (the extent to which one communicates the expectations thus developed). Babad argues that suggestibility is a necessary but not sufficient condition for new information to lead to behavior that affects others. Once convinced that the information is trustworthy, one still needs to act upon it or, as Babad argues, to communicate it. The failure to distinguish between these two conditions, he claims, may account for the many studies in which no expectancy effects were found.

I would like to take issue with Babad's points. First, while suggestibility to experimenters' biasing information may be an important issue in experiments, it may be a far lesser issue in real life situations. People's expectations of others rarely develop in one-shot trials, but rather grow gradually in spiral ways and change slowly as a result of interpersonal contacts that are in turn shaped by expectations. The case of externally induced, suddenly appearing expectations is rather rare. People trust what their schemata guide them to perceive; thus, in real-life situations there is no issue of trust in information. And even, as we shall see below, when schemata are organizationally induced ("minority students are . . ."), they are hardly ever unrelated to experiential data.

Second, and more importantly, expectations are rarely communicated explicitly. The behaviors enacted by teachers with specific expectations may of course "communicate" their expectations, but whether they do depends on the receiver's attributions of intent. When a teacher speaks to me as though I am a child and redundantly repeats her explanations, she may have acquired (so I think) bad professional habits, or she may be trying to put me down. Only if I interpret her behavior in the latter way would I see her as communicating an appraisal of me. Minor (1970) showed that students who were concerned with evaluation by their teachers came to behave as the teachers expected them to behave. Students not concerned with evaluation were not affected by expectations. The former but not the latter students detected the expectancy cues and responded to them.

Specific behaviors of, say, teachers are no more than "raw data" that students have to make sense of on the basis of *their* anticipatory schemata. Thus, while teachers who have developed positive expectations concerning several students because of experimentally introduced new information tend to behave in a qualitatively different way toward these students, the meaning of these behaviors must be ascribed by the latter. Students then respond to the teachers in light of their own expectations. Rubovits and Maehr (1973) found that black (unlike white) students who were labeled "gifted" benefited *less* from their white teachers' behaviors than unlabeled "normal" blacks (the opposite occurred with white students). We may speculate that the black students had different expectations of white teachers than the white students did, and teacher behaviors that were taken as supportive by the whites were seen more negatively by the blacks.

What this suggests is that expectations may be communicated through actions, but the way their nature and meaning are received depends on the receiver's expectations. This continuous process of action and interpretation constitutes the strong schemata-guided interdependence between people in interpersonal contact. Feldman and Prohaska (1979) have shown that *student* expectations translate into behaviors addressed to teachers and affect the teachers' expectations and behaviors. Thus, the behaviors of all parties in an interaction may be schemata-guided and affect each other interdependently.

I have said that students react to teachers' behaviors as a function of the intentions and meanings they attribute to the teachers. Do they react differently when they think the teacher is trying to communicate a personal message? On the basis of the hypothesis of Hovland et al. (1953), the findings of Walster and Festinger (1962), and our own findings, I postulated earlier that events that are perceived as "communicational" and change-intended have a smaller impact than "informative" events. The former are suspected of being biased or self-serving, and thus arouse reactance. It would seem to follow that when labels or roles ("assistant," "student," "slow learner") are perceived to connote impersonal status and expectations (neutral information), one is more likely to adapt to them and fulfill the expectations than if they are perceived as intended to change or control one's behavior.

We now have reason to believe that behaviors toward others that are guided by *negative* appraisals and expectations (teaching less material, less eye contact, more punishment, negative labels, less freedom) affect the receivers' self-concept and self-esteem (Langer and Beneveto, 1978) or perceived self-efficacy (Bandura, 1977a). These, in turn, lead to helplessness, poorer self-efficacy, and the gradual relinquishment of effort (Bandura, 1979). We can suggest, however, that the more the intervening behaviors are perceived as personal messages intended to demean, the less likely they should be to decrease one's self-esteem, self-concept, or perceived efficacy, because one is likely to resist messages that are personal. On the other hand, the more neutrally "informative" such negative expectations are perceived to be, the more trust one should put in them, leading one to adapt to them with less resistance.

Miller, Brickman, and Bolen (1975) tried to teach fifth graders not to litter and second graders to work harder with math. Attributions of neatness were communicated in the former case and attributions of ability or motivation in the latter. Such attributions ("Your class is the cleanest in the building"; "You are a very good arithmetic student") contrasted with direct persuasion attempts ("Don't be a litterbug"; "You should be better in arithmetic"). Results were clear: attributions changed behaviors considerably more than persuasions did. Miller et al. (1975: 438) wrote:

> Attributional statements need not involve persuasive attempt but may instead be [perceived as] simple statement of fact. Indeed, their guise as truth statements may be thought of as their most effective advantage. . . . An appeal to be neat or an appeal to work hard can involve the implicit attribution that the person is not currently the sort of individual who is neat or works hard.

Here we can see how actions that are perceived to convey trustworthy information can become self-fulfilling prophecies more easily than actions that are perceived as intended to change. The latter are more likely to arouse reactance. It is possible to speculate that the opposite would be true when *positive* expectations are perceived as personally intended messages aimed at change; these may be better received than "informative" or "institutional" messages.

Circularity is involved when actions come to modify the behaviors of others to make them conform to expectations. This, it seems, is more likely to take place when negative expectations are communicated and perceived as intended only to convey information, and when positive expectations are perceived as change intended. Do these kinds of effects always take place? To expect circularity we would need to postulate either one of two possibilities. One is that schemata-guided expectations and behaviors lead others to behave as expected, thus confirming the expectations. Alternatively, the others behave in their own way (perhaps only mildly influenced by the expectations) and by so doing modify the expectations. Much of the research on expectations, sex-role typing, and labeling, particularly in education, tends to support the first possibility (see Braun, 1976; Jones, 1977; Cooper, 1979). On the other hand, there is also evidence to support the second possibility. Luce and Hoge (1978) found that students' intelligence and industriousness had no smaller an effect on their achievements than their teachers' expectations. Notice that both possibilities reflect Level III interactions. The first case is a *closed loop* in which expectations, perhaps shaped by past encounters with others, come now to shape the others' behavior in line with the expectations. In the second case, the others' behaviors, instead of conforming to expectations, change them, creating a *spiral loop.*

Brophy and Good (1974) hypothesized that personality differences among teachers may account for the possibility that some teachers are more susceptible to students' behaviors and less inclined to hold to their expectations and make them come true than other teachers. Babad (1979) actually tested "suggestibility" to biasing information as a function of personality traits (such as dogmatism) and found weak though systematic positive relations. Recent developments in personality theory (see Mischel, 1968, 1979; Epstein, 1979; Bem and Allen, 1974) suggest that presently, at least, the search for stable personality correlates of greater or smaller adherence to initial expectations may be unfruitful. It may make greater sense to look at the schemata themselves and the interdependence between the schemata of all participants involved in the interpersonal contact.

The subjects, in the study by Snyder (forthcoming) not only solicited hypothesis-confirming evidence from their interviewees, but also shaped the latter's behavior in line with these hypotheses. They were not necessarily more dogmatic than Luce and Hoge's (1978) teachers, whose expectations had only a mild effect. And Rosenhan's (1973) psychiatrists who "refused" to see the normal behavior of the pseudopatients did not necessarily have more dogmatic personalities than their regular patients, who by and large discovered that the pseudopatients *were* normal. What differentiates between the cases is the nature of the expectation-guiding schemata, that is, their salience (availability) and their centrality. Snyder clearly made the expectation for extravert behavior more salient than Pippert (1969) or Luce and Hoge (1978) did with their induced expectations. The teachers in the latter two studies knew their students (Snyder's subjects did not know each other) and had their competing expectations. And for Rosenhan's psychiatrists, the schemata of "mental illness" and "schizophrenia" were far more central and important than for the patients. After all, such schemata constitute the backbone of the psychiatrists' occupation.

Thus, when schemata are temporarily more salient or generally more central (they explain more of the world, maintain more consistency among subordinate schemata, and the stability of more schemata depends on them), they are "blinder" to contradictory data. And since they translate perceptions into actual interpersonal behaviors, they are more likely to become self-fulfilling prophecies.

However, such schemata do not operate in a social vacuum. Others have anticipatory schemata of their own and expectations and behaviors to match. Teachers have certain differential expectations of black and white students (Rubovits and Maehr, 1973), but the students have their own expectations of teachers and of themselves (Rappaport and Rappaport, 1975; Feldman and Prohaska, 1979). Boys and girls have expectations of each other and act accordingly toward each other (Ickes and Barnes, 1978) and so do sergeants and recruits (Hart, 1978). Now the two sides interact. What happens? Two issues need to be considered here. First we need to consider the nature of the schemata involved, and then we need to consider the social positions involved.

The schemata that help develop expectations in schools come only partly out of one's own experience. A characteristic feature of educational settings (in fact, of all organizational settings) is that they develop, cultivate, transfer, and impose on their members schemata, "scripts" (Mangham, 1978), or "cause maps" (Weick, 1979). Their purpose is to reduce uncertainty, to provide ready-made interpretations, to dictate what goes with what and what leads to what. In effect, organizational schemata or cause maps *are* the organization itself, as Weick (1979: 141) exemplifies with the case of the orchestra:

> The point is, the cause map may *be* the orchestra. If we then ask *where* that orchestra is, the answer is that the orchestra is in the minds of the musicians. It exists in the minds of the musicians in the form of the variables they routinely look for and the connections they routinely infer among these variables. These maps are then superimposed on any gathering where the announced agenda is music-making.

This is so, claims Weick (1979: 157), because "most 'objects' in organizations consist of communications, meanings, images, and interpretations." Thus, educational settings, like other organizational settings, define "disturbance," "success," "proper behavior," "ability," and "desired outcome" and provide causal explanations such as "effort leads to success" or "cultural disadvantage causes difficulties in school."

Another characteristic of educational organizations is that they are *loosely coupled* (see for example Weick, 1976; Meyer et al., 1978). The structure of schools is disconnected from the work done there, and that work is disconnected from its effects. For example, the actual day-to-day classroom activities of teachers are unrelated to declared policies and organizational structures, are uncontrolled, and are hardly inspected; learning outcomes and other effects do not really feed back into the organization and do not change its policies, structure, or procedures. Interestingly enough, the educational activities in which tighter coupling can be found are marginal ones such as certification and general curricular sequencing (Meyer and Rowan, 1978).

To function properly, such loosely coupled organizations need a wide basis of consensus (instead of explicit prescriptions) which gradually emerges between members of the organization and applies to what is central to their common activities. As Weick (1979: 143) writes with respect to orchestras:

> Cause maps are approximations and deal with likelihoods, not certainties. Since residual equivocality remains after individual cause maps are superimposed, it is necessary to gain some consensus among musicians as to what the orchestra is confronted with and how it is to be handled. Members activate *sets of interlocked behavior cycles* to deal with this residual equivocality. Initially, they try to *negotiate* a consensus on which portions of the display are figure and which are ground. When people collectively try to shrink the possible meanings attached to an equivocal input, they essentially are negotiating issues of naming and connection (e.g., "What did we or the composer do that caused that horrible chord?"). Having consensually made the enacted environment more sensible, the members then store their revised and presumably more homogeneous cause maps for imposition on future similar circumstances.

Speaking specifically about schools, various individuals have stressed the impact of school organizational characteristics on teacher behavior (Schlechty, 1976). This impact can readily be appreciated by noting the many ways in which teachers seem to behave in common. While individual differences between teachers in a school obviously exist, the observer cannot help being struck by the similarities—for instance, similar attitudes toward students, work, and administrators, similar ways of responding to problems, and similar feelings of powerlessness and frustration. Such observable similarities have been studied by Meyer et al. (1978), who found high degrees of institutional consensus among teachers instead of formal organizational controls. They conclude, "The process that holds educational organizations together and gives them meaning and value is not the success of the system . . . but rather their structural conformity to prevailing institutional rules" (Meyer et al., 1978: 260).

One function of school consensus is to increase the likelihood of predictable behavior by teachers. When behavior becomes predictable, however, there is a high likelihood that it will become routinized. As Weick (1979) suggests, rules and procedures introduced as means for the accomplishment of ends become ends in themselves. Duke (1978) notes that teachers frequently treat discipline as their primary objective rather than as a means to greater student achievement. If teachers place a disproportionate emphasis on controlling student behavior, they probably do so, in part, because of the nature of school consensus.

There is reason to believe that partly through organizational control, but mainly through consensus, teachers gradually become socialized to use the schemata that are central to the school's functioning (Hoy, 1969), and so do the students. Such socialization then influences teachers' and students' cognitive appraisals of themselves and each other and guides their actual behavior toward each other. When they interact, they utilize (though not exclusively) consensual schemata to understand the others and respond to them.

While such schemata are essential for an organization, particularly when loosely coupled, they leave considerable latitude for self-validation (Weick, 1979). And the more central to the organization the schemata are, the less subject to disconfirmation they become. They become the "real thing." As Monroe (1955; quoted by Weick, 1979: 3) pointed out,

Consensual validation seems to be "common sense" of a high order—the things people agree upon because their common sensual apparatus and deeply common interpersonal experiences make them seem objectively so. It is a critical and cautious term for the reality so often used by other psychological schools.

We might assume, then, that when two or even more subcultures (for example students and teachers), each with its own consensual schemata, come into contact, they have to work out a higher order consensus among themselves. But this apparently is not the case. The relations that develop are *complementary* rather than *symmetrical,* that is, they involve parties of unequal power (Watzlawick, Beavin, and Jackson, 1967). The very nature of school (or family or army) demands complementarity; there are teachers (parents, officers) and there are students (children, recruits), and it is the former's schemata that dominate and prevail. Thus, there is a greater likelihood that teachers' expectations, particularly when they derive from central consensual schemata, will dominate interactions between teachers and students, modify the latter's self-schemata and behaviors, and ultimately become self-fulfilling prophecies.

Some indication of this can be found in Duke's (1978) analysis of disciplinary problems in schools. Faced with certain student behaviors that consensual schemata single out and define as "disruptions," schools develop and enforce an increasing number of disciplinary rules that are perceived by students as unjust and coercive. This then makes the students more disruptive, offering the school confirmation for its perceptions and leading it to enforce even more rules. The school's schemata dominate and prevail. (See also Hart, 1978, for a study carried out in military camps that suggests the same pattern.)

Indeed, we know that students' schemata gradually come to reflect those of school, while their own, if discrepant with those of the school, come to be considered deviant. This is the way specific students or classes of students ("inner city") come to be regarded as "mad," "bad," or "stupid." Regarded as such by dominant consensual schemata that are not easily changeable and are perceived as "real," students learn to behave according to expectations (see Baumeister, Cooper, and Skib, 1979; Weick, 1979).

A colleague of mine in Israel (Adar, 1978) developed a provocative argument pertaining to the identification of certain

students there as "culturally disadvantaged." The official definition of "cultural disadvantage" (C.D.) is demographic. It is
based on the parents' geographic origin (Mideastern countries),
parents' education (low), size of family (large), and the statisti-
cally computed likelihood that any such child will fail in school
(40 percent). First, argues Adar, the definition is long and
complicated and therefore cannot (and *does not*) serve as a
useful mental schema. People condense and simplify it in their
minds. Second, once condensed, the mental label C.D. includes
more students than the legal definition: *all* students from a
certain origin are perceived as C.D., and *all* of them are
expected to fail. Third, when the background that is supposed
to be a sociological cause is linked with outcomes of failure, the
background itself is negatively perceived. It becomes "bad" in
itself to be of Mideastern origin. The result is, as Adar shows,
that cultural origin becomes identified with school failure in
popular perceptions. Every child of that origin is expected from
the outset to become a failure. No wonder therefore that
Bar-Tal (1980) finds that when given the description of an
"Eastern" and "Western" student, teachers immediately predict
for them different learning outcomes and attribute different
causes to their success and failure.

Other studies (Babad, 1979) have shown very clearly that
Israeli teachers approach C.D. students differently from other
students, and similar evidence has been found in the United
States. For example, Williams, Whitehead, and Miller (1972)
found that teachers evaluate their students and predict their
achievements in language arts on the basis of the students'
ethnic dialects. The label C.D. becomes an all-inclusive consensual schema: it is easy to comprehend, appears to eliminate
much uncertainty, and carries with it much predictive power.
While in its original form it may have served as a summary label
for observed phenomena, it thereafter became an anticipatory
schema that applied to too wide a population and provided
ready-made causal attributions and expectations. Most importantly, it placed students in an inferior role, which, as Langer
and Benevento (1978) show, can generate self-induced helpless-

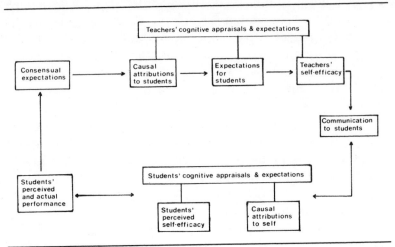

Figure 4.1   Consensual Schemata and Hypothetical Self-Sustaining Prophecies

ness even if students do not experience negative outcomes (which of course they do).

Does the label C.D. then turn into a self-fulfilling prophecy? The answer would be positive if we assumed that consensual schemata are unrelated to external events, in fact create them, as Weick (1979) argues. But it seems more plausible that such schemata gradually develop hand in hand with the observation of a phenomenon. Thus, rather than being a self-fulfilling prophecy, the label C.D. is a self-*sustaining* prophecy (see also Cooper, 1979).

Corno and Duke (both at Stanford) and I attempted to summarize this point in graphic form (Figure 4.1).

Notice that the historical question of whether failure of some students preceded the label or vice versa is unimportant. By now the consensual schema of C.D. is resistant to disproof and maintains the phenomenon as much as the latter maintains the schema.

All this could lead to the conclusion that all schemata, personal and consensual alike, become self-fulfilling or at least self-sustaining prophecies. Does interpersonal contact never modify schemata? Do anticipatory schemata indeed have such uncompromising undirectional influences that, once formed, they cannot be modified by disconfirming behaviors? Recall the study by Luce and Hoge (1978) showing that in the classroom context, students' intelligence played at least as much of a role as teachers' expectations in predicting achievements. Should not such a finding cast strong doubts on the present argument?

A distinction needs to be made between a larger system (such as a school system) and the smaller subsystems of which it is composed (such as specific classrooms). First, following Weick (1980), we might say that each subsystem is more tightly coupled within itself than the larger system. That is, the behaviors (and anticipations) of members in, say, a single classroom are more strongly interdependent among themselves than with those of, say, the district administrators. Similarly, there is more interdependence among two friends in a classroom than in the classroom as a whole, and more interdependence in a school than in a school district. Compare the loose coupling found in schools and even more in districts by Meyer et al. (1978) with the far tighter coupling between grading practices, absenteeism, and climate that Moos and Moos (1978) find in single classrooms.

It follows, that far more communication takes place among members in the subsystem than between them and the larger system. Astin (1977) found, for example, that communicational exchanges and involvement take place more often in smaller schools than in larger ones. The more steps communication must take in a system, the more it is transformed and distorted. And in light of what has been said thus far, the larger a system is, the more events are perceived as neutrally "informative" rather than communicationally intended messages. You are less likely to perceive a policy as a message intended to change you if it is schoolwide rather than a classroom policy. And informative events (even communicationally perceived ones whose sources intend only to convey knowledge) are more effective than change-intended ones.

Glass and Singer (1972) reported on a study by Shaban and Welling that highlights this point. Students were subjected to bureaucratic harassment of two kinds (or to no harassment). Some students were harassed in a way that made them attribute the irritation to a bureaucrat's whims and attempts to control them (the bureaucrat was "personally responsible"), while others were harassed in a way that made them attribute the irritation to regulations ("regulations responsible"). Still others were not harassed at all ("control"). There were clear after treatment differences. Subjects in the "personally responsible" group performed more poorly on a subsequent proofreading task and were more negativistic (showed more reactance) on other tasks than the subjects in the other groups.

Interestingly, subjects in the "regulations responsible" group showed more compliance, resignation, and acceptance of the assigned role of "harassed" than the subjects in the "no harassment" or "personally responsible" groups.

A third consequence of the loose coupling of large systems is that the support for systemwide schemata comes mainly from their consensual nature. They are based less on immediate interactional cycles and more on widely shared beliefs that come to be regarded as "true" by virtue of the fact that others hold the same beliefs. This is not so true of "local" or personal schemata. The policies regarding "culturally disadvantaged," "minority," or "gifted" students are more heavily based on shared notions about, say, educational equality and on statewide test results than ongoing contacts with specific individuals. But a teacher's specific expectations, while derived from the consensual schemata, are also based (in part at least) on the actual behaviors of students in the classroom.

It follows from these three points that systemwide schemata have a better chance of seeming "real" by virtue of their loose connections to daily events, "factual" nature, wide applicability, and superordinate and central place on the consensual hierarchy of schemata. Changing them may entail a change in the whole organizational cause map. Teachers' specific and far more detailed schemata, while related to the consensual ones, can be expected to respond more flexibly to new information. It would be easier to persuade a teacher that the C.D. students in class are "late bloomers" after all than to persuade the school system that the label C.D. is possibly turning into a self-sustaining hypothesis.

A subsystem such as a classroom, home, or neighborhood allows far more personal contact than a larger system and hence more interdependence, in the sense that the participants' schemata undergo more accommodation to each others' behavior. Fancher (1966) found that predicting mental patients' future behaviors correlated negatively with the predictors' reliance on conceptions about personality. The less generalized (central, inclusive) the schemata, the better the prediction. Bowers (1973: 328) observed that "accommodation to the properties of the observed is more likely, the more contact the observer has with the observed."

It appears that the more interpersonal contact there is (hence also more perceived communication) the more specific schemata change can be expected (Amir, 1969). On the other hand, the more systemwide and consensual the schemata are (more "ideological" than those based on personal contact), the more resistant to change they are. The latter have a better chance of continuously providing confirmatory evidence and, to the extent that this is translated into actions, to shape others to be "in line." Returning to the issue of C.D. students, we might say that the system's expectations, translated into role placement, policies of grouping, and the like, have a fair chance of being self-sustaining prophecies, partly because they are so central to the system's consensus and partly because they are perceived as "informative," rather than "communicational." But the day-to-day interaction between a specific teacher and students labeled as "C.D." has a better chance of changing both the teacher's expectations and those of the students.

In sum, schemata-based expectations of people partake in reciprocal interactions. The more central the expectations and the more consensually held they are, the more they make others conform to them. Two factors contribute to this closed loop in educational settings: the centrality of consensus in loosely coupled educational organizations and the complementarity (assymmetry) of the relations in such settings. On the other hand, more experience-based expectations that are developed in daily contacts with others (who also have expectations of their own) are more prone to respond to disconfirming information, since personal relations make the schemata of the parties involved accommodate more to each other. Thus, I have argued, educational systems are more prone to sustain the phenomenon of culturally disadvantaged students than are individual teachers.

There is great similarity between the way schemata operate in interpersonal settings and the way they operate with respect to media exposure and to learning. In each case, hierarchically higher and more central schemata are less susceptible to the influence of external influences, and external events that are perceived as "informative" but not "communicational" may have a better chance of modifying schemata. But schemata play a special role in the interpersonal domain inasmuch as they guide behaviors that may actually shape others' behaviors to conform to expectations. This, I have argued, is more likely to happen when schemata are consensual and serve as a foundation for the functioning of organizations; it is somewhat less likely to happen when more intensive interpersonal contact is involved. Thus, the more interpersonal communication is involved, the tighter the interdependence among the components in Neisser's model (1976) and the more schemata accommodation occurs. On the other hand, the less interpersonal communication there is, the more loosely coupled the interdependence among the model's components, and the statement "I will see it when I believe it" applies more pervasively. In this situation events have a better chance of becoming assimilated into preexisting schemata.

CONCLUSION

The ways schemata operate in school learning, exposure to the media, and interpersonal contacts have four common denominators: First, people's anticipatory schemata bias what they *select* to perceive (as with authoritarian viewers who like TV but avoid Archie Bunker or onlookers who see no situational factors influencing a coerced peer), how it is *interpreted* (reading a story from a particular perspective; finding evidence for "late blooming" in otherwise neutral behaviors of students), and how it is *reacted to* (believing TV, for it is "real"; shaping a student's behavior in line with expectations).

Second, people's schemata are influenced by ongoing events. Thus, TV creates and modifies schemata through "naive changes," "epistemic changes," or "drip effects"; material that is learned in school makes one perceive new material differently; and a student's unexpected behavior can change the teacher's expectations. Here one finds reciprocity between schemata and events "out there."

Third, schemata that are higher up on one's hierarchy, more central, and more consensually shared are less susceptible to change than less central and more contact-based schemata. A paradox follows: we cannot learn from the media (let alone understand anything), learn in school, or relate to each other without anticipatory schemata, yet we become blinded by them. Children learn from TV that blacks are of such and such a character and then apply it to their black peers; children learn that questions in school always have only one correct answer and fail to explore alternatives; and school systems define certain students as "culturally disadvantaged" and then turn out to set the stage so that only confirmatory evidence is marshaled. The more central, general, and consensual the acquired schemata, the more resistant they are to disproof. But the cultivation of ever more general and abstract schemata is what education is all about. The paradox has no simple solution. I will come back to it in Chapter 7.

Last, direct contact with specific events has a better chance of modifying specific schemata (one's expectations of a particular author, one's schema pertaining to botany, one's knowledge of a particular individual). Direct contact with specifics thus facilitates greater interdependence and reciprocity between schemata and events. It follows therefore that general, consensually held schemata ("TV is shallow," "School is a bore," "Whites think abstractly") can more easily lead to self-fulfilling or self-sustaining prophecies than specific schemata.

NOTES

1. That no schemata effects were found in Canada by Vidmar and Rokeach and none in the black sample studied by Brigham and Giesbrecht (1976) suggests that these groups may have employed other schemata than the American or white groups, but these schemata were not measured.

2. However, frequent exposure to events in a negative context, such as seeing a person a few times in a police lineup, results in negative affect (Perlman and Oskamp, 1970; cited by Saegert, Swap, and Zajonc, 1972).

3. There are, of course, claims that schools are not really designed for these purposes, but rather to serve as custodial bureaucracies. However, even if that is their ultimate function, planned instruction is not excluded.

Chapter 5
RICHNESS AND DEPTH IN COMMUNICATION

"That's a window, honey. There are no commercials there."

A message, as we have seen, can be any event to whose source an intent to communicate is attributed. Thus, any behavior or nonbehavior, object, event, or change in the environment, past or present, can be taken in principle as a message. Indeed, some people interpret climatic changes to be messages sent by some superhuman force, while others regard them as natural events of only informative value. Children often attribute communicational intents to objects into which they bump, and some adults treat other people's ways of dressing as messages. Some writers (such as Watzlawick et al., 1967) regard any change in the environment as informative (as opposed to redundant) and hence communicational. But stability (no change) also can and sometimes is considered communicational; this is particularly the case when change is anticipated but does not take place, as when the unchanging condition of a mental patient is understood by the therapist as a message of resistance communicated by the patient's psyche. We may thus say that the number of possible communicational sources is as large as the number and variety of events to which communicational intent can be attributed. In theory, although not in social practice, this number is endless.

There are two aspects to this richness of choice. One pertains to the many things that can be considered communicational messages and sources of communication. I borrow from Goodman (1968) the term *repleteness* to describe this aspect. Goodman used the term to characterize nonnotational symbol systems (others call them "analogic") such as paintings, photographs, and sketches in which every shade, hue, shape, line and color, can be considered meaningful. The term seems to apply to communication as well, since so many things—words, furniture, dress, facial expression, hand movement, pitch—can be seen as communicating something.

The second aspect, which complements repleteness, is *stacking*. It means that within a chosen communication event one can process the information more shallowly or go more deeply into an increasing number of message levels at will. The reader of a text can glance over it to get a feeling for its general gist, probe more deeply into the text to find a developing thread, or go even deeper to discover a hidden agenda, the writer's inner motives, and the like. (This applies not only to communicational events; events that are perceived as informative only can also be processed more or less deeply. But the latter are of lesser concern at present.)

How deeply one processes an act of communication depends on the guidance of one's anticipatory schemata. I am often amazed at how many levels of meaning some scholars find, for example, in advertisements. Thus, Packard (1957) attributed numerous sexual intentions and meanings to ads, while all I usually see in them are their surface features. Clearly Packard is guided by a different schema or a priori mental set than I am, choosing to invest more mental effort in processing ads than do most people.

Repleteness and stacking are *potential* characteristics of communicational events; their realization in any particular case depends on how much mental effort one expends in processing that communication. The handling of repleteness and of stacking thus becomes a matter of choice and skill. The realization of repleteness entails conflict among choices, and the resolution of this conflict demands certain skills in generating and carrying through an epistemic process (establishing, for example, what source of information is more valid for one's present purpose). At least this much skill is involved in the realization of stacking, as it entails the application of increasingly elaborate mental operations.

From a value-laden educational standpoint it would be desirable if youngsters (as well as adults) would address themselves to many alternative sources of information and choose among them with as little a priori bias as possible. It would also be desirable if youngsters would choose to process messages more deeply (albeit selectively), thereby obtaining more information, learning more, and becoming less susceptible to naive schemata changes. But as we shall see below, and because of the effort required by repleteness and stacking, often neither one is fully realized unless special tutoring is provided.

Making use of the potential varieties (repleteness) of communication requires experience and often training. Research done on children's comprehension of metaphors shows that young schoolchildren interpret them literally, sometimes inventing imaginary connections between topic and metaphoric vehicle (for example, "The prison guard had become a hard rock" is interpreted as part of a story in which a witch turns the guard into a rock). Only at age ten can the children make the leap from one domain of metaphor to another (Winner, Rosenstiel, and Gardner, 1976). A similar pattern is found with respect to style sensitivity in art. In the absence of training, only high school and college students can group paintings by style rather than by figurative content. But training makes even seven-year-olds succeed in grouping works of art by style (Gardner, 1972), suggesting that the ability to shift from a salient source to a new less salient source of information already exists at that age, but needs tutoring. (Prior to that age, no training helps.)

What makes the realization of repleteness so difficult is that often it can lead to the experience of at least two kinds of conflict. First there is the possibility of conflict between two or more events to which incompatible meanings are attributed. For example, a child may experience conflict when peers communicate that schoolwork is less important than some group activity, while the child receives opposing messages from parents. A more severe case involves paradoxes ("Be spontaneous!" "I want you to *want* to study") in which two parts of a message, equally logical, exclude each other (Watzlawick, Weakland, and Fisch, 1974). Second, conflict can be experienced when repleteness requires attending to mutually exclusive sources of information (for example, watching TV versus reading a book). Conflict is experienced here in spite of the fact that the meanings arrived at need not be mutually incompatible.

Because conflict between meanings within a message or between different messages is unpleasant, its resolution calls for epistemic behavior—an effortful process involving deeper processing, a more or less difficult solution. Alternatively, one can (and often does) avoid conflict from the outset by the a priori assignment of different weights to messages or sources or by establishing a division of labor between them.

The a priori assignment of different weights to messages or sources (clearly a matter of anticipatory schemata) involves biasing one's choice in favor of a particular class of messages or sources from the outset. We know, for example, that sources whose messages are more compatible with one's pet theories and beliefs, that demand less mental effort, or that offer more useful information when epistemically sought, are assigned greater weights. Similarly, sources that are socially perceived as more like real life, as having messages with greater social status, or as being more valid according to social definitions of reality, are given greater weight. Finally, we are finding that sources whose messages one feels more able to handle are preferred over other sources.

Sources and messages are not only weighted in advance; they are also used to serve different functions, and thus a division of labor among them is established. Schmuck and Van Egmond (1965) have found that teachers have a greater influence on children's attitudes toward school than parents do; parents seem to have a greater influence on children's choices of friends, but peers have a greater influence on relations among friends (Hartup, 1979). Similarly, children learn from their relationships with adults the meanings of dominance, support, and guidance (Whiting and Whiting, 1975; reported by Hartup, 1979). Children learn from their peer relations the meaning of mutual support and also that of aggression and competition (Hertz-Lazarowits et al., 1978). By choosing to rely on different sources for different kinds of information, advice, and support, children avert or minimize conflict.

The decision as to how much weight to give what class of messages or sources is guided by schemata. The same source can be taken as more or less valid, more or less demanding of effort, or more or less informative. No wonder, therefore, that a medium (such as film) can be perceived as serving different needs and offer different kinds of gratification in different places (Katz, Blumler, and Gurevitch, 1974).

This does not mean that weighing and dividing the labor are totally independent of what the messages and sources entail. According to Katz et al. (1974: 26),

> When people associate book-reading, for example, with a desire to know oneself, and newspapers, with the need to feel connected to the larger society, it is difficult to disentangle perceptions of the media from their intrinsic qualities. Is there anything about the book as a medium that breeds intimacy? Is there something about newspapers that explains their centrality in socio-political integration? Or, is this "something" simply an accepted image of the medium and its characteristic content?

The answer is rather simple once interdependence is considered. Sources are composed of different parts (TV carries other things besides "shallow" entertainment, for example), but we selectively anticipate certain parts that are distinctive to a source, often underweighing everything that is not within the selected parts. In this way, school comes to be considered as exclusively print-oriented, newspapers as mainly serving to link one to the wider society, and art museums as providing aesthetic experiences. Each of these sources also serves other functions, but they are often overlooked.

Once certain images (anticipatory schemata) are established, they come to affect not only the ways sources and messages are perceived but what they actually entail. Schools, possibly responding to their public image as the guardians of the print culture, are quick to relinquish any nonprint component (art education) when they are economically pressed. Similarly, TV networks increasingly emphasize those kinds of programs they think are better liked by the public, thereby further reinforcing schemata they helped to shape in the first place.

The realization, then, of potential repleteness in communication is frustrated by the need to avoid conflict between messages. The realization of stacking, while it need not entail conflict, is also difficult, although for other reasons. First, to process information deeply one needs to be epistemically guided by some purpose, question, or unsettled conflict. Such *search* (unlike *exploration*; see Wright and Vliestra, 1975) is a "top-down" process. When you study a painting "in depth" you are guided by some logic, not just random scanning. This is rather difficult for smaller children and effort consuming for adults. Second, probing deeply into a message is a skillful activity. When the skills have not yet been fully mastered, deeper processing becomes inhibitively difficult. For example, Samuels (1970) found that beginning readers got the names of familiar objects off the illustrations that accompany the printed words on flash cards rather than from the print itself, following the principle of least mental effort. Last, much depends on one's perceptions of the value that will result from deeply processing the material, given a certain task, situation, or message. If it requires much mental effort and if one is likely to employ the principle of least effort, then one is not likely to invest much effort *unless* one perceives the resulting value as justifying it. That perception is guided by schemata that anticipate a value from deeper epistemic processing. But unless one has already experienced deeper processing of particular kinds of messages, one is not driven to carry it out, unless tutored. Youngsters may be capable of processing TV programs more deeply, but they need to be shown how to do it and experience the epistemic outcomes of the process before they will actually engage in such a demanding activity (Dorr, Graves, and Phelps, 1980).

In sum, the world is replete with potential communications. However, many conflict with each other, requiring the epistemic process of weighing sources and assigning to them different functions. This process is guided by culturally determined and personal schemata, which are in turn affected by the events themselves. In addition, communications can be processed more or less deeply. That is one can invest more or less mental effort in processing them, depending on one's perception of the value to be gained. This I have called *stacking*. I have argued that both repleteness and stacking are potentialities, but their realization is often difficult and requires training.

In the following sections I discuss in greater detail the issues of repleteness and stacking as they pertain to learning, media, and interpersonal relations. Specifically, the sections on learning and media focus on the investment of mental effort in realizing the potential of deeper meaning and how this affects learning. The section on interpersonal relations deals with the interplay between the content and relational aspects of messages and how these affect the ways people get along with each other.

LEARNING: THE INVESTMENT OF MENTAL EFFORT

In Chapter 4 we saw that the acquisition of specific desirable knowledge is facilitated when the appropriate mental schemata are brought to the fore. But in addition, the learner has to actively process the information. Our common knowledge and daily observations tell us that the more one "concentrates" on the material—the more one thinks about it or elaborates on it—the better one's learning becomes.

Kane and Anderson (1978) have shown that subjects who were given sentences to complete remembered the sentences better than subjects who were given complete sentences. Craik and Tulving (1975: experiment 7) had subjects decide whether a word would more appropriately fit a blank in a simple or in a complex sentence (for example, "the *glove* is torn" versus "the small lady angrily picked up the red *glove*"). When tested for memory, subjects showed better recall of the words when they had made the effort to fit them into the complex sentences. Slamecka and Graf (1978) have found that people learn their own cognitive responses to a message better than they learn ready-made responses. Markus (1977) argued that schemata about oneself are better developed than other schemata, so information related to self and produced by self is more extensively processed and recalled. Rogers, Kuiper, and Kirker (1977) also found that relative to schemata pertaining to others, self-schemata are richer and better differentiated. Such schemata allow more elaborate processing.

One could interpret the latter findings to suggest that self-related thoughts are scarcer and therefore subjectively more valued (see Fromkin, 1973). But such an interpretation would not fully account for the Craik and Tulving or the Kane and Anderson findings where no self/other distinction was involved. Rather, it appears that the common denominator of all these (and numerous other) findings is the amount of mental effort invested in processing. We can generalize that richer and better differentiated schemata allow more elaboration and that learning improves as a function of more elaborate processing (also see Kintsch, 1977).

But what does "elaborate processing" mean and what determines it? Craik and Lockhart (1972) suggested that long-term learning depends on the mental recoding of material at deeper levels. If subjects attend only to the orthographic nature of words, for example, then they are processing them in shallower form than if the words are semantically processed for meaning. Craik and Lockhart's approach implies that processing proceeds from shallower surface levels to increasingly deeper semantic levels, leading to the conclusion that what a learner actually does with material is at least as important in learning as the material itself (see also Kane and Anderson, 1978; Hyde and Jenkins, 1969).

Unfortunately, attempts at using time as the measure by which to assess depth of processing (Craik and Tulving, 1975) have had disappointing results (Baddley, 1978). Even shallow processing may take a long time (proofreading, for example). Nor were clear correlations found between time of processing and learning outcomes (Carpenter, 1974).

Furthermore, one can question the implied progression of processing from surface to deep features. For one thing, even shallow surface features can be processed "in depth" (In what ways has somebody's face changed in the last 10 years?). For another, one can process deeper elements of a message without necessarily reaching them through the more observable ones (for example, one can generate far-reaching inferences from a painting without closely studying its visible features). Indeed, Craik and Tulving (1975) reached the conclusion that what really counts is the amount of material elaboration. Kintsch (1977) presented a similar idea, that the more one mentally elaborates material to be learned, the more contact is made with other mental schemata, thus leaving more memory traces and enriching the meanings arrived at.

Two implications seem to follow from Kintsch's idea. First, more elaborate processing or depth does not have to progress from surface to deep levels of the material. Each such level can be more or less elaborately processed. Second, amount of elaboration is not an adequate concept without at least one other element—non-automaticity of processes. One can perform many or few elaborations of the material more or less automatically. For example, experienced drivers are involved in much mental elaboration when driving, yet they are processing the material quite automatically. A new driver may perform the same number of elaborations but, being a novice, cannot yet carry them out automatically.

Automatic processes, by their very nature, are practically errorless, fast in execution, and immediate (LaBerge and Samuels, 1974). According to Schneider and Shiffrin (1977), once processes become automatic they are triggered by appropriate stimuli and operate independently of one's control. They create less stress (are less effortful) on one's mental capacity than so-called controlled processes. Being automatic, such mental elaborating does not bring the material into closer contact with other mental schemata and so leaves few memory traces, thereby failing to meet Kintsch's criterion. Indeed, while information that is peripherally perceived may be learned, it is being processed quite automatically, and learned less well than "central" information (Kintsch, 1977).

We are thus led to define the elusive concept of "depth" as *amount of invested mental effort* (AIME) in processing material, which itself seems to be composed of two elements: (1) the number of mental elaborations performed, and (2) the degree to which they are nonautomatic. Thus:

$$\text{AIME} = \text{No. of elaborations} \times \frac{1}{\text{automatically}}$$

It follows, for example, that beginning readers process simple printed material more deeply, that is, invest more mental effort in reading, than experienced readers. It also follows that one needs to invest less mental effort in understanding a book's gist than to find logical flaws in its arguments. In the case of the beginning and the experienced readers, the difference between them seems to be the degree to which each masters automatic reading skills. In the second example, the difference seems to lie primarily in the number of elaborations performed on the material.

Thus defined, AIME does not depend totally on stimulus properties (including "objective" message difficulty). Much depends on the skills one has in store as well as on the quality of their mastery. The outcomes of processing cannot therefore be judged as shallow or deep (entailing little or much AIME) without regard to one's prior knowledge and abilities. Furthermore, the extent to which available skills are actually brought to bear upon the material plays an important role. Even material that *should* call for greater AIME can be shallowly processed by people who, for some reason, perceive the material as not warranting it.

Langer, Blank, and Chanowitz (1978) suggested the possibility that when messages are perceived as highly familiar on the basis of structural or grammatical cues, they are responded to quite mindlessly. It is as if people recognize the message as something they have encountered numerous times in the past (such as a typical office memo), and it therefore invokes an overlearned schema. Once invoked, this schema suggests that "this time is just like the last," hence the processing of the specific semantics of the message can be relinquished. That is, Langer et al. (1978: 636) claim that

> attention is not paid precisely to those substantive elements that are relevant for the successful resolution of the situation. It has all the external earmarks of mindful action, but new information actually is not being processed. Instead, prior scripts [schemata], written when similar information was once new, are stereotypically re-enacted.

Thus, Langer et al. found that the same percentage of people (93 percent) will let an experimenter get ahead of them at a copier machine when asked "May I use the copier machine, because I have to make copies?" as when told "because I am in a rush"; they seem to assume that anyone who asks to get ahead of them is in a rush. Likewise, up to 90 percent will return an interoffice memo to a nonexistent office when it contains the sentence "I would appreciate it if you would return this paper immediately to room 238 through interoffice mail." They do not stop to think whether there is such a room or whether the memo makes any sense. Langer's subjects perceived the messages to require extremely little AIME; they behaved *mindlessly*.

We find, then, that AIME depends on what one perceives the stimulus material, situation, or task to require. The importance of perception of task requirements in learning is suggested by the Langer et al. (1978) study described above. It is also illustrated by a number of recent studies reviewed by Clark (1980) in which negative correlations between enjoyment and learning achievements were noted. It appears that high-ability students often choose well-structured instructional procedures and learn less from these than from procedures that put a heavier information-processing burden on them. Perceiving the better structured procedures as requiring less AIME, (and thus being more enjoyable), they invest less mental effort and acquire less information, even when these instructional procedures do call for more AIME. As Clark (1980: 6) points out:

> Students seem to enjoy investing less effort to achieve, and inaccurately assess the effect of investing less effort on their subsequent achievement. They appear to make judgments based on their perceived efficacy. They will report enjoying methods which appear to them to bring more achievement with less investment of time and work.

Perceiving task requirements involves schemata. Children anticipate TV to require less AIME than books; they also know whether a forthcoming exam will tap mainly shallow memory of facts or lean more heavily on inference-making. Usually I do not anticipate much information from, say, political speeches and hence perceive them as deserving only little AIME. But my perceptions would change, and so would my AIME, if I decided to (or were asked to) critique somebody's speech. In that case I would be likely to invest more mental effort in processing the speech material, possibly picking up previously undetected epistemic information.

Perception of task requirements influences not only the amount but the kind of mental effort invested. In a study (Salomon and Sieber, 1970), we showed some subjects a well-structured film and some a randomly structured film. Subjects were asked either to generate many alternative plot lines or to report as many details as possible. The worst performances were by the subjects in the group shown the confusing, randomly structured film and then asked to remember details, and the subjects in the group shown the well-structured film and asked to generate alternative plot lines. Subjects in both groups appeared to have perceived the situation's task requirements in light of what the film entailed: The first group saw a need to resolve the uncertainty aroused by the random mixture of segments, the second perceived a simple film demanding little AIME. Such perceptions of the situation's requirements did not match the instructor's requirements and yielded poor performance. Subjects in the randomly structured version invested AIME in resolving the nature of the plot line but none in noting details, while those in the well-structured version invested hardly any mental effort in processing the simple plot line, and hence could not come up with alternative plots. These findings suggest that achievement of specific learning outcomes is a function not only of the *amount* of mental effort invested but also of the match between the *kind* of mental effort one invests and that which instruction requires. If the learner seeks an understanding of the plot line where recall of details is required, the match will not be close and the teacher-required learning will be hampered.

What determines the perception of task requirements? Schemata theory can help us here. The specific nature of the message has some influence (see Chapters 3 and 4). In addition, past experiences with similar messages and anticipations of future experiences with them play an important role. Related to these experiences is one's *perceived self-efficacy* (Bandura, 1977a, 1977b, 1978) regarding one's ability to process and learn particular kinds of information deeply. What one believes one can do is based on past experiences with messages of particular characteristics. Perceived self-efficacy is one's belief in one's ability to perform certain activities, for example, learning advanced statistics, piano playing, or horseback riding. Bandura found that the greater people's perceived self-efficacy, the more they are willing to invest sustained effort in a task and overcome difficulties.

Only recently have we begun to study how perceived self-efficacy relates to the perception of task requirements in a communicational situation and how this relates to AIME. In one unpublished study carried out in California, we found that sixth graders' perceived self-efficacy in learning from TV[1] correlated negatively (−.49) with subsequent self-reports of AIME in learning from a TV story. In other words, the more efficacious the children felt, the less mental effort they invested in processing the presented information. Moreover, we found that those who felt more efficacious and reported less AIME also learned significantly less from the program. Correlations between AIME and learning from the TV program ranged between .64 and .67.

Such findings do not agree well with those reported by Bandura (particularly Bandura, 1977b). He found higher self-efficacy underlying the investment of more effort, with a greater tendency to overcome difficulties; people give up easily when encountering tasks about which they feel inefficacious. Why should we then find perceived self-efficacy to correlate negatively with AIME and actually to lead to less learning? Apparently, the relationship is a curvilinear one. (The hypothetical relationship is shown in Figure 5.1).

People with a very poor perception of self-efficacy (for example, the phobics that Bandura studied) do not really invest any effort in a task which they are sure is far beyond them. As their perceived efficacy increases, a result of accumulating positive experiences, so does their AIME. If students who are sure they will fail are forced to hand in all assignments, they begin to be successful and experience increased self-efficacy. But this relationship exists only up to a certain point; beyond that, people relinquish the investment of effort, as they are sure the messages or tasks are familiar and easy (recall Langer's findings concerning "mindlessness"). Thus, for example, one is likely to perceive in advance a Walt Disney movie as "easily understood" and forgo any deeper processing of its messages. As it turns out, while Bandura's subjects who began with very low perceived efficacy were on the lower end of the efficacy continuum, our schoolchildren were on the higher end of it. For this reason, Bandura found positive relations between efficacy and effort while we found negative ones.

We may then say that perception of task requirements is strongly related to one's perception of self-efficacy in handling certain types of messages. People who think they are poor at analyzing abstract paintings "in depth" are likely to define the

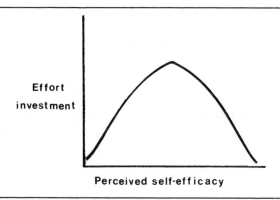

Figure 5.1   Hypothesized Relation of Effort to Perceived Self-Efficacy

situation of looking at an abstract painting as requiring more of them than they can deliver and are likely not to try. Others who consider themselves moderately efficacious might define the situation as requiring mental effort that will yield some value and so may invest more effort in processing the art. And people who "have seen it all" and feel very efficacious might feel, "when you've seen one, you've seen them all" and forego any further investment of effort in processing. The relatively high correlations we found between efficacy and AIME in the study reported above lend support to these hypotheses, particularly when considered together with Bandura's numerous studies on this topic.

In sum, in this section I have considered how stacking relates to learning. Learning is a function of the amount of invested mental effort (AIME) involved in processing the material. The AIME is defined as the number of nonautomatic elaborations performed on the material. The AIME and its specific nature depends on what one perceives as the requirements of the task, situation, or message. Such perceptions are influenced by three related facts: (1) the nature of the encountered message event, (2) one's past experience with and anticipations of future experiences with such an event, and (3) one's perceived self-efficacy in processing such an event "in depth."

An important implication follows. If learning depends on the realization of stacking, (that is, on more AIME), and if AIME depends on perception of task requirements, which in turn is influenced by past experiences and on learners' perceived self-efficacy, then it becomes critical to provide learners with experiences that change their perceptions of certain stimuli and increase their AIME. It stands to reason that as learners acquire the skills needed for deeper processing and learning that the actual application of these skills yields more and more worthwhile information even from sources otherwise perceived as shallow, they will use more AIME on subsequent occasions and thereby learn more from these sources.

The educational issue involved is not just whether material to be learned is deeper, (as even potentially deep material can be handled with little AIME), but whether learners learn to handle material with greater AIME. Clearly, the effort they invest in realizing stacking depends on their anticipatory schemata (perception of task requirements and of self-efficacy), which in turn depend on the value that past investments of mental effort have yielded. As I show in the following section, tutoring in this direction may actually change learners' schemata and improve their selective realization of stacking.

MEDIA: PROCESSING COMMUNICATION IN DEPTH

If people "mindlessly" process office memos because they look so familiar and undemanding (Langer et al., 1978), do they treat other familiar media programs, or media contexts in a similar way? Could it be that for whatever reason, different amounts of stacking are realized in different media, leading to better learning from some than from others?

This question was raised by Singer (1980) concerning the difference between televiewing and reading. Differences were attributed by Singer to the media themselves, that is, to their essential symbol systems (language versus pictures). Singer's argument is that TV is a "crowded" medium which does not permit the transferring of the presented content from short-term to long-term memory. It apparently addresses itself to the right brain hemisphere, and allows only global, "holistic" recognition but no deeper analyses. Further, he claims the understanding of, say, a story requires the generation of imagery, but TV offers a substitute for the active practice of one's own imagery; thus, it stimulates images but does not allow for their generation. In short, for reasons of pace and pictoriality, TV's contents cannot be subjected to much mental elaboration.

Unlike TV, print material, Singer argues, requires readers to draw upon their own memories and fantasies, to invest time in following the drift of a writer, and to conjure up images, a process that requires much effort. Thus, reading may demand more effort or skill for most people, not only in manipulating vocabulary but in producing the necessary private imagery that makes the reading experience so valuable. Some brain research conducted on individuals by Krugman (1976) lends limited empirical support to Singer's arguments.

Hornik (1978) conducted a study in El Salvador in which he followed in a controlled way the effects of introducing television. Although he found television watching had no effect on specific achievement, he did find that it negatively affected more general abilities, including reading. Hornik's data (1978: 14) suggest that the decline in general abilities was caused by a "displacement of attention from more intellectually stimulating activities (reading, interacting with other people and with one's immediate environment) to the watching of intellectually undemanding television programming."

Meringoff (1980) arranged for a story to be read out of an illustrated book to some children and to be shown through animation on TV to other children ages 6 to 8 and 9 to 10. She found that exposure to the TV story was associated more than exposure to the illustrated book with use of visual information in recall and in making inferences. In the book group a complementary difference was found: the children preferred to rely on textual information. Most importantly, though, Meringoff found that the children in the book group based their inferences on their own past experience and general knowledge more often than children in the TV group did. The latter based their inferences more on the visually presented material. If we are to use Kintsch's (1977) criterion, then we can conclude that the book group in Meringoff's study invested more mental effort in generating inferences than the TV group. This seems to lend at least partial support for Singer's claims.

But do such findings suggest that TV, due to its very nature, does not allow (even inhibits) deeper processing? Does it also follow that print requires greater AIME? As we shall see below, the answer is mixed.

Cohen and I (1979) compared the amount of televiewing of 218 Israeli and 160 American fourth and sixth graders.[2] Rather than relying only on self-reported amounts of televiewing, we measured on three occasions children's cued recognition of every 15 minutes of the previous day's programs ("literate viewing"). The multiple choice questions were sufficiently simple that correct answers did not correlate with children's intelligence, socioeconomic status, or school grades. We expected the American children, given the eight channels of color TV in the United States, to receive higher literate viewing scores. After all, that is what personal impressions, popular complaints, and a vast literature suggest. In comparison, Israel at the time had only one noncommercial black and white channel, broadcasting only a few hours every night. But to our surprise we found the exact opposite: Israeli children, particularly fourth graders, received significantly higher literate viewing scores than their American peers. No statistical analyses (controlling for SES, ability, questionnaire differences) washed the difference out. Nor could such differences be accounted for by programing differences, as such hardly existed.

Puzzled, we considered a new idea: Could it be that children in different milieus, and for whatever reason, treat TV differently? Could it be that the Israeli children in our sample took TV more seriously than their American counterparts? While we had no direct evidence to answer the question, we nevertheless found some indirect evidence that at least made the possibility plausible. First, the mothers of the Israeli children had significantly more positive attitudes toward the medium than the American mothers. Second, far more televiewing was done in Israel in the company of significant others, while 39 percent of our American sample had three or more TV sets at home. And as we know from other research (Ball and Bogatz, 1970; Salomon, 1977), the presence of mothers while televiewing changes the context and makes children learn more.

For these and possibly additional reasons, it stands to reason that more mental effort was invested by Israeli children in televiewing, and this may account for their higher literate viewing scores. Indeed, the mastery of specific mental skills was found to be more highly correlated with televiewing in the Israeli sample than in the American one, suggesting that the Israeli children's AIME was greater and that TV's effects on them were greater also.

Such differences cannot be attributed solely to the amount of mental effort required by the medium. With the exception of commercials (absent on Israeli TV), American and Israeli television are quite similar. It seems likely, then, that television allows more choice of depth than we usually think. In other words, the investment of effort in TV seems to depend, in part, on the way one perceives the medium. It may be the case, as Singer (1980) points out, that a certain minimum AIME is required if one is to get any pleasurable information from print media. There is little to be enjoyed in a single word or sentence (whereas on TV you can enjoy a face, a chase, or a setting without processing the whole story). This minimum required by print may be higher than the one required by televiewing, given the differences between their dominant symbol systems. Thus, the "floor" of the AIME required by both media may differ. But this does not mean that we cannot invest more mental effort in televiewing if we so desire. Moreover, given a "ceiling" of mental effort and assuming it is the same for both media, TV should provide more choice of AIME than reading. Such a choice could range from simple recognition of discrete events and characters to deeper processing of plot, relating motives to causes and consequences, and the like. But the size of AIME beyond the required minimum is not determined by the medium. Rather, it should depend on one's skills, one's perception of the requirements for watching television enjoyably and profitably, and one's perceived self-efficacy in meeting those requirements.

Recently some students and I carried out the first in a series of studies to test the hypothesis that the investment of more or less mental effort in media is related to people's anticipatory schemata, and is not just a reaction to the inherent attributes of the media. More specifically, we wanted to know, first, whether schoolchildren tend to invest more mental effort in a printed text than in a TV program of essentially the same content. Second, we wanted to know whether differential amounts of AIME led to corresponding differences in learning. Third, we wanted to know how the investment of mental effort in print and TV related to children's perceived self-efficacy and to their perception of a medium's "realism" (how "true" or contrived its messages are). We included perceived realism because we had reason to believe that the perception of close resemblance to real life is associated with the expectation that little effort is needed. If TV is perceived as lifelike, then its messages are intended to convey information, not to change the viewer, and as we have seen already (Chapter 2), such an attribution implies less effort at interpreting the message.

The study, carried out in the San Francisco Bay Area, involved 124 sixth graders of one school. All children were pretested with a test of perceived self-efficacy (from Bandura, 1977b) in which we asked them how effective they felt at learning about numerous topics from TV and from a book (for example, "How easy would it be for you to learn how to solve math problems/how to build a model/to know the biography of . . ." and the like). There were ten such items covering a wide range of topics, all of which are seen or could conceivably be seen on TV and could be printed in a book. We also measured children's perceptions of the realism of books and TV and asked them to identify reasons why one might succeed or fail in learning from both books and TV. The children were then randomly divided into two groups. The TV group was shown the Canadian film *A Day of a Painter,* a funny, though subtle, comment on how abstract art is produced. The text group received a booklet that presented in print the story of the film. Three graduate students who did not know our hypotheses saw to it that the content of both versions was an identical in gist and story grammar as possible. After the children saw the film or read the text, they were given a brief questionnaire to measure self-reported AIME.[3] Four questions asked how hard the children tried to understand the story, how much they concentrated, how hard they thought their peers tried, and how hard the story was to understand. Since intercorrelations among the answers to the four questions were high, a single score of self-reported AIME could be given.

Results were revealing (see Table 1). Children's perceived self-efficacy for learning from TV significantly exceeded that from books. The correlations between the two were low and on some items tended to be negative. Thus, it seems children express more efficacy in learning from TV than from books, while the efficacy pertaining to the two media are generally unrelated. (As general ability measures were not taken it was impossible to examine the possibility that efficacy with TV correlates negatively with book efficacy in the low-ability group.)

As can be seen in Table 1, the TV group reported the investment of significantly less mental effort than the book group in understanding the story. More TV group members reported the program to be "easy stuff," and more book children reported the text to be "difficult." Intuitively, this should have led to better achievement by the TV group. But this was not the case. It was the book group that achieved significantly higher scores.

It may be that the book group had an advantage over the TV group because it needed to employ fewer mental transformations (Salomon, 1979), since both the material and the achievement test were in written form. While plausible, this possibility is not very convincing, since achievement correlated rather

TABLE 5.1   Selected Means and Correlations for the Two Groups

	TV Group (n=63)				Book Group (n=61)			
	Efficacy	Realism	AIME	Ach.	Efficacy	Realism	AIME	Ach.
Means	38.40[a]	3.25[a]	1.85[a]	5.60[a]	29.12[b]	1.96[b]	2.42[b]	7.45[b]
Correlations: Efficacy	−−	.36*	−.49**	−.34*	−−	.32*	.37**	.52**
Realism		−−	−.28*	−.14		−−	−.31*	−.09
AIME			−−	.67**			−−	.64**

Notes: *p<.05; **p<.01;

Corresponding means (AIME scores in the two groups) with different superscripts are significantly different from each other (p<.05).

highly with both perceived self-efficacy and self-reported AIME, consistent with expectations. In the book group, efficacy correlated .37 with AIME and .52 with achievement. AIME correlated .64 with achievement. Thus in the book group those who felt more efficacious tended to invest more mental effort in reading the text, and those who invested more effort also learned more. Such consistent relations are very much in line with Bandura's (1977) formulations.

The TV group, on the other hand, displayed a different pattern. It will be recalled that its mean efficacy score was higher than that of the book group. This relatively high efficacy correlated negatively with reported AIME (−.49), and with achievement (−.34), while AIME and achievement intercorrelated .67, similar to the correlation in the book group. It appears that children in the TV group who felt highly efficacious in learning from TV tended to invest less mental effort in the program (relative "mindlessness"?) and thus learned less from it.

In addition, it is interesting to note that more "realism" was attributed to TV than to books, and this attributed realism correlated positively (.32 to .36) with perceived efficacy but negatively (−.28 to −.31) with AIME. In other words, messages that were perceived as more lifelike and less contrived were perceived to be "easier" and to demand somewhat less mental effort.

Finally, significantly more children attributed failure to learn from books to external causes ("Books are difficult"), and failure to learn from TV to internal ones ("They aren't smart"). The converse was the case with the attribution of success: More children attributed success in learning from books to internal causes ("They're smart") and success in learning from TV to external ones ("It's easy stuff"). These findings suggest that TV is perceived to be an easy medium ("You must be dumb not to understand TV") and books a hard one ("You're smart if you understand books").

The results of this study suggest that children's expectations about the medium's demands and their beliefs about their own efficacy make them invest more or less mental effort in processing the content. Differential investment of effort in turn influences how much learning takes place. The greater attribution of "realism" to TV serves as a possible and partial explanation of the observed differences. If TV, apparently due to its pictoriality, is perceived as more lifelike, it is taken to require less mental effort (see also the section in Chapter 6 on media).

The findings of the study just reported do not refute Singer's (1980) general argument that AIME differences between TV and print are due to symbol system differences. But the results show that aside from what is medium determined, one's perception of the effort required to process a media communication has an effect on AIME. One could argue that perceptions and attributions simply reflect the true nature of the media: that TV inhibits deeper processing and this fact is correctly reflected in children's attribution, while print requires more AIME and is perceived accordingly. But while children's perceptions and attributions may reflect the real demands and characteristics of the different media (the media cultivate, if you wish, certain anticipatory schemata), they apply these schemata to new material even when this is inappropriate. By treating the film *A Day of a Painter* as a typical, and thus easy-to-master, TV specimen, the children in our study relinquished the investment of more mental effort in it and hence learned less from it.

But this did not have to be the case. Assume we told the children that a test on the film was to be given, thereby changing their perception of the task's requirements. It is reasonable to expect that they would have felt less efficacious in "easily" succeeding on the test, would have invested more mental effort in viewing the film, and would have scored higher on the test than the TV subjects in our study actually did. In other words, the hypothesis is that stacking or processing in depth is not just a direct function of what the media actually require and inhibit but also of what one *thinks* they require and inhibit.

Once such perceptions have been learned from encounters with media, they guide us in our differential investment of mental effort. By treating a medium such as TV shallowly, that is, by relinquishing the investment of much mental effort in its messages, we obtain only little and stereotypic information from it and thus "prove" the shallowness of the medium, even when we could experience more depth in it if we chose to.

Moreover, it can be hypothesized that the depth people anticipate in a medium influences their selection of messages from it. Hence when people treat TV as a shallow medium (Furu, 1971, found that Japanese fourth graders felt guilty about watching TV), they learn to disregard its potentially more demanding contents and so further reinforce their anticipatory schemata. The circle is thus closed.

Thus far I have argued that different media, due to the nature of their inherent symbol systems, require the investment of different minimum amounts of mental effort to obtain pleasurable information. However, AIME expended beyond that minimum is determined not by the medium, but by anticipatory schemata. The schemata, rather than the medium, determine how deeply messages can be processed beyond the necessary minimum. Two classes of schemata appear to be involved here. One pertains to the specific content that is presented; the other—a more general kind of schema—pertains to the medium in general. The same division appears in connection with reading. Butkowsky and Willows (1980) found that poor readers, while no less intelligent than average or good readers, expressed helplessness with regard to reading and blamed themselves for failure in reading. They were also less persistent in reading and invested less effort in overcoming difficulties. Evidently they were guided by far more general schemata than the ones that pertain to the specific content of what they read.

If such general schemata guide the amount of mental effort invested, then a change in the schemata should lead to a corresponding change in AIME. Such a change could be temporarily achieved by changing the perception of the immediate context by a co-observing mother, by changing the perception of the task ("There will be an exam"), and the like. The change could, however, also be a more lasting one if it involved one's general schemata. Moreover, if one were to learn to perceive a medium differently, and thereby to invest more mental effort in its messages, one would also have to experience through practice the worth of deeper processing and thus experience a more appropriate level of perceived self-efficacy.

Corder-Bolz and O'Bryant (1978) had a kindergarten teacher co-observe a thirty-minute TV program with pairs of children and either elaborate upon the televised content or offer general and unrelated comments. The children in the "intervention group" acquired more knowledge from the program than the children in the nonintervention group. They also displayed their newly acquired knowledge a week later, thus retaining their advantage over the untutored group. To the extent that better learning is a function of AIME, the tutored children can be said to have invested more mental effort in processing the program. But whether they learned anything beyond the program's content, such as how to learn more from TV, and whether they were likely to apply such knowledge in other televiewing situations is unknown.

Prasad, Rao, and Sheikh (1978) taught the mothers of 8 to 10 year old boys to volunteer information that countered a toy commercial either by "reasoning" or by "power-assertiveness."

Control children received no counter-information. The children's purchasing behavior in a simulated store was subsequently measured. Again, indirect evidence suggested that both types of counterinformation increased children's mental effort investment in processing the information, as judged by the longer time the experimental children needed to make their "purchase" decisions. (Interestingly enough, the "reasoning" treatment reduced the percentage of children who bought the advertised toy in comparison to the percentage of control children. But the "power-assertiveness" treatment increased that percentage dramatically, offering additional evidence for the distinction I made in Chapter 2 between messages with the perceived intent to convey and those with the perceived intent to change.) As in the study by Corder-Bolz and O'Bryant (1978) it is unknown whether the children learned anything that was transferable to other encounters with TV ads.

Dorr, Graves, and Phelps (1980) attempted to teach children about TV and thereby modify their more general TV-related schemata. They designed two TV curricula, which they taught to kindergarten and second and third grade children. One curriculum focused on the realism children attribute to TV and attempted to decrease it. It emphasized such issues as TV's nonrealism as well as the economic motives behind the TV industry. The second curriculum was designed to teach children TV processes, but mainly how to compare TV messages with other sources of information. Posttreatment measures showed that the children learned the contents of the curricula to which they were exposed. Learning about TV production and economics helped children to discard wrong information they apparently had before the classes, while the "process curriculum" successfully taught the children about sources for evaluating the realism of TV. More importantly, though, when children's reactions to a transfer situation (an episode of *The Jeffersons*) were measured, indications were found of carryover effects. That is, children's judgments concerning the reality of the program showed treatment effects as compared with a control group. But when measures of racial attitude change were taken, mixed and nonsignificant differences emerged. Thus, Dorr, Graves, and Phelps (1980: 80) concluded that

> young children can clearly, in as short a time as six hours [of training] learn much about television and about how and where to seek alternative sources of information. Moreover, they can apply the acquired information when asked to reason about the reality of television content. They do not become junior sophisticates, but they improve markedly.

The three studies just described provide evidence for two arguments. First, the studies of Prasad et al. (1978) and of Colder-Bolz and O'Bryant (1978) show that children's AIME in TV messages can be temporarily increased through guidance and tutoring, suggesting that TV, while requiring little AIME yields more information when more mental effort is invested. The study by Dorr, Graves, and Phelps (1980) shows that children's more general perceptions (schemata) of TV's demands and offerings can be changed, thereby possibly laying the foundations for a more lasting change in the AIME they selectively expend on TV. Unfortunately, no direct measures of AIME, efficacy, or perceived task requirements, were taken and we can only guess, at present, that these were changed.

It seems, then, that the realization of stacking in media messages apparently is greater in some media than in others. Some are shallowly dealt with and are therefore perceived as shallow media. Tutoring suggests that this shallowness is not an inherent nature of the media, since children can learn to get more from them. Still, more studies of the Dorr, Graves, and Phelps type need to be done to provide more evidence for the plausibility of this approach.

INTERPERSONAL RELATIONS:
THE TWO ASPECTS OF HUMAN CONTACT

Whatever has been said in the preceding sections about increasing stacking through greater AIME also applies to interpersonal contacts. This section, however, is devoted to the issue of repleteness, because it plays such a central role in the development and maintenance of interpersonal contacts. The nature of such contacts heavily depends on how many potential sources of communication are recognized as conveying messages. For example, the nature of interdependence developing between me and a student of mine will depend on whether we perceive messages only in what each of us says or also in what each of us expresses nonverbally, possibly including dress, facial expressions, spatial proximity, even the tidiness of my office.

One way to examine repleteness in interpersonal relations is through the interesting distinction between two aspects of communication proposed by Watzlawick, Beavin, and Jackson (1967), following Gregory Bateson's earlier work. One is the *content* (or "report") aspect, typically carried out by words that have agreed-upon denotations in a specific field of reference ("This chair is broken"; or, "You weren't too successful on the last exam"). The other is the *relational* (or "command") aspect that pertains to the nature of the relationships among the interactants ("I was just joking"; or, "This is a warning!" implying an asymmetrical nonfriendly relationship). The relational aspect, as Watzlawick et al. maintain, provides information about the information in the message event; thus it is a *metamessage*, putting the content into a context.

More often than not, the relational aspect of a communication is carried by nonverbal means (a frowning face, a smile, close proximity in a conversation), in which case it can be easily separated, relatively speaking, from the communications content. For example, the psychiatrist who sits above and behind the patient on the couch establishes a particular kind of relationship that provides a context for their conversation. So does the teacher standing in front of her classroom and the principal seated behind a heavy desk. In all these cases the relational aspect, although not independent of the content aspect, can still be separated from it. Such separation becomes even more easily observed when there is a mismatch between the two: a lover who yells "I love you" into the ear of his deafened sweetheart, or the drill sergeant who whispers in a begging voice the order "attention!"

But there are other occasions in which the separation is more delicate, mainly because the relational aspect is not carried by any observable separate means. For example, parents may tell their child "You're still just a child" and that the child should behave accordingly. Since the child knows this all too well, there is hardly any novel content in that message. There is for the child only a relational aspect to the message (a demeaning one at that), disguised as denotational content. One can easily think of the kind of interaction that may now develop between child and parents. The child is likely to respond with some resistance to the relationship read into the message, while the parents are likely to see nothing wrong with their statement of a factually correct content and may even expand on it to show *how* correct it is.

Content aspects of messages are usually more conventionalized than relational ones and follow better known and stricter rules of semantics and syntax. Words allow the generation of new combinations of "characters" into sequences (words and sentences), and the meaning of each can be gauged against a public, shared understanding of meaning via dictionaries, grammar books, and the like. This is quite impossible with nonverbal elements. You cannot really make an elaborate statement by combining in any grammatically accepted way a frown, high voice pitch, and arm raising, followed by a lowered voice and eyeblink. Nonverbal elements can denote or depict, but mainly they *express* in a variety of ways, and their meaning cannot easily be judged by correspondence to a referent (do tears express joy? sorrow? frustration?). For this reason the relational, usually nonverbal, aspects of communication are far more difficult to express explicitly than the content aspects (see Watzlawick, 1978; Zajonc, 1980).

We could draw an analogy between the relational and content aspects of messages and oral and text manifestations of language:

> Oral language is a flexible, unspecialized, all-purpose instrument with a low degree of conventionalization in which the meanings of sentences must be negotiated in terms of the social relations, the

content and the prior world knowledge of the participants [Olson, 1977: 10].

On the other hand,

> Written language, by virtue of its demands for explicitness of meaning, its permanence as a visible artifact compatible with repeated scrutiny and reflection, and its realignment of social and logical functions, serves the intellect in several ways. It is an essential means for the abstract true statements that constitute objective knowledge; it is critical to the particular mental achievements we designate as conceptual intelligence; and it is a predominant instrument of formal schooling [Olson, 1977: 11].

The analogy between the relational aspect of communication and oral language and between the content aspect and written language becomes quite clear. It highlights the greater difficulty in explicitly handling the former. For example, I cannot easily ask a student of mine if in her behavior she wishes to express disinterest in our conversation, as she is likely to deny it and may even suggest that I am projecting my own feelings onto her.

Some research findings could be interpreted as reflecting the difficulty in handling relational aspects in educational settings. It has been found that boys display more disruptive and undisciplined behaviors in school than girls (Duke, 1978). But we also know that girls' disruptiveness is more verbal whereas that of boys is more behavioral (Maccoby, 1966). Verbal disruption is usually perceived as less damaging (Brophy and Good, 1974), possibly because it can be handled more easily. Behavioral disruption is more expressive than denotative, and as we shall see below, the behaving person is less aware of what is really being expressed.

The differences between the relational and content aspects of messages and between the symbol systems that carry them lead to yet another difference. The two classes map upon, relate to, or simply represent different fields of reference. Thus, as Watzlawick et al. (1967) and Zajonc (1980) point out, translation from one system to another is difficult and, when attempted, often frustrating and ridiculous. When relations are expressed solely by words (assume no softness or hardness of voice, no stress, no change in pitch), they leave one with the feeling that the most important thing has been totally left out.

It is for these and similar reasons that Von Bertalanffy (1965: 41) stated that

> if the meaning of Goethe's *Faust,* of Van Gogh's landscapes, or Bach's *Art of the Fugue* could be transmitted in discursive terms, their authors should and would not have bothered to write poems, paint, or compose, but would rather have written scientific treatises.

The same, in even stronger terms, could be applied to interpersonal contacts. If we would express our mutual relations in words we would not bother to hold hands, frown, maintain eye contact, change voice pitch, and the like.

Recent research suggests important correlates of the repleteness of communication in human interaction. Lord (1980) studied in two experiments the possibility that self-schemata (schemata that people hold about themselves), though richer than schemata pertaining to others, entail mainly propositional, verbally or semantically coded information; the schemata people have concerning others are more imagery based. In other words, we think about ourselves in terms of verbal propositions and about others in images. Lord found empirical support for this possibility. In line with schemata theory, Lord assumed that people are better able to remember new information that fits more easily into preexisting schemata. He found that people showed better recall of specific trait adjectives when they had to decide whether the adjectives described themselves rather than others. In a second experiment he showed that people who were asked to generate images on the basis of given nouns involving either themselves or somebody else (father, Walter Cronkite) showed better memory of images involving others than themselves. And while self-images turned out to be more vivid, they were usually less salient and less active than the images of others.

Lord's findings can be interpreted on the basis of a point made by Jones and Nisbett (1971), namely that we have more opportunity to see others than ourselves, thus use in our cognitions more images of others than of ourselves. Self-schemata summarize much experiential information across a wide range of situations and dimensions in abstracted and well differentiated ways. But these schemata are not based on perceptual data, as are the schemata about others. The latter are more gestalt-like, impressionistic, and nonverbal, involve fewer dimensions, and are less differentiated. People were more likely to answer "it depends on the situation" when asked if a trait described themselves than when they were asked if it described their fathers (Nisbett et al., 1973).

Being able to interact with others and obtain perceptual data about them leads, then, to the imagery basis for the schemata we hold about others and may make us more aware of the relational aspects involved in the messages of others. Indeed, there is evidence to show (Watzlawick, 1978) that we are more aware, even more sensitive, to the relational aspects in other people's messages than to those in our own.[4] I may be quite unaware of the nonverbal cues I give while teaching, but my students are quite sensitive to such cues and attribute to them communicational, relational meanings. The converse is the case with respect to the students' messages. I see facial expressions and hand movement and I hear voice inflections and changes of pitch to which I attribute relational meanings, but my students are not much aware of what their nonverbal behaviors are expressing.

This low self-awareness is highly consistent with Lord's findings. People are bound to have great difficulty in recognizing what nonverbal relational cues they are claimed to emit if their self-schemata are mainly propositional. "You know," I am often told by my American colleagues, "you communicate in your tone of voice much hostility." This indeed may be the case, and I am inclined to believe them, but I am not really aware of this behavior of mine. I also know that I do not intend to communicate any hostility or one-upmanship, but this is beside the point, as others attribute such an intent to me on the basis of what they read into my tone of voice.

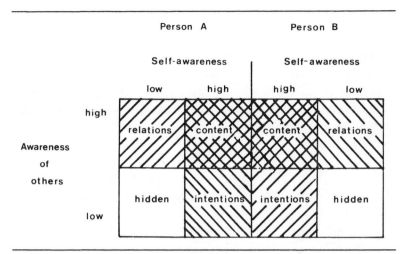

Figure 5.2   What Persons A and B Are Aware of When They Meet

It is for this reason that self-viewing on videotape or film is so helpful in teacher training and therapy (see Salomon and McDonald, 1970; Walz and Johnston, 1963), as it may be the first time that trainees and patients come to see themselves as others usually see them, and thus to apply to themselves standards they usually apply to others (Nielsen, 1962).

An interesting image of interpersonal contacts emerges on the basis of the above. People are more aware, sensitive, and responsive to the relational aspects in the messages of others and less aware of the relational aspects in their own messages. Yet people are more knowledgeable of their own communicational intents than of the intents of others. The latter they attribute on the basis of past experience, expectations, and ambiguous cues. The image that emerges can best be shown in graphic form, based in part on the well-known "Joe-Harry Windows" (Figure 5.2). Let us divide each person's awareness of two personal communicational aspects into a high and low region, and use the same division for awareness of the two aspects in another person's messages. Having created a 2 x 2 matrix, we can now identify four cells: One cell represents the cases in which persons are aware of both themselves and of others. Specifically, this is the cell where people know what they are saying and what the others say in an interaction. The *content* component of their messages fits in here best. The second cell represents the case in which people are not much aware of their role in the communicational exchange but are aware of the role played by the others. That is where the *relational* component of messages fits in. The third cell represents the case of great self-awareness but little knowledge of the others; that is where *intentions* fit in. (The fourth cell in each matrix represents the case where neither person is aware. It thus is a mutually hidden area of no concern to us in this context.)

Now persons A and B come into contact. Person A is aware of and addresses the content and relational aspects of B's behavior and generates attributions about B's intentions, but A is unaware of personal relational cues (of which B is of course quite aware). B behaves like A; thus, as can be seen in Figure 5.2, the two matrices show mutual awareness in only one of the four cells (the darkly shaded area) and leave room for much misunderstanding that results from one-sided awareness in the other two cells of interest.

Why misunderstanding? First, because each person makes self-generated attributions about the other's intentions and proceeds to interact with the other on such a basis without necessarily checking the attributions of the other (as is the case with those who attribute to me hostile intentions which I *know* I do not entertain). Second, each person responds to both content and relational aspects of the other's messages without the other being fully aware of the messages to which the first person is responding. Thus one of two things often develops. In some cases an argument develops in which the content of each person's message is debated, while in effect the disagreement pertains to the relations between the two. This can be called a *dispute on a marginal level,* as both sides are disputing something other (but more easily dealt with) than what is really in dispute:

Student: "I *really* don't know what I should do after graduation. Perhaps go into business or industry." (This old uncle of mine is so out of touch with me.)

Uncle: "Computers! That's where the future is. Go there young man! Where's the phone? Two phone calls and it's all arranged." (Finally I can show my nephew how powerful I am.)

Student: "Actually, I don't think this is good for me. Perhaps I'd better continue with graduate school. Never mind, forget it." (I won't let him control my life.)

Uncle: "What's wrong with computers?"

Student: (It's not the computers, it's *you*.) "I hate numbers . . ."

In other cases the two sides feel that the relational aspects of their contacts are unsatisfactory, but when each of them confronts the other with a verbal account of the latter's unpleasant relational cues ("Don't speak to me this way!"), the other is likely either to deny speaking that way or to say that even assuming this mode of speech *was* used, nothing was intended by it. This can be called a *self-sustaining dispute,* as the more the two confront each other with verbal reports of what is hidden to either one of them, the more there is to be disputed:

Teacher: "You're not listening to me." (She disregards me.)

Student: "I *am* listening to you!!" (What on earth does she want of me? She's putting me down.)

Teacher: "Don't speak to me this way." (She's disrespectful and communicates this to me.)

Student: "O.K., What do you want of me?" (Let's get out of this trap; I hate the way she speaks to me.)

Teacher: "First I want you to *listen,* and listen *well!*"

Student: "O.K., I *am* listening." (My God!)

The kind of interpersonal contact described above is character-ized by weak reciprocity or, if you wish, weak coordination or "loose coupling" among participants. This is manifested in a number of ways: (1) Participants are not aware of the same elements in the communicational exchange; they "bracket" or "punctuate" the exchange in rather different ways. That is, what person B picks up from person A's behavior and interprets as communicational and relational is A's blind spot, and vice versa. (2) Even if A and B attend to the same elements (A has explicitly pointed out to B that B's silence is "disturbing" A), they do not ascribe the same meanings to that element (A thinks the silence is rejection; B sees it as concentration on a task). (3) Most importantly, even if they do share the meanings (they may agree that B's silence means that B is threatened by A), the relational meaning is either rejected ("You shouldn't feel threatened by me . . .") or, worst, ignored. One way or the other, it is not *accepted* (Watzlawick, Beavin, and Jackson, 1967). In contrast, when we speak of "intimate" or "harmoni-ous" relations we usually imply strong interdependence whereby "bracketing" of both the content and relational aspects of the interaction are shared, meanings are shared, and expressions of relations are mutually accepted.

At this point it is useful to distinguish between *circular* and *spiral* interactions (more on this in Chapter 7). Even in loosely coupled relations there is some interdependence. The content and relational cues of A's message are responded to by B; even when B totally misunderstands A, A is likely to correct B, to withdraw or repeat the message; whatever A and B do is interdependent (recall the fights between Martha and George in *Who's Afraid of Virginia Woolf*). But such relations are likely to create vicious circles as the participants respond only to what they perceive, excluding their own blind spots, and thus inter-preting the perceptual data in light of unchanging anticipatory schemata.

Consider the following example. Person A, a teacher, seeks advice from person B, à colleague. While the content of the request is commonly understood, the relational cues are not. As Glidewell's (1980) research suggests, B, on the basis of consen-

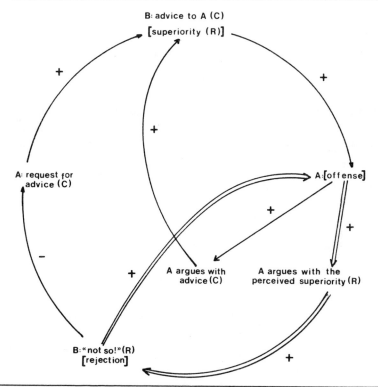

Figure 5.3   Circular Possibilities Resulting from Teacher A's Request for Advice from Teacher B

sual schemata, is likely to attribute to A's request some weakness and inferiority and to attribute superiority to herself. (For this reason, apparently, Glidewell found that over a ten-day period, 37 percent of the 121 teachers observed neither asked nor offered advice. Without exception, no advice was given if not preceded by an explicit request, and most teachers believed that asking for advice reduced one's status.) Person B responds to both the request and the relational inferiority implied. Person A is likely to be hurt and respond to the latter aspect by rejecting it. Person B, unaware of what A has picked up, is likely to do more of the same—namely, to elaborate her advice, thereby confirming her relational interpretation. This then develops into a dispute on a marginal level. Alternatively, B may

address A's offended feelings by rejecting A's own interpretation, thereby entering a self-sustaining dispute. Ultimately,
A is likely to withdraw and never request advice again. Figure
5.3 describes the vicious circle involved.

Such relations (as far as they last) are circularly interdependent. The participants are "stuck" in either the content or
relational aspects of their contacts. If person B would become
more aware of what her nonverbal cues communicate to A, if A
would accept B's expressions of superiority, if B would perceive
A's hurt, or if both could step out of the loop and examine it
from a meta level (change of the second order), then this
relationship would lead to *spiral* interdependence. That is, each
person's schemata would be more accommodating to the other's
inputs (rather than seeking self-confirmation), thereby leading
to a mutually shared way of handling both aspects of the
contacts. The developing interdependence would be spiral inasmuch as it would develop rather than get stuck in closed loops.

The shift from circular interdependencies to spiral ones
should interest us most. What are the correlates of such a shift?
One important factor is the shift from using general, undiffer-
entiated cues to more specific, multidimensional cues as a basis
for interpreting relational messages. Indeed, first encounters are
strongly dominated by global perceptual cues which often lead
to errors of interpretation. Individuals who are perceived as
talking more in a conversation are also seen as "moving forces"
in interactions (Taylor et al., 1979); discussants who are more
brightly lit are perceived as more inner-directed (McArthur and
Post, 1977); and discussants who face an observer are perceived
as more important in setting the tone of the discussion than
discussants who face away (Taylor and Fiske, 1975). Taylor and
Fiske (1975: 252) generalized the case and argued that "the
casual attributions people make, the opinions people express,
and the impressions they form of others in work or social
situations are often shaped by seemingly trivial but highly
salient information."

This "trivial but highly salient information" is actively sought
out, guided by one's anticipatory schemata (such as teachers'
assumption that colleagues who seek advice show inferiority).

Initial encounters are dominated by general, often stereotypic expectations (see Miller and Steinberg, 1975). Being general and culturally or otherwise consensually based, such anticipatory schemata are poorly differentiated and allow for only shallow, undemanding processing of relational cues (Kendzierski, 1980). Thus during early encounters, when each participant is guided by general, consensual schemata, neither repleteness nor stacking are much realized.

The change occurs when, among other things, participants begin to read the relational cues in each other's behavior on the basis of better differentiated schemata and are guided less by a priori consensual schemata. (Referring back to the section on interpersonal contacts in Chapter 4, one can easily see why teachers and students, having much daily contact with each other, are less likely to fall into the trap of self-fulfilling prophecies than personnel whose arena of work is the larger educational system.)

Two mechanisms appear to be involved in the shift from little to more realization of repleteness. These are *self-disclosure* (Miller and Steinberg, 1975) and *feedback* ("These are my true intentions" and "That's how your behavior makes me feel"). Taken together these mechanisms are what Miller and Steinberg (1975) have termed the "Siamese-twin" strategy. For such a strategy to occur, two conditions need to be met. The *necessary* condition is that the participants perceive themselves to enjoy equal status or symmetrical relations.[5] The *sufficient* condition, it seems, is that the participants share a desire to realize more repleteness in their relations, that is, to employ the needed mechanism to achieve better interdependence.

This is where the realization of repleteness in interpersonal contacts between educators and students faces its greatest difficulty. There appear to be at least two sources for this difficulty. The first involves the status differences that are built into educational systems. The second involves the strategies used by educators to maintain their status, role, and mission.

To begin, let me consider the difficulties arising from status differences. Awareness of the relational aspects in the messages of another person is not equally distributed. Individuals who are assigned a relatively lower status are more sensitive to the relational aspects of the messages they receive from their superiors (see Tjosvold, 1978). Subordinates, more than their superiors, try to assign meanings to the content of their superiors' messages by embedding them in the relational context, apparently due to the desire to equalize status, avoid relative inferiority, and reduce perceived nonreciprocal dependency (Kipnis, 1976). Thus, students, children, lower level employees, patients, and soldiers are particularly attentive to how their teachers, parents, bosses, physicians, or officers relate to them. Subordinates have more to gain from closing the status gap than do superiors. The ones who enjoy a higher status and to an extent dominate the type of relationship that develops are far less sensitive to the relational aspects in the messages received from their subordinates. As Tjosvold (1978) points out, people with higher status show little sensitivity to relational cues, particularly to "invitations" for more reciprocity and relational interdependence, as if they were trying to defend their status by ignoring or rejecting such messages.

Thus, we can see that because of status differences, symmetrical relations in education are difficult to achieve, making the shift from more formal to more interdependent relations face built-in hurdles. When conflict arises (which is often the case, as we well know), there is a greater chance that it will be "resolved" by withdrawal into the content aspect of the messages or by self-sustaining, circular disputes of the "Don't speak to me this way" type. The alternative would require the realization of more repleteness in the form of more self-disclosure, honest feedback, and so forth (Roloff, 1976). But this shrinks the status gap and renders the superior person more vulnerable to the advantages that the "inferior" may now take.

The second source for difficulty in realizing repleteness in educational settings is partly related to this issue of status differences. Educators are given the authority to educate, hence also the legitimacy to employ more or less coercive strategies in controlling the behavior of their students. This is particularly needed in schools in which, as Duke (1978) points out, disciplined behavior has become an end in itself rather than a means to some other ends. When coercive means are used, the power-holders gradually devaluate the subordinate's performance, ability, and autonomy and more insistently maintain the status gap (Kipnis et al., 1976). They become increasingly less sensitive to both their own and their subordinates' relational cues; that is, relational cues are ignored or, at best, acknowledged and rejected (Kipnis, 1976).

A related characteristic is that schools rely heavily, nearly exclusively, on verbal communication. The reasons for this are numerous (such as, the single educator having to handle many students, the tradition of the word in education). The difficulty arises in the shortcomings of language in handling relational aspects of communication. For whatever reason, the expression of relations is more trusted when nonverbally expressed than when transmitted verbally. Thus, students are more likely to put trust in their teacher when her behavior is taken to express trustworthiness than when she (only) says, "You can trust me." Verbal statements pertaining to relations need to be validated by nonverbal behavior. A school's claim that rule enforcement is "just, equal, and consistent" is checked against the staff's actual behavior. And as Hargraves, Hester, and Meilor (1975) point out, students are quick to note when the behavior does not bear out the statement.

Given these difficulties, it becomes quite possible that educational settings cannot easily develop spiral interdependence, of the kind described earlier, without great effort.

More likely, educational settings (though, as I have argued in Chapter 4, not necessarily the individual educators) easily enter circular interdependencies and specifically self-fulfilling and self-sustaining prophecies. Consider two illustrations. Dykman and Reis (1979), it will be recalled, found that children with poor self-images chose low risk seats in the classroom and also did poorly in school, thus maintaining their poor self-concepts. We know from the work by Tjosvold and Kastelic (1976) that teachers are not likely to focus much attention on such children of little promise. Thus, relational aspects in the children's messages (on the few occasions they do speak up) are often ignored or interpreted in light of general negative expectations. At the same time the little attention given to these children and the less-than-supportive attitudes toward them by their peers and teachers (Tjosvold and Kastelic, 1976) are likely to be picked up by the children (given *their* expectations), only to further reinforce their poor self-concept. If their classroom plight were discussed in the school, it would most likely be in terms of their performance (content), not in terms of others' response to their relational cues.

A more pervasive case pertains to school discipline. Duke (1978: 116) points out that

> a standard response to increased misbehavior has been to create more rules and/or make the consequences for disobeying existing rules more harsh. Each year, however, the "crisis" in school discipline continues. It would appear that the strategy of combatting misconduct with more rules and stricter punishments has not proved very effective.

Duke notes that although both students and teachers are concerned about behavior problems, the problems that worry teachers are not the same ones that concern students. (The former are more concerned with attendance-related behavior, the latter with fighting, theft, insult.) Such a mismatch is an important contributor to feelings of injustice (see Hart, 1978) and leads to reactance by the students who are disciplined (Brehm, 1966). Duke also suggests that many of the school rules are neither consistently nor (as subjectively seen by students) justly enforced, particularly since many of them are not really explicitly communicated (Hargreaves et al., 1975). Under such conditions misbehavior actually increases (Hart, 1978).

Why should misbehavior increase? Given the context of this chapter, we might say that as more rules are enforced (Alschuler et al., 1977, counted more than a hundred in a typical school), students experience greater loss of control (Fisher, 1976) and more inequity and threat to freedom (Brehm, 1966). They are likely to interpret the enforcement of such rules as communicating to them a relational message with which they disagree. Rejecting it, they respond in kind by trying to redefine the relations in their own terms, that is, by "misbehaving." But school authorities, unaware of their own expressions of relations, perceive such student behavior in light of their own schemata as "misbehavior." They also see in students' misbehavior a relational threatening message (defiance) and respond with reactance in kind: more rules and harsher enforcement. Both sides are now stuck in the relational aspect, each seeing only the other's "input" (not their own), which each side rejects. Thus a self-sustaining, circular dispute develops.

How could such circularity be avoided and more repleteness allowed to develop? Dimmitt (1970) has shown that when teachers are trained to observe student attending behaviors, the teachers become far more accurate observers and the students become more attentive. Teachers who observe inattention could raise their voices and call for attention, but then they would often lose students' attention (Kounin, Gump, and Ryan, 1961). What Dimmitt showed, on the other hand, is that when teachers become aware of and control their own relational cues (for example, maintain more eye contact with more students) and realize more repleteness, students reciprocate. This kind of behavior was missing in the classrooms observed by Dykman and Reis (1979), leading to the circular interdependence they have noted.

Concerning the disciplinary cycle described above, one procedure that appears to break it is shifting the responsibility for rule-making and enforcing to the students themselves (Duke and Perry, 1978). Although this may have several undesirable side effects, it at least removes one element that facilitates the typical circularity. Rules designed and enforced by peers are less likely to be perceived as demeaning relational messages, and are more likely to be taken as specific content prescriptions that pertain to specific behavioral referents. This may not result in spiral interdependence, but at least it helps to avoid circularity.

CONCLUSION

Given the attributional nature of communication, any behavior, event, or act can be taken, in principle, as communicating something. Whether it does communicate depends heavily on one's anticipatory schemata. This rich potential of communication sources and messages can be arranged along two dimensions: (1) the number of communicational sources to which people can address themselves ("repleteness") and (2) the number of "levels" within a message which people can process ("stacking"). Repleteness and stacking are not preexisting facts but potentialities that can be realized. One can address more or fewer sources and process messages more or less deeply. Choice, conflict, and skill are involved in such realization; thus, one is likely to introduce a division of labor among potential sources and messages, thereby realizing more stacking in some media than in others and realizing more repleteness in other people's behavior than in one's own.

I have equated stacking with "depth of processing" or, more accurately, with the amount of invested mental effort (AIME), which itself is a function of the perceived requirements of the stimulus, task, or context and of one's perceived self-efficacy in processing information deeply. AIME is positively related to learning and curvilinearly related to perceived efficacy. Thus, students who perceive a medium such as books as very demanding and do not believe in their efficacy to process its messages deeply are likely to invest little effort in them, and hence learn less from them than students with more perceived self-efficacy. It is suggested (Butkowsky and Willows, 1980) that in such cases children's perceived self-efficacy should be increased through tutoring. On the other hand, students who perceive themselves to be highly effective in processing the messages of a medium (such as TV) because of the medium's attributed realism and undemanding nature are likely to forego the investment of effort and thereby learn less from it than students who feel less effective and therefore invest more effort. Following Dorr, Graves, and Phelps (1980), it is suggested that such students can be tutored in processing the medium's messages with greater AIME by learning how unrealistic the messages are and how much more information can be gotten out of them.

This chapter also dealt with the realization of repleteness in interpersonal contacts. Following Watzlawick et al. (1967), I tried to show that such contacts entail both a content and a relational aspect, the latter usually being of a nonverbal nature. I claimed that we are more aware of other people's emission of relational cues than of our own, which leads to misunderstandings. As relations become more intimate, people become more aware of their own relational cues, perceive the relational cues of others less stereotypically and globally, and process them in more differential ways. As global anticipatory schemata come to play a lesser role, the chance for vicious communicational circles and for self-fulfilling prophecies diminishes. Thus, I argued, many school problems (including discipline and under-achieving learners) occur when interpersonal repleteness is not realized, each side seeing only its own responses.

NOTES

1. Children were asked how effective they felt they could be at studying a range of topics from TV. Reliability of the measure over time was .87.

2. Amount of televiewing was one of the independent variables of a cross-cultural study of TV's effects on the cultivation of mental skills. For more details, see Salomon (1979).

3. We are presently involved in developing other, less obtrusive measures for AIME.

4. However, we can become more aware of the noncontent aspects of our own behavior when we see ourselves in a mirror (Duval and Wicklund, 1973: study 2).

5. This does not mean that symmetrical relations cannot lead to *less* realization of repleteness. Symmetry is but a necessary, not sufficient condition.

Chapter 6

CONTEXTS AND MESSAGES:

Containers within Containers

*Inside every large problem is a small
problem struggling to get out*

Hoare's Law

Events and acts perceived as communications are hardly ever discrete and disconnected. Not only are they connected to each other, appearing as a continuous flow, but they are also embedded in each other such that some come to serve as contexts for others. A specific utterance occurs in the context of an ongoing conversation, a movie is seen in the context of a theater, and a counselor interviews a student within the contexts of their respective social roles and the more general setting of the school.

What is context? A context is usually seen as anything that offers meaning to something else and is perceived to be on a higher level of generality than that "something else." Any behavior, place, time, symbol, organization, role, spatial arrangement, expression of a relationship, or the like can serve as a context, provided it meets these two conditions. For example, a drawing of a wild flower can be taken as an expression of beauty, the symbol of the state of California, an add for a new perfume, or an illustration of a botanic specimen, depending on whether it appears on a brochure of the Sierra Club, on a highway sign, on a small bottle, or in a botany book. Each of these serves as an alternative context for the drawing inasmuch as it is (alleged to be) on a higher (meta) level of generality than the drawing and offers specific meanings for it.

Related to this is the notion that contexts are hierarchically ordered like Chinese boxes, with each superordinate context including the ones below it, which include the ones below them, and so on. Thus, an intermission between class sessions permits certain behaviors (such as yelling) not allowed during class sessions and offers them specific meanings. The same yelling means something else during class hours. But the meaning of the intermission itself represents notions of relative freedom, equality, and relaxation within the wider cultural context of time allocation and time budgeting in school. This cultural context is subsumed under an even wider or more general context of the institutionalization of education and the bracketing of activities in the flow of time.

A special class of contexts is *behavior settings* such as public lectures, churches, basketball courts, youngsters' hangouts, and restaurants. Barker (et al., 1978: 195), who coined the term and initiated much research in this domain, defined the context of behavior settings as mixes of physical and human components (ecobehavioral phenomena) and ongoing occurrences (programs of events). According to this viewpoint, "Behavior settings are components of larger, more complex social systems such as communities and institutions" (Wicker, 1979: 758). Thus, this special class of contexts, which is anchored in part in physical locales, is also hierarchically ordered.

Common to everything that functions as a context is that it does not exist "out there" as context. It does exists perhaps as a place (schoolyard), a symbol system (the alphabet), a time (morning), a role (student), and the like, but these do not become contexts until expectations, ascriptions of meaning, consensual norms, and plans of activity are associated with them. The context of a textbook (unlike that of a source book) will only suggest a different approach to the text to someone who knows that different assumptions underlie the two kinds of books.

Webb (1980) studied the effects of group versus individual contexts on achievements. He found that it was not the context that had an effect but rather what happened within it. Some students learned more in groups (particularly when their errors were corrected and explained by able peers), but other students did not. The amount and character of the interaction was determined by status perceptions: Students who refrained from active participation were those who feared criticism and further loss of status. The group context was perceived by them as inhibiting rather than facilitating any request for help. In general, then, a context affects people's behavior according to how the people *perceive* the context. Contexts are "in the minds" of people. When they are not, they seem to have no effect (Saegert, Swap, and Zajonc, 1972). Precisely the same thing is true of mental schemata. They serve as storehouses of knowledge and programs for execution that are brought to bear on specific events, are hierarchically ordered, and are interrelated among themselves (see Chapter 3).

Once we consider the affinity between contexts and schemata, we can see how contexts function. Contexts are mentally employed as anticipatory schemata to assimilate specific events, thereby giving them meaning. Both context (that is, what we bracket out from the surrounding to serve as context) and schema are *devices of prediction.* Once an event has been perceived in light of a particular context (schema), much is already known about it (Weick, 1979). The argument that contexts are akin to mental schemata is nicely illustrated by recent research on manning (briefly, the number of, say, workers available to do a job). Wicker (1979) found that people in overmanned conditions reported less involvement than people in undermanned conditions. But it was not the sheer size of the working group that made the difference. Rather, much depended on the people's previous experience, which shaped their perception of the manning context. Workers who were shorthanded on one group task judged the following task to require fewer people than workers who were overstaffed. (Recall Parkinson's law, according to which work expands to fit the time, resources, and personnel available for its completion.)

The argument that contexts serve as devices for prediction (where context A helps to predict the behavior of B) is well illustrated by the studies of Langer et al. (1978) on mindlessness. As will be recalled, Langer et al. showed how people, upon encountering a message of highly familiar, overlearned structural cues, forego the processing of its content. These cues invoke learned "scripts" (schemata) that predict, in the person's eyes, nearly all there is in the message. Report Langer et al. (1978: 641):

> These studies taken together support the contention that when the structure of a communication, be it oral or written, semantically sound or senseless, is congruent with one's past experience, it may occasion behavior mindless of relevant details. Clearly, some information from the situation must be processed in order for a script to be cued. However, what is being suggested here is that only a minimal amount of structural information may be attended to and that this information may not be the most useful part of the information available.

The identification of contexts with schemata leads to a number of implications. For whatever has been said thus far about schemata in preceding chapters also applies to contexts (for example, that the meaning of communication events depend on schemata-derived attributions; that schemata bias the gathering and structuring of, and meaning assigned to data; that a schema can be replaced by another; and more).

In understanding communication, three parallels between contexts and schemata are particularly important. First, all messages are perceived in a context (just as they are perceived in terms of one's schemata). Second, contexts, like schemata, are hierarchically ordered, and the cognitive distance between context and event determines the role of the context. Third, context and message can, under specific conditions, reverse roles, turning the former into message and the latter into context (while the bench in the park lends special meaning to the loving words of the young couple, their words also lend specific meanings to the bench and the park). Thus, contexts not only affect the nature of messages, they are also affected by them.

Let us consider these three points in more detail. Messages cannot be perceived outside of a context, in the same way that events are meaningless when no mental schema is applied to them. Contexts as schemata tell us what is to be anticipated and how to understand it. They also tell us, as we shall see later, what kind of message is legitimate and what we can afford to say or do, given the place, time, people, role, and so forth that we are facing. What happens, then, when we face an event that is at odds with its context (a professor who suddenly explodes in anger during a lecture) or that cannot be automatically embedded in a specific context (a statement uttered "out of the blue")? In such cases we "force" the event into some context that makes sense to us. If the angry behavior of that professor cannot be attributed, say, to observable student disruptions, we would tend to assign it to his alleged traits ("He's nuts"), to his hidden dispositions ("I've heard he fights with his wife"), or to his yet unknown plans ("He's trying to prove some kind of point—you'll see"). Given the prevalence of the "basic attributional error" (Ross, 1977), we are most likely to assign the professor's strange behavior to his traits or dispositions rather than to situational factors such as his students' subtle expressions of unfriendly relational cues.

Contexts can serve in numerous roles. They can explain actions, as when the professor's anger is "explained" as a result of his angry nature. Contexts can also serve as *justifications* for events. Salancik (1975) argues, for example, that when the outcomes of actions are ambiguous (when it is unclear how much "school success" one has achieved or whether one has made a "wise choice of a career," for example), stated intentions become a context within which the meaning and worth of all kinds of preceding actions are judged.

One could go on to enumerate a long list of roles frequently assigned to contexts, but the list can be collapsed into two major kinds of roles. Contexts serve a *normative* function by legitimizing some messages and prohibiting others. And contexts serve a *meaning* function by suggesting what specific denotative and connotative meanings should be assigned to events. To understand this division of labor between contexts we need first to discuss the issue of *context hierarchies.*

Contexts, like schemata, are hierarchically ordered. What determines the hierarchy? Again, the parallel with schemata suggests an answer. We have reason to believe that schemata are hierarchically ordered in terms of *generality* (the schema one may have of "communication" is higher in the hierarchy than the schema of "media research") and *typicality* (the more typical case contextualizes the variant). Generality determines inclusiveness. Thus, for example, our concept of time is more general than our concept of morning and includes it. Typicality implies stability or "anchorness" (Tversky, 1977), the baseline from which variants depart. For example, a new speech on the economy is a variant that is considered more or less typical of the President's established position on the economy. Similarly, a musical theme is a baseline context for the variations that are played on it. All variants take part of their meaning from their similarity to or difference from a stable, "basic" expression. It follows, then, that whatever is more general and/or more typical in people's minds, serves as a context for the more specific and variant. Furthermore, given that contexts or schemata are hierarchically ordered, it follows that their cognitive distance from a specific event may differ. This is particularly important for contexts of generality. The classroom is more general than a particular lecture in history, which is more general than the specific argument that the teacher presently develops. The more general context of the classroom is farther away from the teacher's specific argument than the topic of that class session. The context of the educational system is even farther away from the teacher's thesis than the classroom setting. (Notice that we are dealing here with a cognitive distance between schemata, not any "objective" distance.)

The farther away a context is from a particular event the less it can offer specific meanings to that event. The knowledge that this is a book with an interactional viewpoint does not much help the reader in interpreting the last sentences. Similarly, the knowledge that the teacher's utterances are embedded in an educational system does not directly offer any meanings to the teacher's smiles. But such general contexts accomplish a normative function. The title of this book renders some arguments more relevant than others, and the context of education suggests that certain utterances (gossip about the principal's private affairs) are "illegitimate."

Specific meanings for an event are suggested by contexts that are cognitively much closer to it. The meanings of these sentences should be better understood in light of the present chapter heading and even more in light of the opening sentence of the preceding paragraph. The kind of meaning likely to be given to the teacher's statement that "the students better do their homework" is influenced by the history of class compliance, and even more by the teacher's immediate nonverbal communication of that statement. The greater the cognitive distance between context and event, the more a normative function is accomplished; the smaller the distance, the more a meaning function is accomplished.

For example, the context of summer camp implies that certain behaviors are more permissible than in the context of the classroom. But aside from legitimizing some behaviors and forbidding others, such contexts do not directly influence the meanings of any specific behavior or utterance. They may have an indirect effect on specific meanings through intermediary contexts subsumed under them, but the specific meaning is left to be influenced by the context closest to the event. Thus the meaning of "You're losing the game" will be understood on the basis of specific and immediate cues (scorn or sympathy in the caller's voice).

Distance between context and event is, of course, relative. The context of an educational system is far closer to the idea of compulsory education than to a class in home economics and thus can accomplish for the former more of a meaning function and serve for the latter in a normative capacity. But this does not mean that in actuality such a division of labor is systematically followed. Contexts do not accomplish anything by themselves; people attribute to them whatever role they accomplish. Thus, people's attributions may violate the distinction I have made.

For example, Safer (1980) showed psychology students Milgram's film *Obedience* and then asked them to predict the shock levels that uncoerced subjects would voluntarily administer. By and large, Safer's students overestimated the shock levels (when compared with one of Milgram's studies), apparently attributing the obedient behavior of Milgram's subjects to their general "evil character" rather than to situational factors. By so doing, the students apparently invoked a remoter context ("character"), disregarding a situational context closer to the observed behavior. The situational context could have offered a more accurate interpretation of the obedient behavior, suggesting that when no pressure is exerted on the subjects, obedience drops drastically. Having invoked a context which is cognitively closer to the event and more readily available, they used it to provide meaning and erred dramatically in their predictions. (This is another example of the "basic attributional error" of attributing the cause of a behavior to a trait or disposition rather than a situation.)

Not all events regarded as contexts are necessarily more general or typical than events taken as messages. The smile which is supposed to contextualize the verbal statement "You're really something!" is neither more general nor more typical than the statement. The roles of smile and statement could have been reversed. Indeed, Sommer (1959) found that more interaction takes place among people who sit close to each other, particularly when they sit side by side. The context (seating arrangements) affects the kind of messages that are exchanged. But in another study, Sommer (1965) found that influence can go the other way: The desire for a specific kind of interaction (competition, cooperation, informal chat) influences the preferred seating arrangement. Figure and ground have reversed their roles, as both are more or less equally general and prototypic.

If message and context can sometimes reverse roles, it follows that the perception of what is context and what is message may often depend on one's choice of perspective. Is my angry response to be forgiven within the context of a hostile atmosphere that you created by your tone of voice, or is your tone of voice to be understood in the context of my expressed anger? Clearly, the answer is neither one nor the other—they are circularly or reciprocally related. Classroom climate is a context for teacher grading practices and student absenteeism. When the climate is positive, more learning takes place, more reinforcements are given, and there is less absenteeism. But then, as Moos and Moos (1978) suggest, more liberal grading practices may be the context (or ground) and a supportive climate the specific event (or figure). We can generalize the case by proposing that the closer "message" and "context" are to each other on the hierarchy, the more they become interdependent, lending meaning to each other.

This interchangeability of context and message has important implications for the understanding of interpersonal relations, because many "abnormal," or "disturbed" (or desired) behaviors of students are perceived as specific variants within a wider, stable context of personality. The possibility that these behaviors and their alleged context are interchangeable is rarely entertained.

Contexts, like schemata, should accommodate to the events they contextualize. For example, the context of an organization influences the flow of messages within it, but it does not determine that flow absolutely. Employees who have more autonomy in an organization with only few bureaucratic levels (typical of schools) depend more on each other and less on their supervisors. Over time, their specific goals come to dominate the more general goals of the organization. Sensing this, supervisors are likely to introduce tighter controls, limit the autonomy, and establish more coordination. The context has thus been changed by a communicational pattern initially influenced by the context.

Similarly, one would expect the family context of tele-viewing to "legitimize" the avoidance of conflict resolution in the family (Rosenblatt and Cunningham, 1976). At the same time, one would also expect the escape from conflict resolution by televiewing to influence the way families watch TV together (Walters and Stone, 1971). Televiewing patterns and conflict resolution behaviors in families are close enough to each other to reverse roles over time.

In what follows, I take some of the ideas presented above and apply them to issues related to learning, interpersonal relations, and media. As in previous chapters, no attempt is made to exhaust the topics but only to illustrate them.

CONTEXTS AND LEARNING: EXCHANGING ROLES

Learning, the cognitive processes whereby new knowledge and skills are acquired, can be seen as the innermost box in a hierarchy of contextual Chinese boxes. Placing learning in such a position is, of course, just a matter of perspective. If we were concerned with, say, classroom climate, we might focus on *it* as the focal point of other contexts, including learning achievements. But as the focus here is on learning, the question of how its contexts affect it is of greater interest. One general context for learning (though not the most general one) is "schooling," that is, the whole culture that surrounds the institutionalization of education, the division of labor it imposes, the rules it sets, the attendance it requires, and the like. As Silberman (1970: 9) points out,

> Children are taught a host of lessons about values, ethics, morality, character, and conduct every day of the week, less by the content of the curriculum than by the way [teachers] talk to children and to each other, the kinds of behavior they approve or reward and the kinds they disapprove or punish. These lessons are far more powerful than the verbalizations that accompany them and that they frequently controvert.

Numerous cognitive outcomes, such as abstract modes of thought, have been attributed to literacy, that is, to the acquisition of a shared written language (Greenfield, 1972; Olson, 1977). However, abstract thinking is more strongly linked to schooling in general than to literacy per se. Scribner and Cole (1978) showed in a unique study carried out on the Vai tribe in Liberia that literacy without schooling had certain highly specific outcomes that were limited to the range of practices afforded by the Vai script. But abstract thinking was not affected by literacy without schooling, which affords the repeated practice of many skills in many areas (Scribner and Cole, 1978; see also Luria, 1976, for a longitudinal study in Central Asia that showed how "schooling" a rural society led to profound cognitive changes).

Of a somewhat less general nature are the contexts of the school system, for example its degree of organizational centralization. Less centralized systems, like the ones in America, are described as "loosely coupled" (Meyer and Rowan, 1978). They are seemingly more adaptive to local demands, but also vulnerable to manipulation, powerless in everything but ritual classifications, and remain relatively unchanged by what actually happens within the schools. In contrast, "schools observed in Britain show much more internal coordination. Evaluation and control are exerted under the authority of the headmaster, whose role in school and in British society is substantial and is rooted in established tradition" (Meyer and Rowan, 1978: 84). The differences between more and less tightly coupled systems affect the autonomy of principals and teachers and also the system's ability to adapt to changing societal conditions.

We do not know as yet in what ways the communicational networks of coupled and decoupled systems differ. But it is reasonable to hypothesize that there are more "vertical" messages flowing up and down the more tightly coupled system and more "horizontal" messages flowing in loosely coupled ones. It would follow from Tyack's (1974) analysis that large educational bureaucracies (in loosely coupled systems) shield the teachers from outside demands of accountability. But at the same time, their very existence depends on consensual agreements (as has been shown in Chapter 4), and hence on tight interdependence between colleagues.

On a less general level one may find the school itself. Schools differ from each other within tighter or more decoupled systems in terms of their size (see Astin, 1977), the cohesiveness or isolation of their physical designs (Myrick and Marx, 1968), overall social climate (Moos, 1979), and their overall control ideology (Willower, 1975). Concerning the latter context, Rafalides and Hoy (1971) reported on the basis of a large-scale study of teachers and administrators that student alienation seems to result from authoritarian control systems in which students are expected to accept teacher decisions without question. DeCecco and Richards (1974) pointed out that more than half the conflicts in schools are resolved by school personnel, and the decisions are then coercively imposed on students. This, they argued, escalates additional conflicts. Willower (1975), among others, has shown that a control ideology goes hand in hand with teachers' custodial attitudes toward students as people who cannot discipline themselves and are irresponsible. Jones (1969) found that teachers with custodial attitudes are more frequently found in centrally controlled schools. The attitudes and beliefs of teachers are quite different in open schools, with the effect, as Duke and Perry (1978) have argued, of fewer disciplinary problems and, as Thomas (1980) showed in his review, greater student capabilities of self-management.

Control contexts affect "lower level" contexts such as classroom management and climate. Tjosvold and Kastelic (1976) had teachers teach students whose behavior had been labeled as either "highly motivated" or "unmotivated." The teachers were led to believe that their respective principals valued either collaboration with students or control of students. They found that teachers who thought their principals wanted control taught unmotivated students in more directive ways with less rewards, lower grades, and less support than did teachers who thought their principals wanted collaboration. This teaching style has already been shown to affect classroom climates and learning outcomes negatively (Dunkin and Biddle, 1974). The impact of the principals' values on teachers' behaviors was smaller when "motivated" students were taught, suggesting to

Tjosvold and Kastelic (1976: 773) that teaching under pressure to control may result "in poor grades and negative teacher opinions, both of which can reduce the unmotivated students' future opportunities."

Another important context is the classroom social context. Some studies show that teachers' management strategies and classroom social atmospheres are interrelated (see Moos and Moos, 1978) and could be seen as contextualizing each other. Similar interdependence seems to characterize the classroom social context and learning outcomes (see Schmuck, 1978). It has been shown that classrooms with supportive friendship patterns enhance academic learning, while classrooms with more tense relations inhibit learning (see Schmuck, 1971). Lewis and St. John (1974) studied the impact of racial integration on 154 black sixth graders in 22 white-majority classrooms. When the blacks were accepted into the white peer group of the classroom and when the class held a norm stressing academic achievement, the achievements of the black students increased. It stands to reason that the improved achievements of black students affected, in turn, the classroom norms.

Other specific contexts that affect learning include: the teacher's adherence to or deviation from her own rules of accepted and unaccepted correct answers (Mehan, 1974), the classroom seating and furniture arrangement (see Getzels, 1974), the introduction of advanced organizers, a priori perspectives and objectives (see Chapter 4), and more.

The abbreviated hierarchy of learning contexts presented above is far from exhaustive, but it illustrates the complex web of contexts in which the process of learning takes place. Such a hierarchy of contexts must be part of people's schemata hierarchies, or the contexts are powerless. This opens up numerous new issues. One that I want to consider here has not received much attention in the literature, and pertains to the reciprocal relations between context and learning.

To begin, learning, while perhaps the "lowest event" contextualized by many other contexts, affects some of them reciprocally. It would be unreasonable to expect learning outcomes to

change contexts such as schooling or the organizational structure of the school system, because, being relatively loosely
coupled, such remote contexts are not easily affected by messages from "lower down" Sarason, 1971). Other, cognitive less
distant contexts are affected by the learning they contextualize.
According to Schmuck (1978: 234),

> The pattern of peer-group friendship and influence relationships
> within the class had an impact upon the students' self-concepts and
> attitudes toward school, which, in turn, affected the students' aca-
> demic performance—or so at least could go one plausible explanation
> of my correlational data.

Another plausible explanation of such data is that learning
outcomes themselves have an effect on peer group friendships
and self-concepts of students. These two explanations are not
mutually exclusive. Classroom climates, self-concepts, and
achievements simply affect each other reciprocally. Mehan
(1974) found that while teachers gave their students relatively
explicit rules (instructions), they very often adjusted them to
ongoing events during actual teaching (creating "double
binds"?). Mehan (1974: 124-125) concluded,

> Rule use in a social situation is an interpretive process. The "correct-
> ness" rule had to be interpreted against a constantly changing
> background of features of the setting which might include the child's
> behavior, the teacher's expectations, the question structure. Because
> the rule cannot anticipate those background features, the formal
> statement of the rule is incomplete.

In sum, immediate classroom contexts, instructional messages, and learning outcomes are close enough to each other to
exert reciprocal influences. But proximity does not explain *why*
such reciprocal influences take place. This process seems to
occur because, unlike remote contexts which suggest general
norms of behavior, closer contexts suggest specific meanings,
and meanings are sensitive to everything occurring in a specific

situation. For example, Webb's (1980) low-ability students who failed to solve math problems within a learning group stopped seeing the meanings of the prescribed group activity as learning and thereby changed the immediate group context. They did not, however, change, behaviors prescribed by the wider school context. Like math achievement and group learning, many other pairs of context and outcomes can reverse their positions, including achievement and classroom atmosphere, student time spent on the task and the teacher's way of talking to her students, students' ability for self-management and peer interaction, and students' motivations and their achievements.

Thus, the question is not just, for instance, how a relaxed classroom climate leads to learning for some students while a more tense climate leads to learning by others. One would also need to ask the reverse: how the learning *processes* (for example more or less AIME, more or fewer exchanges of ideas among students) affect the *climate.* For example, Tjosvold (1978) reports findings that in classrooms with more differentiated statuses (less cohesiveness) and a less dense communicational network, less learning takes place. It is reasonable to assume that in such classrooms the students most affected are the social "rejects" whose learning performance deteriorates the most. But suppose that, for whatever reason (such as special help), such students begin to demonstrate improved learning achievements. What would this do to the loose classroom cohesiveness? Similarly, aptitude-treatment-interaction (ATI) research shows that different learners excel in different learning contexts. Snow (1977), who examined a number of ATI studies, found a common thread suggesting that instructional contexts that put a heavier information-processing burden on students ("open" instruction) benefit mainly the abler ones; more didactic, "closed" contexts that provide explicit guidelines mainly benefit the less able students. But as some students show poor performance in one or another context, more instruction is directed to them. Consequently, the less didactic "open" contexts become somewhat more prescriptive to accommodate the unsuccessful poor ability students, while the more didactic context is "opened up" for the able students who do not fare well in too controlled a context.

Notice, however, that such a reciprocal process can only take place under one condition: when students' achievements are seen as responsive to context rather than predetermined by traits. In the latter case, contexts are kept stable (as they are considered inconsequential) regardless of the learning they produce in some learners, and thus they cannot be changed by their own outcomes. I will discuss in greater detail the issue of contextualizing (attributing causes to) students' behaviors in the next section.

INTERPERSONAL CONTACTS: HOW TO CONTEXTUALIZE STUBBORNNESS?

People generally try to adapt their behaviors to the perceived requirements of contexts so they will not be perceived as "troublemakers," "deviants," "mad," "bad," or "stupid." Thus, for example, Bem (1979) describes the use of a Q-sort method whereby idealized "types" of people are described (as "critical, skeptical, not easily impressed"), and judges score people according to these types in various situations. These scores are then correlated with other items and with the actual performance of subjects in specific contexts. Bem and Funder (1978; reported in Bem, 1979) used this method to test competing social-psychological theories ("dissonance," "self-perception," and "self-presentation demands of the setting") in the classical setting of the forced-compliance experiment. (In this kind of experiment, subjects are asked to advocate a view they oppose, with the frequent result of their attitudes changing in the direction of the advocated view.) Bem and Funder found that the best predictor of attitude change was the self-presentation theory, supporting the view that individuals adapt their behavior to situations as they understand them.

Bem also reported the use of the Q-sort method to predict children's delay-of-gratification behavior. Specific Q-sort items showed positive or negative correlations with delay-of-gratification behavior in *one* experimental setting, but in another, conceptually equivalent experiment, a very different portrait of the long-delaying child emerged. According to Bem (1979: 10):

> The important point to be emphasized here is how this Q-item portrait points rather directly to the properties of the situation that appear to be salient to the children and functionally controlling. Thus it would appear that the presence of the experimenter and the implicit social desirability of delaying are as salient to the children in this setting as the differential attractiveness of the two food items, the stimulus that, on theoretical grounds, is supposed to be the controlling variable.

Many more such observations pertaining to the considerable variation in people's behaviors in different settings have been noted time and again in recent years (see Endler and Magnusson, 1976).

People also ascribe meanings to others' behaviors in light of the contexts they perceive for the behaviors. For example, one attributes different meanings to failure in school depending on whether one sees it in the context of poor ability or of bad luck (see Bar-Tal, 1978). In general, then, interpersonal contexts influence the kind of communicational exchanges that take place. Furthermore, these exchanges, as I have suggested earlier, influence the immediate context in turn. For example, Glidewell (1980), in a study mentioned in Chapter 5, found that 82 percent of the 121 teachers he surveyed were committed to the belief that teachers have equal status among themselves and are autonomous; 80 percent believed that asking a colleague for advice implies a lower status; and 74 percent believed in both. Given such a context, it becomes clear why those experiencing it did not ask for advice. Instead, another communicational pattern was found to take place: "experience swapping" through informal storytelling. Such a substitute for explicit requests for advice by teachers who needed support created a new context for interaction.

It would be impossible to render a catalogue or taxonomy of interpersonal contexts. As Nuttin (1977: 201) has pointed out, person and situation cannot be "considered as two autonomously preexisting units interacting with each other at a given moment"; rather, they "function and exist as two interdependent poles of a unitary behavioral process." Thus, while we could study how communication patterns develop within contexts of symmetrical or complementary relations, we must remember that these contexts are in people's minds and that ongoing exchanges gradually change the context. Mischel (1977: 338) similarly has warned us that "it is important to avoid emerging simply with a trait psychology of situations, in which events and settings, rather than people, are merely given different labels. The task of naming situations cannot substitute for the job of analyzing *how* conditions and environments interact with the people in them."

Such interaction is generally ignored when behavior is seen in a context that emphasizes simply, rigidly defined characteristics, either of situations or of traits. For example, three studies illustrate the dangers of explaining behavior through traits alone. Asch (1955) found in a classic experiment that 37 percent of his subjects conformed to group pressure against their own judgment. In Milgram's (1974) "basic" study, 60 percent of the subjects obeyed absurd and cruel demands by a "scientific" authority. Barnett, Matthews, and Corbin (1979) defined a game for children aged 3 to 13 as being either a competitive or cooperative game. Subsequently, when asked to donate some of the earned rewards to handicapped children, the children whose game was defined as competitive were far less generous than those in the cooperative game.

If we had not known the contexts of these experiments, we could have easily (and erroneously) attributed the behaviors of Asch's, Milgram's, and Barnett's subjects to such traits as "conformity," "cruelty," and "stinginess." And this is precisely what people tend to do, committing the "basic attributional error," particularly when they are only partly familiar with the others whose behaviors they contextualize (Monson and

Snyder, 1977). Harvey et al. (1980) studied different conditions under which unsolicited comments attributed causes to interpersonal events. They found that regardless of experimental condition, between 75 percent and 95 percent of the attributions were dispositional. As Safer (1980) has shown, disregard for situational contexts and for the adaptability of people to them leads to grave attributional errors by which people are perceived as "obedient," "disadvantaged," "lazy," or "uninvolved," as if these were permanent, omnipresent, and context-free behaviors (Moos, 1979; Jones and Nisbett, 1972). Moreover, there is evidence to show that we are particularly apt to disregard contexts and attribute negative traits to people we only partly know (Lingle and Ostrom, 1979).

Here, then, we face a paradox. On the one hand people are flexible in adapting their behaviors to situational demands, as perceived by them. On the other hand, people assign each others' behaviors to dispositional contexts. The preference for personalogical attributions to others is apparently so strong partly because the context (schema) of "personality" is so well learned, so widely shared, and so easily available, while the changing demands of situational contexts can more easily be disregarded. As Epstein (1979: 1099) points out, "(a) it is emotionally satisfying to believe that behavior is predictable, particularly when it is someone else's; (b) it is simpler to classify behavior by people than by situations, [and] (c) people have implicit personality theories that assume stability in personality, and their theories bias their perceptions."

The difficulty of perceiving a situational rather than a personalogical context is also great because the attributor is often part of the other's context and hence exerts an immediate influence on the other. Should the other's behavior be "strange," unexpected, or undesirable, it is far safer to attribute this to "dispositions" than to one's *own* inputs. Consider three examples one might find in schools. The possibility that Johnny's "disturbed" behavior is a response to the classroom context dominated by the teacher is a threatening one to the teacher, because if that were true she would have to consider the way *she* contributes to Johnny's undesirable behavior. The same applies, of course, to the hypothetical Johnny. He also is more likely to explain the teacher's undesirable behavior as part of her disposition. Seeing her "in context" would make Johnny share the responsibility. But when that behavior can be framed within the context of the student's (teacher's) own personality dispositions ("poor upbringing," "vengeful," "restless"), the context which the teacher (student) helped to shape can be disregarded. Whatever the teacher (student) does is thought to be just a response to the *student's* (or teacher's) input.

Another example: I tend to explain the defiance of a student who constantly disagrees with me as the student's "resistance to authority," to see him as a "resister," and to try to "treat" that disposition of his. He (quite understandably) resists such treatment, but this only proves to me that I was right in labeling him a resister in the first place. As a well-socialized member of the educational community, I am unlikely to examine influence of my own behavior on the student's defiance. Similarly, when students' cheating on exams is perceived as part of their dishonest disposition, they are handled punitively (which only teaches them to cheat more carefully). If they were seen within a situational context, the effective "treatment" would not be punishment but making a change in the context. But the situational context includes the very people who want to stamp out the cheating, a fact they are not likely to acknowledge. Hence, they prefer to address themselves to cheating as a disposition of the students. This however is not likely to be the way the cheating students would contextualize their own behaviors.

The paradox described above (a mismatch between the ways people contextualize their own and others' behaviors) leads to certain actions, or "treatments." Consider a treatment designed to change a student's disposition. Such a treatment creates a new interpersonal context that is likely to entail, in the present illustrations, suspicion, threat, fear, and reactance, and these are likely to influence the nature and specific meanings given to acts within the new context. Moreover, it is a context within which one is unlikely to be very much aware of one's own relational cues but extremely sensitive to those emitted by others (see Chapter 5). Most importantly, disciplinary (or supportive) acts can be perceived by the receivers as messages. And because these are addressed to undesirable behaviors and attributed dispositions ("We won't tolerate cheating!" "Cheer up, life is so much nicer than you think"), one is likely to infer that one indeed has such a disposition. After all, when a new context has been created, one tends to adapt to it.

Two related consequences follow from such a situation. One is that attributing the cause of behavior to a disposition is an act not easily refuted. Given the great variability in people's behaviors, there are always *some* behaviors that confirm a dispositional attribution. People who are considered to have the trait of being "influential" are most attentively listened to and their messages more deeply processed. As their words are taken more seriously, these people are afforded greater influence (recall the treatment of "Chauncey Gardiner" in Jerzy Kosinski's *Being There*).

A related consequence is that intervention focuses on the alleged dispositions rather than on the situational context which gave rise to the undesirable behavior. Thus, for example, rather than examining the possibility that one's depression is interdependent with the attempts of others to cheer the depressed person up, attempts are made to change another context—the *disposition* for depression (Watzlawick et al., 1974). Increasingly intensive interventions may then be employed with, alas, little success.[1]

Many kinds of punitive and "corrective" interventions show such small success because they do not change the immediate situational contexts which maintain the undesirable behavior far more strongly than other contexts such as "dispositions." When increasingly harsher, deeper, or more extensive measures are taken (more "serious talk," more punishment, more interpersonal aid), they do not change the context; they only become more interdependent with the behaviors they were designed to change. Thus, for example, the clumsy child is constantly warned to be careful, and as her clumsiness does not disappear, she is not even given a glass of water to hold. The more her clumsiness becomes an issue of concern, the clumsier she becomes, as by now she is afraid of her own movements and of the others' reactions. The possibility that the child's increasing clumsiness comes to be maintained by her parents' behavior is often overlooked.

A study by Zigler and Butterfield (1968) can serve as a partial illustration. They confirmed the hypothesis that culturally disadvantaged preschoolers perform less well on IQ tests under standard testing conditions for motivational reasons. Still, low IQ scores are usually attributed to poor upbringing and poor ability rather than to standard testing conditions that have been shown to have adverse motivational effects. The more that "disadvantaged" children are labeled as such, then, and singled out for special treatment, the more the labels and treatments may come to *maintain* their "poor ability."

This is not to say that personality dispositions, prior preferences, skill deficiencies, and the like do not affect interactions. Obviously they do, as I have emphasized all along. However, once an interaction takes place, it serves as an immediate and powerful context which often overrides to a significant extent initial dispositions. Each person brings to the situation dispositions (personal contexts or schemata) with which to approach, interpret, and react to others. However, as a relationship steadies over time, more interdependence of perception and behavior develops (see Chapter 5) and more routinized strategies and tactics set in, so "certain patterns of interaction tend to recur with only minor variations from one sequence to the next" (Peterson, 1979: 37). The relationship becomes a salient context on its own right: "At any stage in the course of a relationship, the pattern of recurrent interactions that takes place between the participants *is* the relationship" (Peterson, 1979: 37). And the influence of this context on the participants' behaviors becomes much stronger in maintaining these present behaviors than the participants' initial dispositions (also see Bandura, 1978).

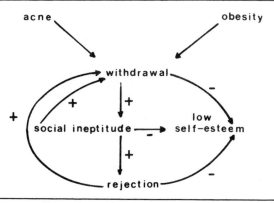

Figure 6.1 How a Loop Becomes Independent

Weick (1979) provides a number of relevant illustrations. One based on Wendner's (1968) work on "vicious and virtuous circles" is particularly pertinent here. Imagine a youngster who is fat and pimply, conditions that apparently lead him to withdraw socially in embarrassment. He experiences (or so he thinks) social rejection while displaying social ineptitude, which leads him to experience poor self-esteem and further withdrawal. Figure 6.1 describes the events. This youngster is in an ongoing interpersonal context. Withdrawal, lowered self-esteem, and social ineptitude have already been routinized to become part of a familiar context and are mutually interdependent. Within that context neither social ineptitude nor social rejection are single causes. Rather, each maintains the other in an already functionally autonomous circle. As Weick (1979: 82) points out, "an outcome produced for one reason may continue for other reasons due to amplification."

Others might try to help the youngster with his ineptitude by helping him cope with social interactions. Such an approach appears sensible, since the continued misery is now assigned to the context of the youngster's social ineptitude, and correcting a deficiency by doing its opposite sounds reasonable enough (Watzlawick et al. 1974). But there is a chance that the youngster will interpret such aid as a demeaning message that he is weak and dependent which only worsens his self-esteem. The more he then tries to "make it" without help, the more he proves his social ineptitude. On the other hand, aid could be perceived as a sign of social acceptance rather than "superiority," thereby breaking the vicious circle. But regardless of the ultimate outcomes, the important point to note is that the youngster's misery is maintained or changed more by the others' behaviors, which his withdrawal keeps maintaining, than by the initial causes.

Patterns of interpersonal contacts develop in distinctively different ways depending on whether the behaviors of others are seen as determined by (that is, contextualized in terms of) traits or affected by interaction. When the cause of another person's behavior is attributed to personality traits ("He's stubborn and won't listen"), the attributor is likely to try to change the undesirable traits or reinforce the desirable ones. This is particularly the case for educators, who often feel an obligation or desire to change a student. Thus, if an educator sees a student as "stubborn," there is a tendency to use ever stronger measures to overcome the alleged stubbornness; attempting to change the trait itself ("Don't be stubborn").

In light of what has been said in earlier chapters, it is reasonable to expect that when one tries to change another's traits, the other perceives such attempts as personal messages that call for a response. For example, when a teacher tries to make me, say, more decisive or assertive, I will tend to see such action as intended to communicate the teacher's dissatisfaction with my indecision, and I will tend to reciprocate in one way or another.

Attempts to change a student's dispositions can be perceived as either benevolent or malevolent. For example, a student can perceive a teacher's explicit attempts to foster her self-esteem as helping her or as demeaning her in her peers' eyes. In either case reciprocity may take place, but its nature will differ. Perceived *benevolence* is reciprocated with benevolent actions (Kruglanski, 1975) in the form of greater acceptance of the other's definitions and attributions. For example, Baumeister, Cooper, and Skib (1979) found that when it was publicly announced that a subject had a particularly desirable trait and it was then stated that people with such a trait perform poorly on a specific anagram-solving task, the subject solved significantly fewer anagrams. They "took a dive" to adapt to the trait context.

Malevolence is likely to be perceived when one's "traits" become a target for change against one's will. People are likely to see in the attempts to change them implications that they are not what others think they should be. This leads to reactance (Miller, Brickman, and Bolen, 1975). In such cases, the change target is likely to respond by revolting against the educator's definitions, by performing the forbidden behaviors behind the other's back (Hart, 1978), and the like. Baumeister et al. (1979) found that when it was announced that subjects had an undesirable trait, they tried hard to disconfirm the attributional context by performing *better* than expected.

The important point to note is that whether the effort to change one's traits is perceived as benevolent or malevolent, one responds reciprocally. In the case of perceived benevolence, the context is accepted, thus leading to possible self-fulfilling or sustaining prophecies: students come to believe that they are able (or indecisive) and behave accordingly. In the case of perceived malevolence, the context is rejected and vicious circles develop and are reinforced: The student becomes "uncooperative," which calls for increasingly stronger countermeasures, and so on.

It is quite a different story when an educator sees student behaviors in an interactional context. First, the attributor is more likely to address personal inputs and the interactional context, and less likely to attempt to change directly the other's behavior underlying disposition. Thus, with my "stubborn" student I might test the possibility that my style of communication makes him behave "stubbornly" and then might change my own behavior. Or I might express frustration, thereby changing the whole interactional context, raising the contacts to a meta level.

A second difference is that the student is less likely to see the educator's behaviors as messages intended to change "badness, madness, or stupidity" and more likely to see them as actions that are aimed at changing the context. For example, when a parent tells a child, "I can see why you wouldn't want to listen to me" (Knudson, Sommers, and Golding, 1980), the object of the statement is not the child or the child's "traits." Rather, it is the parent's perception of the relationship between the two; that is, actions and messages are addressed at a higher (meta) level. Knudson, Sommers, and Golding (1980: 761) showed that when couples successfully engaged in conflict resolution they expressed increasingly higher level perceptions. These led not only to greater agreement about content per se, but also to greater "access to the perception of the other: under- standing . . . and realization of understanding." In other words, when communication concerns the context of interaction and not individual personalities, people respond more positively. This may occur because they see themselves as responding to a particular situation and not as expressing undesirable person- ality traits. When others see this also, they feel their motivations and actions are understood, and they do not feel they have to defend their own view of what is happening. Once this approach is taken and one participant moves to a meta, context level ("I think we misunderstand each other; is this what you're trying to say?"), one can expect the other participant to respond with similar attempts.

In sum, I have argued that interpersonal contacts are influ- enced by contexts, but as these are like schemata, it is difficult to generate a taxonomy of context independent of the ways they are perceived. I focused on the differences in interaction between two extreme cases on contextualizing another's behav- ior: assigning behavior to a trait or disposition context and assigning behavior to an interactional context. The former usually dominates in people's perceptions, leading to the "basic attributional error" and making people ignore the situations within which they and the others interact.

This issue is of particular relevance to education, since educators try to mold the behaviors of students according to whether they assign students' behaviors to trait or interaction contexts. In fact, educators are not very likely to assign behaviors to interactional contexts because the educators would have to acknowledge that they themselves influence these contexts by their actions. I have argued that assigning behaviors to a trait context leads to attempts to change (or reinforce) the trait. The change agents usually fail to see their own contribution; they think they "only respond" to the other's behavior. Such attempts are perceived by the other either as benevolent intentions to communicate, leading to acceptance and to self-fulfilling prophecies, or as malevolent intentions, leading to rejection and development of vicious circles. Assigning behaviors to an interactional context, a much less frequent case (particularly in education) involves changing one's own behaviors or the whole interactional context. This happens when communication is "raised" to meta levels, inviting reciprocal change instead of repetition or escalation of the same kinds of behavior and perceptions. Research (Knudson et al., 1980) and case studies (Watzlawick et al., 1974) suggest that desirable changes in interpersonal relations are more likely to occur when behaviors are seen in the context of interaction rather than the context of personal traits. I discuss this issue at greater length in the next chapter.

<h2 style="text-align:center">CONTEXTS AND MEDIA:
THE APPLICATION OF "PICTORIAL STANDARDS"</h2>

As with learning in school and with interpersonal relations, the contexts in which exposure to the media takes place affect the way in which media exert an influence. In studying the cognitive effects of *Sesame Street* on Israeli children (Salomon, 1977) I found that when mothers in families with low socioeconomic status watched the program with their preschool children, the latter learned nearly as much from it as middle-class children did. (Asking middle-class mothers to watch the program with their children did not affect the latter's learning, possibly because nothing new was introduced by our manipulation; middle-class mothers generally watch such programs with their children anyway.) Another example: Mialaret (1966) hypothesized that because people feel anonymous in darkened movie theaters, they can afford to express their emotional reactions to the movie in less inhibited ways and thus can experience stronger emotions. Unfortunately, this hypothesis was never put to a test.

The contexts depicted in movies or described in books also influence how something is understood. Edgar (1977) found that Australian children are more disturbed by violent acts on TV when these acts are seen within contexts that can be related to their own lives. Collins and Zimmermann (1975) showed that when children saw aggressive acts on TV in an experimentally induced context of negative motives and consequences, their subsequent violent responses were more inhibited.

The medium itself serves as a context as well. It is an untested, yet reasonable hypothesis that a show such as *Backstairs at the White House* would be treated with greater AIME when shown on "serious" public television than when shown by a commercial network whose stock in trade is light entertainment (assuming we could control the composition of the audience and prevent differential self-selection).

Such contexts can be ranged in a nested hierarchy ranging from the remoter ones, such as the general perception of a medium's function, to the more proximal ones, such as the specific contexts of events described or depicted in specific media presentations. Somewhat less obvious is the notion that the most essential contextual differences among media (yet the ones least studied) are their modes of gathering, packaging, and presenting information, that is their dominant symbol-systems.[2]

Elsewhere (Salomon, 1979) I have argued that neither contents nor modes of usage constitute the essential difference between media: Stories are read in books, read aloud, and dramatized on TV; scientific experiments are read about, seen in the lab, and shown on screens; and motorists consult maps or gas station attendants for directions. Similarly, movies are seen in darkened theaters, but so are opera and ballet shows; reading is done in solitude and so is the examination of a stamp collection.

What does serve as an essential difference among the media is their symbol systems - the unique blend of picture and sound, program and commericial in TV; printed formal language in books; cartography in maps; and the like. These different modes of presentation serve as meaning contexts in at least two ways. First, we have reason to believe that different symbol systems, and the different symbolic components within them, are processed by different kinds of mental skills (see Salomon and Cohen, 1977). Second, the same content presented via different symbol systems appears to yield somewhat different kinds of information (see Meringoff, 1980).

Here, however, we face a problem: How does one come to treat differently coded messages in different ways? After all, as Roupas (1977: 51) points out, a picture, musical notation, piece of writing or map is just an object, "be it canvas covered with pigment, some splotches of ink, a sequence of sounds or something else," and "in order to function as a symbol capable of communicating information *it must be interpreted in some way*" (italics added).

As TV figures so prominently among the media, and as it is dominated by pictures, I will elaborate the argument with reference to pictures and TV. And since TV is so often seen by children to be lifelike (Leifer et al., 1974; Greenberg and Reeves, 1976), I will concentrate mainly on how the context of a symbol system affects the perception of "resemblance" and "realism."

Symbols, as Goodman (1968) argues, are quite meaningless unless seen as part of a *system*. When a curved line belongs to the pictorial system, every twist, every variation of width, strength, and color counts; when it is part of the system of graphs, only the variations among coordinates are relevant. It would seem that the assignment of a symbol, character, or sign to the context of a particular system determines its status as symbol or sign, as well as its more specific meaning. The same also applies to subsystems: The letter U has certain sounds in the context of the English language and different ones in German. And within each language, the sound is influenced by the context of the word (compare "use" with "utterance").

We could say that each symbol system has its own intrinsic properties, to which we have learned to be sensitive, and that we differentially apply mental skills of processing to them. We have also learned to seek out different kinds of information depending on the symbol system into which we contextualize a message. Thus, we know that pictures are "analogs" and then look for resemblances between them and their referents, and we know that words are arbitrary signs and do not seek any resemblance between them and their referents.

This is precisely where symbol systems as contexts and people's schemata as contexts may differ from each other. People put messages they recognize as pictures into a pictorial context that indicates to them that some measure of "resemblance" or "realism" must be involved. But as Goodman (1968) so nicely shows, pictures represent their referents without necessarily resembling them. He argues persuasively that certain qualities (to be discussed in the following pages) do distinguish pictures from other symbol systems, but realism (or resemblance) is not one of them. Thus, we may contextualize lines, shades, patches of color as pictures but then apply to them the wrong expectations. And it is these expectations, not the "true nature" of a symbol system as semioticians know it, that determines how we handle a message. So the context that determines our way of handling messages in the media is more strongly influenced by our mental schema than by the medium's symbol system.

Goodman (1968) analyzed symbol systems in the arts and differentiated among them along the dimension of *notationality*. The differences between notational systems (musical scores, language) and nonnotational systems (nonverbal expressions, pictures) are well articulated by Gardner, Howard, and Perkins (1974: 31):

> A notational system consists of a set of separate, discontinuous characters (for example, a musical score) correlated with a field of reference which is similarly segregated (sounded pitches) so that any character in the system isolates the object or objects it stands for, or, conversely, an object isolates the character that is correlated with it. Notationality contrasts with a continuous, unsegregated (for example, pictorial) system for which no alphabet or set of disjoint characters exists.

Such a distinction implies, contrary to popular common sense notions, that nonnotational representations (such as pictures) are far from closely resembling their referents, in an "analogic" sense. For to be "analogic" each and every discrete element or "character" in a symbol system (say, the letter O) ought to map upon one parallel element in the field of reference (the sound "O"). Pictures, frowns, or body movements, while having apparent "similarity" to their referents, do not map upon them in any unequivocal way.

Goodman argues that a picture resembles itself to the maximum and yet is rarely taken to represent itself. Resemblance is (philosophically speaking) a matter of symmetry, whereby if A resembles B then B resembles A. But this is not the case in art or media depictions. *The Jeffersons* may resemble a familiar neighboring family, but the family does not resemble the program. (As Tversky, 1977, has shown, perceived resemblance is asymmetrical—the number 13, the variant, resembles the number 10, the "anchor," but not the other way around.) A picture (or TV program) may *resemble* one thing but *represent* another. For example, a painting of Churchill as lion resembles one thing (lion) and represents another (Churchill). Thus, according to Goodman (1968: 5):

> The plain fact is that a picture, to present an object, must be a symbol for it, stand for it, refer to it; and that no degree of resemblance is sufficient to establish the requisite relationship of

reference. Nor is resemblance necessary for reference; almost anything may stand for almost anything else.

Why, then, are pictures perceived to resemble their referents (even when the latter do not exist, as in the case of a painting of the devil)? Why are Rockwell's paintings "more realistic" than many of Picasso's? The naive answer is that the former paintings provide greater amounts of pertinent information. However, if we replaced each of the colors in a Rockwell painting by its complement it would still yield the same amount of information, but would now be regarded as less "realistic." Thus, as Goodman concludes, informational yield is no test of realism.

What *is* a test of "realism" is the perceived resemblance between a denotative depiction and what we, as the picture users, have in mind as template, schema, or context. Old Japanese drawings look quite unrealistic to us, as old European paintings must have appeared to the Japanese. But each culture would swear that *its* depictions are realistic (as did the sixteenth century artist who drew a locust as a flying horse). Similarly, many of us who saw the "neorealistic" Italian films of the fifties (such as *La Strada*) would not regard them as such today, although the films themselves have not changed. However, the schemata into which we assimilate such films to give them meaning certainly have changed.

Everything we encounter and perceive as communicationally intended is, by necessity, also seen as representational or symbolic (see Chapter 2); that is, it is coded. And if an event is taken as coded, then we have to translate it from its communicational symbol system into a cognitive one, for we represent the world to ourselves in symbolic forms (see Kosslyn and Pomerantz, 1977). These may partly but not wholly replicate the ones used in communication (Bruner, 1964; Salomon, 1979). Thus, we think in images that resemble perceptions of events (Shepard, 1978), we think in terms of verbal propositions (Paivio, 1978), and possibly we think in other symbol systems as well.

It follows that communicational symbol systems can be closer to or farther away from the cognitive symbol systems one employs at a given time, for a particular purpose, and for specific contents. It is reasonable to assume that most of us think of spatial relations in terms of images, and thus a drawing will come closer to such mental representations than words. And it is equally likely that the reader of this book (whose schemata concerning "realism" and "resemblance" are now attacked with discrepant information) counterargues with Goodman or me via internal propositions, not images. Thus, the text here comes closer to the reader's mental mode of elaborating the material than cartoons would.

When a coded message is encountered and translated (that is *re*coded, not *de*coded), the number of translation steps it requires depends on its "distance" from the context of the symbol system with which one eventually understands it. If I had used cartoons rather than the English language, so many more translation steps would be required that many readers would give up in frustration. It is apparently for this reason that numerical exercises are "easier" than math problems in words, and that stories with illustrations improve comprehension by beginning readers compared with stories lacking illustrations (Pressley, 1977).

Certain representations appear to be more "realistic" because their symbolic form comes closer to the way users represent the depicted entity to themselves. The less recoding something requires, the mentally "easier" it is to experience and the more "real" it appears. This applies even to representations of ideas that cannot be seen or touched. As Goodman (1968: 36) argues,

> Just here, I think, lies the touchstone of realism: not in quantity of information but in how easily it issues. And this depends upon how stereotyped the mode of representation is, upon how commonplace the labels and their uses have become.

For a representation to issue the information easily it must be quite stereotypic. In other words, it must fit into the context of developed schemata with minimal recoding. If such representations have been frequently encountered in the past, thereby cultivating appropriate anticipatory schemata, and if a new representation (another crime drama on TV) looks in symbolic structure very much like the previous ones, then it is considered "stereotypic," as it easily fits into the preexisting mental context.

Indeed, as Goodman (1968: 39) points out, "That a picture looks like nature often means that it looks the way nature is usually painted." The same, even more strongly, applies to images and conceptions we have acquired from the media. "Naive" and "drip" effects of the media (see Chapter 4) cultivate anticipatory schemata that serve as contexts into which new messages are assimilated. The media-cultivated images then come to serve as the "real thing," for in most cases one does not have much else to base an image on. (Are not the reader's images of Soviet classrooms, coal mines, galaxies, the double helix, British aristocracy, and the Holocaust based on media presentations?) To the extent that new encounters with depictions happen to fit neatly (to require only little recoding) into one's images, they are likely to be seen as "realistic."

Here, then, is a perfect case of spirality: Exposure to media depictions cultivates images which then are used as contexts that give meaning to new depictions. The "closer" the symbolic form of the new depiction is to the symbolic form of the context image, the more "realistic" the former appears. When the depiction deviates from the context, the latter is likely to accommodate itself to the deviant depiction, thus changing our schemata for "realism" (see Chapter 3). For example, it seems that Japanese paintings appeared "unrealistic" to the first westerners who encountered them, but continued exposure to such paintings made them seem more "realistic" in the eyes of Europeans (Gombrich, 1960).

I have argued that if a representation comes close enough to one's preferred cognitive symbols, it will be seen as both "easy to understand" and "realistic." But while this may be the case with pictures, maps, and even diagrams, it is *not* the case with, say, words. Even the most verbal, proposition-inclined readers of this book will not treat this text as "realistic" or as "resembling" the referents, even if they need only a few steps of recoding to comprehend the text. Similarly, people are more likely to think of TV's pictoriality as "realistic" when they do not have to recode it, but are not likely to think that TV dialogue is "realistic," even if it requires little recoding. So what I have argued regarding "realism" seems to apply only to nonnotational symbol systems.

It also follows from my argument that when a mode of presentation requires much cognitive recoding it will not be seen as "realistic." But as Roupas (1977) correctly points out, an X-ray does not in the least resemble our perception of the human body, but it is still a "realistic" picture for us. Similarly with television: Viewers would be quite likely to believe that a picture of a kind they have never encountered before (such as a vastly enlarged photograph of a cell nucleus) is "realistic."

"Realism," as we have seen, is very much a matter of expectations and shared assumptions, not necessarily a function of what a representation really is. But why does this pertain only to nonnotational systems and not to notational ones? Why are TV productions often seen as lifelike, but texts, statistical analyses, and musical scores are not? A possible answer is that nonnotational systems are taken to *depict* their fields of reference while notational ones are taken to *describe* them. A Bosch painting of hell depicts hell; Sartre's play *No Exit* describes it.

Goodman (1968) postulated that in a representational system that depicts rather than describes, continuous variations along some dimension of the symbol correlate with corresponding variations along some dimension of the referent. This does not hold for notational systems that describe a referent. For example, the size of the letters in the word "five" has no bearing on "fiveness," regardless of how small, bold, or spread the letters are. But the size of a tree in a painting does bear on our idea of "treeness." Thus, nonnotational systems have certain properties, such as continuity, seemingly absent from notational ones. It is true that every symbol, including a printed letter, has some continuity, but this continuity often indicates nothing to the perceiver.

When do we know whether continuity (or other properties) should be considered in mentally recoding a symbol? As Roupas (1977: 69) argues, we need to apply an interpretative standard of a special kind: a "pictorial standard," meaning simply "a rule that declares when a symbol is to count as faithful to an object." Then, when we note one or more properties associated with the "pictorial standard" in a particular symbol, we assume that other properties are relevant and yield meaningful information about the referent. Thus, for example, we apply the pictorial standard to a word and to a drawing and decide that the word does not have the properties of a picture but the drawing does. Therefore we know that examining continuous variations in the thickness of a letter will not tell us anything about its referent, but examining such variations in the lines and shades of a drawing will.

Notice that the "pictorial standard" serves as a context. It tells us what properties in a symbol to look for, what they indicate, and what meaning to give to the information the symbol yields. Most importantly, this standard often tells us that one of the properties indicated by depiction or continuity is "resemblance" to objects or "realism." And this can easily lead to errors. Maps, I have found (Salomon, 1968), are often perceived as pictures (that is, a "pictorial standard" is applied to them) and are therefore seen as "realistic" depictions. Eighth graders, and to a lesser degree adults, perceive the color green on a map (elevation 0-100 m.) to depict cultivated land, the color yellow (elevation 100-200 m.) to depict desert, and circles that represent cities to depict "round, walled cities."

Such errors suggest that the symbol system of maps is incorrectly perceived; a "pictorial standard" is applied to them, while in fact many of their properties are quite notational. But once maps are seen in a pictorial context, certain map properties are singled out as indicative of "realistic depiction."[3]

In the case of TV, once its messages are contextualized as pictures, the application of the "pictorial standard" leads to the conclusion that events on TV are "realistic." But the same is not done with the dialogue because a different standard is applied to it. The influence of the pictorial standard is so strong that it can cause people to see a resemblance even when the depiction does not resemble anything, not even another image (as is the possible case with X-rays).

In sum, symbol systems serve as contexts in two ways. People recode messages into their internal modes of representation, and the number of recoding steps determines the "ease" of a message and how "realistic" it appears. These internal symbol systems are contexts that serve a *meaning* function. In addition, there are the standards one applies to a message. When such a standard is a "pictorial standard," certain properties of the message become relevant and indicate the existence and importance of other properties. Such standards are contexts that serve a *normative* function, as they suggest which message properties are relevant and what they indicate.

All this implies two things. First, if the ultimate nature of a medium presentation depends so heavily on how its modes of presentation are contextualized by the receiver, then the kinds of mental contexts children bring to bear on media presentations should be of concern to educators. Television, as I have shown in Chapter 5, is approached as an "easy" medium, and this, it appears, is very much due to its pictorial symbol systems. Not only are TV programs seen as depictions, these depictions are seen as "realistic," with the added expectation that no great AIME is needed to understand TV's messages. Attempts to change children's perception of the medium, like the one by Dorr, Graves, and Phelps (1980), are in this respect attempts to teach children to contextualize TV differently. More specifically, children were taught that the property "depiction" does not necessarily indicate realism. Thus, the training may have created a dissociation between the "pictorial standard" and the assumption concerning realism. The same kind of instruction would be needed with other symbol systems in the media.

Second, it is reasonable to assume that previous encounters with media presentations provide children with particular images into which new events are then contextualized and judged for realism and correctness. It has been hypothesized

(Salomon, 1979) that children learn from their heavy exposure to TV to think in terms of TV's symbol systems. Although there is some experimental evidence to support this hypothesis, as yet we do not have evidence to show that such internalized symbol systems are then applied as contexts to new events.[4]

Assume for the moment that we had such evidence. The "language of TV" that children would come to use in cognition (much like "internalized speech") is only one way to store, process, and contextualize new events. Other ways are equally useful as schemata and contexts, but heavy televiewing may make them less accessible. One should be able to think of mathematical relations in terms of spatial vectors, propositions, and formulae interchangeably. This, as Olson (1978) points out, is one of the indications of good comprehension. Likewise, children should be able to think of other people in terms of words, images, sounds, and the like. (Recall the findings of Lord, 1980, suggesting that we often tend to think of others in terms of images and of ourselves in propositions, a tendency that may be reinforced by heavy TV viewing.) The purpose of teaching children to contextualize new events in different symbol systems would not be to strengthen one cognitive mode at the expense of others, but to help children use symbol systems interchangeably and to see other people and events in many contexts.

Similarly, one would want to teach children to apply to coded media messages alternative standards, not only the "pictorial standard." For example, it should be possible to teach children how to look at a picture as a metaphor or as something that expresses rather than depicts. Indeed, as a study by Gardner (1972) shows, children can be taught to apply other than the simple "pictorial standard" to works of art, and thus to deal with properties such as artistic style and expressivity.

CONCLUSION

Communicational events are always contextualized by other events that are more general and can offer them meaning. But contexts are not entities "out there." They are places, roles, behaviors, and so forth to which people assign specific meanings, properties, and expectations. In this sense, contexts are akin to anticipatory schemata, and what applies to schemata applies also to contexts. Contexts as schemata are "arranged" on a hierarchy according to generality and typicality and contain each other. They serve two major kinds of functions. The ones farther away from the contextualized event serve in a normative capacity by prescribing the legitimacy and desirability of behaviors. The contexts that are closer to the event offer meanings to it. For example, the context of school prescribes how to behave; the context of a teacher's nonverbal behavior offers meaning to her verbal instructions.

Contexts and messages, when close enough to each other in people's perceptions, can exchange roles and influence each other reciprocally. This point is discussed in some detail in the section devoted to learning. Learning can be seen as a process that is contained in a number of more general contexts ranging from schooling in general to classroom climates. However, I emphasized the interchangeability between learning and some of its closer contexts: climate, classroom management, social cohesiveness. I concluded that one should ask not only how, say, classroom climate gives meaning to specific interactions that promote or inhibit learning, but also how learning outcomes change the meanings of interactions and the classroom climate.

In the section on interpersonal contacts, I argued that people adapt themselves to contexts quite flexibly, and yet when we attribute causes to others' behaviors we prefer dispositional over situational ones. Thus, we tend to ignore people's flexible adaptation to contexts. This is a paradox inasmuch as most people actually behave situationally and explain their own behaviors as such. The question, then, of how others' behaviors are explained (contextualized) is of great importance in education, since educators try to change student behaviors. When they see the context of these behaviors as the student's traits or dispositions (the more frequent case), the undesirable "disposition" is then the target of change. This creates a new "treatment context" to which the student adapts; accepting the attributed "traits" (self-fulfilling prophecies) or rejecting them, becoming noncooperative and inviting stronger treatment and thus moving the educator and student into a vicious circle.

When the context of behavior is seen as a situation involving interaction, one does not try to change a "trait" or "disposition"; one is concerned with the interactional context. The latter then is seen as a force stronger than the remote context of "disposition" in maintaining the behaviors of the participants. Thus, the interactional context is the change target, promising more desirable results.

In the section on media, I argued that of the many contexts nesting media exposure, perhaps the most essential but least studied are the media's symbol systems. I focused mainly on TV and the issue of pictoriality.

Two main points were made. First, the meaning of a coded message seems to depend on one's own mental symbol system, into which the message is recoded or translated from the medium's symbol system. The less recoding needed, the more "realistic" the message appears. But this seemed to explain too much: Language is hardly ever seen as "realistic," while pictures of unfamiliar objects frequently appear as such. Thus followed the second argument according to which pictures are seen as depictions at which point a "pictorial standard" is applied to them. This standard implies the existence of other properties that indicate "resemblance" or "similarity," even when such do not exist or cannot be determined. (And as the philosopher Goodman postulated, resemblance is unnecessary and insufficient to make something into a picture anyway.)

The "pictorial standard" turns out to be a normative context, but it is often taken as a context that provides meaning, and meaning contexts influence judgments of "realism." I suggested that children be taught to use both kinds of contexts flexibly: applying "pictorial standards" (without expecting pictures to be "realistic") interchangeably with nonpictorial standards.

NOTES

1. Watzlawick et al. (1974) devoted a whole book to these issues which strongly influenced me in writing this section.

2. By "symbol systems" I mean any collection of signs or characters, such as musical notes, shapes, and colors, or the alphabet, which are used to convey information in a referential way (Roupas, 1977). See more on this in Goodman (1968), Perkins and Leondar (1977), and Salomon (1979). The latter more directly deals with symbol systems in the media. Also see Chapter 5, the section on interpersonal contacts.

3. Similar errors occur when people treat abstract art as depictions and then search for "similarities" to familiar objects, often not knowing that expressive art need not be correlated with resemblance.

4. The only evidence we have regarding this tendency, to the best of my knowledge, comes from one of our earlier studies showing that a sample of children experimentally exposed to *Sesame Street* subsequently learned more from a science film, suggesting that film-relevant skills had been improved by *Sesame Street* and successfully applied to the science film.

Chapter 7
LOOPS AND SPIRALS

*If you have a genuine causal circuit, then
any change made anywhere will
eventually itself be changed by the
consequences it triggers.*

(Weick, 1979:77)

This book relates communication to education by means of a reciprocal paradigm. The paradigm postulates that personal dispositions, attributions of intent and meaning, communicational behaviors, and educational outcomes are reciprocally related to each other. We are influenced by others' messages, but it is our (often a priori) interpretation of the messages that influence the *way* we are influenced. It is logically consistent to derive from such a perspective the conception that communication is a consequence of attribution and attribution is a consequence of prior communication. No wonder, therefore, that throughout the book I often return to circular and spiral processes. I could even find empirical evidence to support (at least partly) my claims.

How curious! Once you choose a particular paradigm, perspective, or vantage point, provided you adhere to it, you are quite likely to marshal the necessary evidence to support it. I am sure that it would not be too difficult to find a sufficient number of real-life examples and research findings that could be interpreted to support an alternative viewpoint. To paraphrase Wagar (1963; quoted by Jones, 1977), the ultimate function of a paradigm is not to describe the world but to make it.

The purpose of pointing out my vices is to highlight the cyclical nature of communication, as I see it. The world around us, particularly its social reality, is sufficiently "raw" and rich to permit us to interpret it according to our a priori assumptions, hypotheses, and expectations (our schemata) and even to change the world around us to fit our beliefs. Thus, it would seem, we are moving in loops—some more vicious, others more virtuous. But then, not everything yields to our expectations, allowing us to assimilate it without any accommodation by our schemata. Other people have their own expectations and want to interpret our behavior, even change us, in light of *their* schemata. Research findings, likewise, can be selected and interpreted in light of an initial paradigm, but only to a point. Beyond that point, research findings begin to revolt. Not everything moves in loops or closed circles. Some processes are more akin to *spirals,* whereby external events change schemata which, once changed, handle similar stimuli in new ways.

The reciprocal nature of interaction—its circularity and spirality—has emerged throughout the preceding chapters. We have seen how closed loops take place. Children with poor self-concepts select "uninvolving" seats in classrooms and cut themselves off from the mainstream of ongoing events (Dykman and Reis, 1979). They attribute pejorative meanings to relational aspects of messages addressed to them, and consequently maintain their self-concepts. We have seen how labeling a person as "mentally ill" (Rosenhan, 1973), "assistant" (Langer and Benevento, 1978), "culturally disadvantaged" (Adar, 1978), or "late bloomer" (Meichenbaum et al., 1969) can turn into a self-fulfilling or self-sustaining prophecy. We have seen how people solicit only confirming evidence and make others behave in accordance with expectations (Snyder, forthcoming). We discovered how the initial perception of television, itself based on TV's apparent realism, leads to the investment of little mental effort, which then "proves" TV to be shallow. We have also seen how people's initial expectations help them avoid the ideas of *All in the Family,* and how the consensual conceptions that educational systems hold can become resistant to disproof and possibly become taken for the "real thing" (Weick, 1979). Similarly, we have considered how contextualizing another's behavior as the result of a trait or disposition can influence the other to adopt the disposition (Baumeister et al., 1979).

We also observed the escalating intensity of closed loops. Among these, we included the relationship between disciplinary actions and undisciplined behaviors (Duke, 1978), and we observed how teachers' expectations of students' low motivation depress motivation even further (Tjosvold and Kastelic, 1976). We saw that disputes can intensify when interactants are unaware of their own relational cues, reject or ignore the other's interpretations, or base their own judgments on global schemata.

More virtuous circles were also discussed. Interdependence among individuals can grow in intimacy, leading to even closer contacts; successful experiences lead to enhanced self-efficacy, leading to the investment of more effort in tasks (Bandura, 1977b, 1978). Children influence the way TV influences them, and changes in the former lead to subsequent changes in the latter, which again change the former.

We have considered not only closed and escalating spirals but also the possibility of larger changes of whole conceptual and interactional systems. Such changes differ from relatively smooth spiral movements in their discontinuity and "jumps" from one level to a meta level of discourse or relations. For example, we briefly considered ideological conversions as an example of breaking out of closed loops, and we considered how to avoid the paradoxical role of schemata as promoters and then inhibitors of learning. Following Watzlawick et al. (1974), we distinguished between changes of the first and second order, the latter typically being more of the discontinuous kind.

All this is of marginal interest unless we accept the possibility that communication, as conceived here, is prone by its very nature to create, become part of, and sustain loops and spirals. For the circular nature of communication follows logically from its interdependence with the attribution of specific intents and meanings. Thus, you see what you believe (a loop); but you may also come to change your beliefs in light of new encounters (a spiral). Similarly, in social interaction you respond to other people in light of your expectations, but your way of responding to them is influenced by the way they respond to you in light of their expectations. In some cases each party sticks to personal expectations, attributions, and interpretations (loops); in other cases, these change (spirals).

Most important, what one sees, says, and does depends heavily on the information and understandings one has stored, that is, on prior education. Subsequent encounters with one's surroundings either remain unchanged, being totally determined by the stored education (as is the case with some idealogues and entrenched experts), or gradually change (as is expected of scientists), or they undergo more dramatic changes (as when one experiences important new insights).

Given such loops and spirals, it becomes necessary to ask what characterizes the former, what characterizes the latter, and how they differ from each other. Then we will have to ask what kinds of communicational procedures can educate one to break out of existing loops and to avoid them sometimes in favor of spirals.

CLOSED LOOPS: "I WILL SEE IT WHEN I BELIEVE IT."

Loops are recurring chains of events which persist, unless stopped or broken. Although each loop has a starting point, once the loop is set in motion the event that began it can become quite peripheral as the loop comes to sustain itself. For example, as will be recalled, the expectation that another person is an extravert causes the expecting person to solicit mainly confirmatory evidence and even to shape the other's behavior to conform to expectations (Snyder, forthcoming). Thus, the initial expectation is reinforced by the solicited evidence. The original "cause" for the expectation (personal experience, a shared stereotype, an experimenter's suggestion) gradually becomes irrelevant, while the loop becomes self-sustaining.

Perceptual Loops. But while all loops become self-sustaining, they differ from each other in method of operation. We can speak of at least two kinds of closed loops, one of which is *perceptual.* Simply put, the way I expect something or someone to behave shapes how I sample and interpret information they yield. Shumsky and Mehan (1973; quoted by Lancy, 1978: 126) illustrate such a loop, reproducing a conversation among teachers and a principal during a faculty meeting.

Principal: And Mrs. Neal, do you have kids that you don't think should go on to second grade?

Mrs. Neal: Well, Mike Brandon for one.

Mrs. Susan: He's on my list.

Mrs. Neal: Oh, he's on your list?

Mrs. Jones: Did he take the reading test?

Mrs. Susan: Yeah.

Mrs. Jones: How did he do?

Mrs. Susan: Wait a minute, I've got it here (pause). I think he did OK, yeah, oh, he got a 1.7.

Mrs. Pollen: That's good.

Mrs. Neal: Yeah, but I was surprised by that. He can't read that good. He must have guessed a lot. I still have him in the Bluebirds (slow reading group).

As we see from the example above, in perceptual loops, schemata do not easily accommodate to experience. People resist modifying their perceptions and behaviors in the light of new information if the price of accommodation is too high; that is, if strongly held assumptions are threatened. Weick (1979: 156-157) points out that such may particularly be the case in organizations, in which goals, rules, and structures are consensual and are therefore perceived as the "real thing." Nobody questions them; thus they restrict "unorthodox" explorations and encourage the gathering of confirmatory evidence only.

> Any idea that restricts exploration and sampling will come to be seen as increasingly plausible by the very nature of that restriction. If a person has an idea and looks for relevant data, there's enough complexity and ambiguity in the world that relevance is usually judged more plausible. One of the prominent characteristics of schemata is that they are refractory to disproof.

Perceptual loops are particularly likely to repeat themselves unchanged when one party to the interaction is an organization, event, or object that does not have expectations of its own. Hence it is easy if you expect TV to be shallow entertainment to ignore everything else it may present and continue to treat it with minimal AIME. Unlike your friends or colleagues, TV is not likely to impose *its* anticipatory schemata on you.

Perceptual loops are exemplified by the dangers of "group-think," as analyzed by Janis (1972). The more cohesive and consensus-driven the group, the less it will allow the introduction of discrepant information that may disturb harmony by changing shared schemata. Being true believers in a shared schema, group members perceive only what can be assimilated into preexisting schemata.

Perceptual loops of a similar kind occur when potential employees are interviewed for a job (Tucker and Rowe, 1979). Interviewers read letters of reference which create in them either positive or negative expectations. Equipped with such expectations, they then give the interviewees more or less credit for past successes and hold them more or less responsible for past failures. Hiring decisions are then influenced by such attributions.

Reactive Loops. If stimuli are active instead of passive, they tend to change the nature of the perceptual loops and make them more reactive. In reactive loops, one person's expectations influence another person to conform to those expectations. Kelley and Stahelski (1970) illustrate the case rather clearly. They brought people to play the well-known Prisoners' Dilemma game, in which cooperation between participants can yield high scores for both; however, competition by both leads to losses for both unless one remains insistent and the other becomes "chicken." The participants in the Kelley and Stahelski study first expressed a desired relationship with partners. Each competitor was then matched with a cooperator. As expected, after a few games, most competitors judged their partners (initially cooperators) as equally competitive. As it turned out, competitors turned their initially cooperating partners into competitors without realizing that they were the ones to cause the shift, thus making the prophecy come true.

What makes a prophecy self-fulfilling? Merton (1957: 423) defined it as "in the beginning, a *false* definition of the situation evoking a new behavior which makes the originally false conception come *true*." Two conditions would seem to be needed. One is the false expectation and the other that the "object" of the expectation begins to behave in new ways. But is the false nature of the expectation indeed a necessary condition? When teachers were told that several students were "creative," "late bloomers," or "promising," they behaved toward them differently than before (see Chapter 3), thus making the prophecies come true. However, these prophecies could have been correct (based, say, on real tests), yet initially unknown to the teachers. Incorrectness does not seem to be a necessary condition to make a prophecy fulfill itself.

As for the second condition—eliciting new behaviors from the expectation target—it seems to be necessary for self-fulfilling prophecies but not for self-sustaining ones. In Snyder's studies (forthcoming), people whose behavior was shaped to become more extraverted exhibited new behaviors and thus made a prophecy come true. However, "culturally disadvantaged" students may exhibit learning difficulties from the outset, and the way in which schools treat them may only sustain the failure without eliciting new behaviors (see Chapter 4).

Self-sustaining expectations are a particularly potent force in education, and often cause confirming behaviors to be repeated. Other behaviors are prohibited, never given the opportunity to be evoked, or simply ignored. Thus, the people who have experienced failure at a task (such as studying math in high school) have a self-perception of ineffectiveness at similar tasks (statistics), relinquish any sustained effort in mastering them, and so maintain their perceived poor self-efficacy. The educational system "knows" from past-experience that inner city minority children are poor at school, labels all of them accordingly, places them in the "Bluebird group," teaches them less, treats them in more controlled ways, and thus ends up with the expected poor learning outcomes. Neither the math failure nor the failures of the inner city children were *produced* by expectations, but expectations may have prevented failures from turning into successes. They maintained previous behaviors at the expense of new ones.

ESCALATING LOOPS

Closed loops, with the exception perhaps of self-sustaining prophecies, are relatively short-lived. In the case of perceptual loops, only so much discrepant information can be evaded or distorted. Either the anticipatory schemata become further entrenched ("There's *really* nothing of value on TV") or have to accommodate somewhat to the information. In any event, they do not stay unchanged for long. In the case of self-fulfilling prophecies, one's own expectations or the others' behavior, or both, gradually change. Thus, the "assistant," "culturally disadvantaged," "gifted," and "mentally ill" either reinforce by their behavior the others' expectations and strengthen them, or else they change their behavior and change the expectations. Spiral reciprocity is clearly involved.

The relative instability of closed loops easily (though not exclusively) turns them into *escalating loops.* These are loops in which the reciprocal relations between the expectations of person A and the behavior of object or person B do not change in essence but in magnitude. Thus, the dog chases its tail increasingly faster, but the tail "escapes" correspondingly faster. The school board imposes ever harsher rules, which are followed by increasing student transgression. While the magnitude of the events changes, their nature continues as "more of the same."

Weiner (1976; quoted by Weick, 1979) provides a typical example of how a chain of events becomes a loop which then amplifies itself. In 1971, a Citizens' Advisory Committee of 67 people was appointed in San Francisco to study how desegregation in education should be implemented. The committee started meeting quite frequently, making it increasingly more difficult for black male members to attend all meetings. Such a minor difference in attendance begins to amplify itself, since, as Weick (1979: 158) states:

> The participants who show up repeatedly produce an environment of sophisticated analyses that requires more participation from them, which makes them even more informed to deal with the issues that are presented. A vicious circle is created in which the regular participants of the advisory council enact the very sophisticated and subtle issues that their new-found competency enables them to deal with.

As a consequence, some participants select themselves out, thereby leaving even more responsibility to the more active and increasingly more competent participants. The loop amplifies.

Weick (1979) described such loops in terms of sets of relations among variables. For example, the less one understands a discussion, the less one listens and the more boredom one experiences. As boredom increases and attention decreases, that individual understands the discussion even less, and so on. Such relations among variables can be either positive (increases in one lead to corresponding increases in the other) or negative. Whenever there is an even number of negative relations in a loop, or when there are positive ones only, the loop escalates. (Obviously, a loop cannot escalate infinitely; it has its natural upper limits. Totally dropping out of the advisory committee or falling asleep during the boring discussion are examples of such limits.)

A loop cannot escalate when an odd number of negative relations is involved. For example, the more discussants there are who want to contribute comments, the greater the number of expressed ideas. But then, as the field of talkers gets crowded, the number of commenters decreases (a single negative relation in the loop). In such a case the loop becomes stabilized, that is, "corrects" itself. When fewer people volunteer comments, the "crowdedness" decreases, and this again encourages more people to volunteer comments.

When a loop escalates and its effects amplify, its components become more strongly interrelated. Fewer outside forces are allowed to exert much influence on the loop; the loop becomes more independent. For example, participation in a committee's work and contribution to its work become strongly interrelated to such an extent that prior intentions, well-meaning as they may have been, exert no more influence on the escalating loop. The loop becomes functionally autonomous.

This kind of development is of great relevance to education. First, as we shall see, education is easily trapped in escalating loops, both virtuous and vicious. Second, educational interventions in the form of communications come to *intensify* the escalation of spirals where they are designed to impart knowledge, to overcome difficulties, to strengthen or weaken certain behavior tendencies, or to establish patterns of interrelations. The addition of "didactic" instruction to the spiral of knowledge acquisition can intensify it. So can the expression, say, of mutual trust and liking between teacher and students; the more they trust each other and express it (through relational cues), the more interdependent their relations and the less dominated they are by global schemata. This in turn leads to even greater closeness.

Similarly, the attribution of a communicational intent to parents' attempts to control the amount of their teenager's televiewing may easily increase the latter's televiewing behaviors, as similar attributions to anti-smoking campaigns seem to increase youngsters' tendency to smoke (Evans et al., 1979). In short, communication in education can intensify both virtuous and vicious spirals.

However, matters are somewhat more complex. Educational communications can also weaken a loop, even break its spiral movement. When, does an educational intervention intensify a spiral and when does it weaken it? Specifically, when would some kind of instruction make children be less influenced by, say, TV commercials and when would such instruction make them *more* vulnerable to ads?

Watzlawick, Weakland, and Fisch (1974) developed a theory of change and persistence. They argue that solutions to a difficulty (which is sometimes unavoidable, such as the "generation gap") often turn the difficulty into a bigger problem. While the solution is maintained by the "problem," the "problem" is maintained by the "solution." Further, they argue that each side sees the other as the stimulus and itself as only a response. Each side fails to see how its own actions come to maintain the other's actions. Thus, since the "solution" does not work (in spite of its obvious logic as it is the opposite of the "problem"), more of the same actions are employed: the sad (by now depressed) person needs more cheering up, the teenage smokers need more intensive anti-smoking campaigns, the "disturbed" child needs more treatment. "Problem" and "solution" become interdependent, and escalate.

Such a pattern is described by Hart's (1978) study, mentioned earlier in the book. Hart set out to examine whether punishment of new recruits in military units deters transgressions or reinforces them. Hart studied fifty army companies, using cross-lagged panel correlation methods. He found three conditions where punishments are perceived as unjust and create possible reactance and more lawbreaking: (1) where there is little consensus between superior and subordinates over offense rates, (2) where superiors punish as a response to lawbreaking labels, and (3) where superiors feel that punishments are effective.

Watzlawick et al. (1974: 46) offer the following conditions under which "solutions" become interdependent with "problems" and escalate each other. First, they argue, loops are created when action is needed but is not taken, as when a difficulty is denied and the denial itself is denied. For example, the teacher who asks for an advice from a colleague feels talked down to (see Chapter 5) and expresses her feelings. If the colleague rejects the teacher's feelings as "invalid," a loop escalates. This happens when "(a) acknowledgment, let alone attempted solution, of the problem is seen as a manifestation of madness or badness; and (b) the problem requiring change becomes greatly compounded by the 'problem' created through its mishandling."

A second condition, according to these authors, is action which is taken when it should not be, for the difficulty cannot be eliminated (there will always be some youngsters who smoke), and its treatment makes it into a far more serious problem. The more anti-smoking campaigns there are in a school, the more curious youngsters become about smoking and the more room they have to spite their teachers.

Third, escalating loops develop when action is taken at the wrong level. Such is the case when instead of trying to change interpersonal contexts, one tries to change others' attitudes, let alone their dispositions and traits. In such a case, particularly when the change targets refuse to cooperate, their refusal itself becomes a target of change escalating the loop further. Thus, a change of the first order from within the system is attempted, rather than a change of the second order which would handle the whole system from a meta level.

Underlying these conditions is one common denominator: termination of the escalation (before its natural upper limits) is not part of the system. When *is* termination part of a system? Weick's (1979) "mathematical" calculation provides a possible answer: When the relations in a loop cancel each other out or balance and correct each other (an *odd* number of negative relations), the loop has a built-in braking mechanism. Thus, for example, one can terminate an escalating loop by prescribing to a disruptive student "new" kinds of disruption (rather than continual punishment), thus arousing reactance and spiteful nondisruptive behavior.

All this, however, does not specify the conditions under which escalating loops are bound to happen. The conditions just mentioned help us to identify existing loops and to analyze them, but not to predict them. It is still unclear when, say, cheering up sad children will brighten their day or when it will depress them further. Similarly, it is still unclear when criticism ("constructive criticism," to be sure) improves work quality or when it taxes one's patience, thus gradually reducing work quality over the longer run.

Predicting escalating loops is beyond the scope of this book, but it is possible to identify one factor that enhances the escalation of loops. It serves as a facilitator or catalyst (without being either a necessary or sufficient condition for the development of escalating loops). This factor is communication, as conceived in earlier chapters.

HOW COMMUNICATION AFFECTS SPIRALS

To begin, recall the study by Prasad et al. (1978) in which schoolchildren watched toy commercials on TV while their mothers volunteered information that countered the toy commercials. The mothers were instructed to do so by either "reasoning" with their children or by expressing "power-assertiveness." While "reasoning" decreased the number of children who bought the advertised toy in a simulated store, "power-assertiveness" increased that number. Thus, in one case an educational communication changed children's behavior, while in the other case the intervention increased the very behavior it was designed to curb. It is reasonable to speculate that under more natural conditions, and when the interaction between mother and child is observed for some time, mothers who are unhappy with the results would intensify their "power-assertiveness." Provided the children have sufficient freedom of behavior, one would expect them to reciprocate by asserting themselves as well. Mothers' and children's "power-assertiveness" would become interdependent in an escalating spiral.

The "reasoning" treatment, designed to serve as a negative feedback (to reverse the direction of a behavior), came to function as such. But the "power-assertiveness" treatment, which was also intended to function as a negative feedback, ended up as a *positive* feedback (maintaining the direction of the behavior). Somewhere along the line a negative feedback was made (surely not by the mothers but by the children) into a positive one. It is not very reasonable to assume that the children who experienced the "power-assertiveness" treatment brought with them any a priori expectations that were different from those of the children in the other treatment. It is more reasonable to assume that the two groups of children differed with respect to the attributions of intent they made to the mothers' volunteered information: The children in the "reasoning" treatment seemed to have attributed to their mothers an intent to inform and those in the "power-assertiveness" treatment—an intent to control. The latter attribution may have led to reactance.

An attribution of intent that leads to reactance can reverse the direction of a feedback. Reactance is experienced by individuals who feel their free behaviors are threatened with change, leading the individuals to try to restore their control (Brehm, 1966; Wortman and Brehm, 1975). Such restoring is expressed in spiteful behavior. Repeating one's behavior in spite of counteractions is very much an expression of reactance to the (attributed) intent to change. And repeating counteractions are, likewise, an expression of reactance. The more actor and counteractor repeat their behaviors, the more they become entrenched, counterargumentative, "stubborn," withdrawn, evasive, or just plain spiteful.

The finding by Prasad et al. (1978) that the "reasoning" treatment decreased the percentage of toy buyers suggests that the children may have attributed to their mothers an intent to convey information rather than to change them. Thus, no reactance developed and the educational communication changed the behavior without becoming interdependent with it in an escalating loop.

Earlier I described the escalating loop of the advisory committee in which participation and involvement were positively interrelated. The less some members could afford to participate in the frequently held meetings, the less involved they felt and the less they contributed to the work, turning frequent absence from meetings into real marginality. Now assume that some of the members who have to support their families begin to blame the more active members for scheduling the meetings too frequently. They attribute to the latter an intent to keep them out, even to alienate them, and see in the way meetings are scheduled a message designed to force them to participate more often or to become marginal members. Once such attributions are made, rather than perceiving the situation as an unfortunate natural "given," these members may respond by attending even fewer meetings ("protest"). By so doing they escalate the loop faster. It is easy to see how the loop would escalate even more intensively if the active members see a message in the others' absence. The attributions of communicational intent to change give such a loop, which would escalate anyway, further impetus.

An important point to notice is that often actions are not initially related to the behavior that eventually causes them to continue. Actions or events such as poor school performance, social withdrawal, or excessive devotion to TV programs may be originally caused by all kinds of factors: low motivation, acne, shame, love for entertainment, and whatnot. But attempts are made to change these and reactance develops; the "solutions" can come to replace the original causes in maintaining the problems.

Consider another complication. When a self-serving motive is attributed to the source of a communication, even intended changes that one welcomes might lead to reactance. A depressed girl knows she is unhappy and would perhaps welcome being cheered up. Being depressed, she is far more sensitive than usual to others' minute behavioral cues and makes finer attributional distinctions among the motives of others (Pittman and Pittman, 1980). She is also more likely to attribute self-serving motives to others (such as the unconscious feeling, "It makes me uncomfortable to see negative feelings; I want you to act happy for my sake"), and she is likely to find "evidence" for that in the way the others cheer her up (a perceptual loop). As in an argument, she wants her feelings recognized, not denied or labeled as not valid. Consequently, she might respond with reactance. Not sensing why cheering up does not yield the desired results, her friends might now try even harder, depressing her further (and creating an escalating spiral).

This view of interaction suggests that educational "solutions" often worsen the "problems" they try to alleviate. This may happen when students attribute to educational communications an intent to cause either a change in them that they do not want or a change that they think reflects self-serving motives of the educator. Under these conditions, reactance develops and spite may take place, and the more spiteful behavior occurs, the more vicious circles escalate.

In fact, it can be argued that education is both easy prey for and beneficiary of loops of all kinds, as well as a possible safeguard against vicious ones. Education becomes involved in loops and spirals because educational settings are specific behavior settings or contexts to which the "subjects" have to adapt. Adaptation entails the use of contexts as mental schemata, and the better one acquires these, the more "appropriate" one's behavior becomes. But educational contexts often (though certainly not always) attempt to achieve this adaptation by controlling students' behaviors through rule setting and telling them what is and is not appropriate. This often generates reactance, particularly in higher grades, leading to poorer performance (Wortman and Brehm, 1975) and hence to increasing external control. In contrast, there are many examples to show that students respond more positively to educational actions that are perceived as intended not to control them but only to convey information. Rokeach (1975) shows that students' values can be changed by giving them feedback concerning discrepancies in their values and by showing them where they are relative to reference groups which they select. Even computers can serve as such change agents. To create such a change, mediated by students' arousal of dissatisfaction with their own value system, the feedback they receive must be perceived by them as truthful.

However, actions perceived as intended only to convey information, devoid of an intention to change, are not frequently found in typical educational activities. Teachers, parents, commanders, and many a therapist do not just impart neutral knowledge; they see it as their mission to cause change and see to it that their efforts are perceived accordingly ("You see? Didn't I tell you so from the very beginning?"). I suspect that educators, for a number of reasons, are more likely to *tell* students how inconsistent their value systems are and who their reference group should be, rather than use Rokeach's (1975) method. Educators are also likely to punish, reinforce, and persuade children to improve in some behavior domain, rather than to use positive attributions of the kind employed by Miller, Brickman, and Bolen (1975), whose statements about student neatness and ability led to increases in neatness and achievement. Little wonder, then, that communication as often practiced in education leads to spirals, many of which are less than virtuous.

A related issue concerns the consensual nature of the schemata that guide the activities in educational systems, schemata which for numerous reasons are not easily changed. Given the loosely coupled nature of educational systems and the fact that they could not possibly operate without consensual schemata, schools inevitably develop perceptual loops and self-sustaining prophecies. Thus, students are labeled, placed in slow or fast learning groups, and generally treated in accordance with consensual expectations. Edelman (1977) has even argued that the agreed-upon language of education defines roles, expectations, and behaviors and so creates a new reality. Students become "deviates," "obsessive-compulsive," or "hostile" as a function of teachers' and counselors' labels and treatments, given in response to students' misbehavior (Cicourel and Kitsuse, 1963).

All this suggests that education, which builds upon many change-intended communications, consensual labels, and schemata, contributes to many spirals and loops that apparently cannot easily be avoided or even observed. It is hard to be aware of them, partly because education (like so many other fields of social activity) is usually seen as a chain of short, linear cause-and-effect links: small-group teaching is expected to lead to better learning, humor to increased involvement, and a supportive climate to cooperation. But to see how education becomes part of spirals, one needs to examine clusters of links as they develop over an extended period of time. The circular or spiral consequences of many activities do not appear right away (Weick, 1979). For this reason, apparently, education is more concerned with changing people than with changing inter-dependent relations. You may "see" that a student's old and worn shoes are evidence of attempts to win the attention of school authorities, or that tardiness is "a means of avoiding success" (Cicourel and Kitsuse, 1963: 112-113). It is more difficult to see how the student's behavior and the school's reactions become interdependent over time.

BREAKING UP LOOPS: GIVE ME A
FULCRUM AND I WILL MOVE THE WORLD

But education need not be just the "victim" or beneficiary of communicational loops; it can also help students learn to avoid loops. For example, when students learn via modeling or other techniques how to resolve conflicts (see Bar-Tal, 1976) they learn, in fact, how to avoid potential self-sustaining disputes. And when teachers learn to observe student attending behavior more closely, thereby making their students more attentive (Dimmitt, 1970), they learn how to avoid potential vicious circles and generate virtuous ones.

In both of these examples, some educational communications lead to educational outcomes which then come to serve as desirable foundations for new kinds of communications to take place: more cooperative, less conflict-riddled interactions. The alternatives are, as we well know, escalating disputes and spirals of inattention, anger, "ripple effects," and progressively less attention in classrooms.

Notice two important elements in the examples above. First, students and teachers not only solve or avoid a specific loop, they may also acquire a strategy to avoid such loops in the future. (It is quite a different question whether they are likely to employ the strategy when a new loop is about to develop.) Second, this strategy is *external* to the real or potential loops which they can now avoid, leading to a change in the whole structure of these loops.

More specifically, the spiral of conflict and nonresolution that children often become involved in does not itself include its own resolution (unless one simply yields to the other), nor does the spiral of students' inattention and teachers' punitive actions include its resolution. Teaching the children, say, to share or to take turns entails the introduction of a behavior external to the spiral of conflict. Similarly, making teachers attend more carefully and more evenly to students' nonverbal cues entails introducing a behavior pattern that is not originally part of the spiral.

Such imports do not just magnify or demagnify a behavior (how forcefully a child fights in an argument) or a relationship (how dependent the "ripple effect" becomes on teachers' calls for attention). Rather, they change the behavior itself, remove it altogether (no entrenchment), or change the whole nature of a spiral relationship (students' inattention is not followed, as is usually the case, by teachers' disciplinary actions). Imagine our advisory committee classifying some of its work as preparatory tasks to be done at home by some members, while other work, based on the preparation, would be done during committee meetings. Such a division of labor is not part of the already escalating loop described earlier; it may change the nature of the behavior (absence from meetings is not, then, a behavior that must be negative) and change the relations that have escalated the spiral before (absence from meetings does not increase marginality).

The movement of a loop or spiral now becomes discontinuous, and such discontinuity constitutes a change of the second order, or a *change of change* (see Chapter 3).

It follows that there are two different types of change: one that occurs within a given system which itself remains unchanged, and one whose occurrence changes the system itself. To exemplify this distinction in more behavioral terms: a person having a nightmare can do many things *in* his dream—run, hide, fight, scream, jump off a cliff, etc.—but no change from any one of these behaviors to another would ever terminate the nightmare. . . . *This kind of change [is a] first-order change.* The one way *out* of a dream involves a change from dreaming to waking. Waking, obviously, is no longer a part of a dream, but a change to an altogether different state. *This kind of change* [is a] *second-order change* [Watzlawick et al., 1974: 10].

Watzlawick et al. (1974) and Palazzoli et al. (1978) describe a number of such second-order changes which I will mention only briefly. One kind entails the removal of the "solution" that has become interdependent with the "problem" and now sustains or even escalates it. Thus, for example, rather than urging the ambivalent change-resisters to change (which often make them even more entrenched), eliminating the "solution" should at least discontinue the already escalating spiral. If one would also behave paradoxically and discourage the resister from changing ("There's really no justification to try a new method"), then the developing reactance could lead to spite and paradoxically, to less resistance.

Aside from using less of the same "attempted solutions" or introducing a paradox, one could also try to reframe the situation, spiral, or relations in new terms, that is,

to change the conceptual and/or emotional setting or viewpoint in relation to which a situation is experienced and to place it in another frame which fits the "facts" of the same concrete situation equally well or even better, and thereby changes its entire meaning [Watzlawick et al., 1974: 95].

For example, Dorr, Graves, and Phelps (1980) reframed TV for their young subjects as a nonrealistic (rather than true-to-life) medium, thereby apparently making them expend more mental effort in processing its messages.

Having been invited to consult with a school about excessive televiewing by the students, I found a well-developed spiral in which much televiewing on the one hand and teachers' urging to watch less TV on the other reinforced each other. I first suggested that the teachers stop urging the children to limit their TV time. After a while, teachers started to urge the children to watch *more* TV, and then began to assign homework based on the most popular programs. Televiewing was now reframed as a legitimate source for knowledge. Not only did the children start watching less TV, they also learned (it seems) to gain more knowledge from it by expending greater AIME in its programs.

Removing an attempted "solution," introducing a paradox, or reframing an issue can apparently break vicious spirals. However, our concern here is not just with the practical employment of such strategies (see Weick, 1979; Watzlawick et al., 1974, and Palazzoli et al., 1978, for excellent suggestions). Assuming that education is both an outcome of communicational spirals and the basis for them, it should also serve as a basis for avoiding spirals. In other words, we not only want to resolve loops and spirals when they occur but also to train educators and students to use such strategies so that the interactions that follow will not escalate vicious spirals.

Common to all kinds of changes of the second order (which break spirals) is the employment of procedures, mental schemata, attributions, or behaviors that come from outside the spiral. Employing them entails stepping out of a situation and examining it from afar. How else would we realize that our well-intended message is perceived by our listerners to be ill intended, that an attempted solution comes to sustain a problem, or that our ostensibly justified *responses* are, in effect, *stimuli* for further escalation?

To step out of one frame of reference and move into another, to break a conceptual or interpersonal loop, or to recontextualize something, it is necessary to use higher order mental schemata which (1) guide and supervise the movement from one frame of reference to another ("I may be caught in a loop, I'll obtain a better view of the whole situation"), and (2) provide the specific alternative perspective or procedure ("What if I *agreed* with my adversary's view?"). The first kind of schemata is more superordinate and general than the second and might be referred to as *fulcrum schemata*; the second, more specific and subordinate kind of schemata might be referred to as *lever schemata*. One needs the former to be able to use the latter. An example of a fulcrum schemata is entailed in Weick's (1979) suggestion that managers should come to realize that the organizations in which they operate are cognitive cause maps. Examples of a lever schemata are entailed in his suggestions of how to break specific loops.

The fulcrum schemata concerning us here involve people's knowledge, or awareness, of how they operate on the world and how the world operates on them. This is what Flavell (1978) calls *metacognitions*: knowledge and belief about the kinds of factors that act on me and on which I act. In this respect, it appears, metacognitions contrast sharply with the "mindless," automatic, and little-AIME-involving behavior discussed in Chapter 5.

Wilson (1980: 291) discusses the same idea under the label of *insight* within a therapeutic framework:

> Insight, stripped of its surplus psychoanalytic meanings, has always been one of the nonspecifics of behavior therapy. An effective means of gaining insight or developing awareness about one's psychological functioning is self-monitoring. Specific thoughts and feelings can be monitored in addition to overt behaviors. These private events can then be consciously reflected upon or evaluated in terms of one's reciprocal interaction with the social environment.

The use of such higher order insights, fulcrum schemata, or metacognitions should be a possible safeguard, if not guarantee, against vicious spirals. As Howard (1971: xx) observed: "If a person comes to 'know' a theory about his behavior he is no longer bound by it but becomes free to disobey it." Ross, Lepper, and Hubbard (1975), as will be recalled from Chapter 3, have shown that subjects who were taught about the perseverance phenomenon (that is, how people tend to develop a "theory" about their own behavior and then adhere to it even in the face of invalidating data) became far less persevering than others who were only given the invalidating information. The former acquired a fulcrum schemata (metacognition) from which they could observe themselves and thus avoid the trap of perseverance in which the latter subjects were caught.

If communication is so much a matter of attribution and mental constructions of meanings, then the very recognition that this is the case is itself a fulcrum from which one can observe how relativistic and reciprocal communicational events are. Once we accept the idea that events are reciprocally related to each other, we can try to control the relations and, in cases of undesirable circles, employ specific lever schemata to break them up.

For example, it has been shown that unresponsive actions in an interaction, particularly disqualifications (actions that are perceived to invalidate one's messages, such as changing the subject, failure to respond by ignoring the message, and the like) create dysfunctional relations (Danziger, 1976). In light of a number of points made in earlier chapters, it is easy to imagine how, say, teacher and students can develop such dysfunctional relations which, unless terminated by an outside factor, will gradually escalate. But, then assume that the teacher (or we could start with the students) who originally blames the students for disqualifying her messages comes to realize that the students and her ways of interacting are mutually dependent (Peterson, 1979). This is a fulcrum schema, as it is on a meta level, above and outside the interaction itself. Once realizing that, the teacher may decide to become more responsive; that is, to increase the number of her responses to the students' behaviors, increase the proportion of her responses that are related to the content of the students' behaviors, and introduce a more positive, agreeing tone to her messages. Using such specific levers, which follow from the new fulcrum she has chosen, she might now find that the initial vicious circle has disappeared and a more virtuous one that includes growing mutual attraction begins to develop (Davis and Perkowitz, 1979).

But acquiring fulcrum schemata is not the same as acquiring an overall tendency to employ them in daily communications. Situations that appear highly familiar, as we have seen already, are dealt with quite automatically and "mindlessly," even by people who have mentally stored higher level schemata and are perfectly capable of employing them[1] (see Langer and Imber, 1979). After all, behaving in overlearned, "mindless" ways frees one's limited capacities to be used elsewhere. On the other hand, entertaining the general idea that events can be reframed, that what events are is very much a matter of perception and construction, or that people are involved in reciprocal relations (rather than always identifying misbehavior with badness or madness), are rather demanding fulcrum schemata. Once you take them seriously and employ them as fulcrums, you also have to search for new lever schemata that might offer specific alternative views and modes of action.

In short, being taught how to step out of a communicational situation to examine it from afar (from a meta level) is no assurance that it will become a common and daily routine. The knowledge people have that movies are staged, that scary scenes are well rehearsed, and that the characters are acting, does not prevent them from becoming scared by horror movies. They either choose not to use that knowledge as a fulcrum or else are carried away and fail to use it. No wonder, therefore, that Watzlawick et al. (1974) argue that people who are part of a vicious interdependent spiral cannot step out of it on their own and need an outsider to "pull" them out. The fish, indeed, may be the last to discover the existence of water.

Such a discouraging conclusion would be warranted only if we assumed that the acquisition of stepping-out strategies is an all-or-none, once-in-a-lifetime event and that if these strategies are not acquired "on time," one is trapped inside all subsequent interactions. But the conclusion is less warranted if we conceive of education and communication as an *ongoing* reciprocal process. The children in the Dorr et al. (1980) study may not have become "junior sophisticates" after six hours of instruction, as shown when they failed spontaneously to use a new metacognition in viewing an episode from *The Jeffersons*. But the experiment was terminated at that point. Children and adults alike would need far more training in stepping out of their routine way of interacting with TV, let alone social interaction, to be able to examine the interaction from another perspective.

Flavell, in his review (1979), quotes recent research that suggests how central metacognitions are in oral communication, reading comprehension, writing, problem-solving, and various kinds of self-control and self-monitoring. But these metacognitions must have come from somewhere. Educational communication, not necessarily limited to its formal forms, may contribute something to the development of such metacognitions, thus serving as a foundation for subsequent communications. Writes Flavell (1979: 910):

> I can . . . imagine trying to teach children and adolescents to monitor their cognition in communication and other social settings. . . . Perhaps it is stretching the meanings of metacognitions and cognitive monitoring too far to include the critical appraisal of message source, quality of appeal, and probably consequences needed to cope with these inputs, but I do not think so.

Brown, Campione, and Day (1981) trained educable retarded children in self-testing strategies for checking their readiness in recalling without error rote lists they had learned. Not only did the use of such metacognitions lead the children to assess their learning better (rather than claiming to be ready when they were not, failing, and then possibly repeating the cycle), they even used these metacognitions a year later, introducing modifications of their own.

Although research into the teaching of fulcrum schemata or use of metacognitions is still in its infancy, a few examples suggest that it is possible and desirable. Clinicians who are trained in the MRI approach (for example, Watzlawick, 1978) and who view "pathologies" as often sustained by "attempted solutions" become quite proficient and creative in reframing conceptions of these "pathologies." And teachers and other professionals who are trained by means of self-viewing on videotape or film become better at examining their own reciprocal commerce with others as they are seeing it through the eyes of the others (Walz and Johnston, 1963; Braucht, 1970).

Clearly, acquiring the ability and the tendency to step out of a situation, to examine it from another perspective, to select a new lever of action, and to employ it is not a matter of a few hours; it is a long and tedious process. Moreover, we would want the student to be able to use fulcrum and lever schemata *selectively* rather than become a "feckless obsessive, paralyzed by incessant critical evaluation of his own judgments and decisions" (Flavell, 1979: 910).

All in all, it may well be one of education's most important objectives to train students, whenever possible, in stepping out strategies, in wording and rewording, in framing and reframing, and in exploring alternative interpretations of the "obvious" in order to prepare them for communication that moves (when appropriate) in discontinuous spirals. Communication would be the beneficiary as well as the means for such educational achievements.

The behavior of one of my professors illustrates my point in a nutshell. Israeli undergraduates, by and large, are never too eager to read background material for their courses, particularly if such material is in a foreign language (English). In fact, they avoid the readings as much as possible, frequently turning class sessions into a constant conflict of interests between them and their professors. In most courses professors give up in frustration (which turns the lists of assigned readings into ceremonial symbols); but in some courses they become involved in escalating disputes.

These disputes, as many readers may have experienced themselves, become functionally autonomous. Professors' demands and students' evasions escalate into anger and absenteeism, totally detached from anybody's initial intentions and interests. Mutual dislikes often develop, and the courses tend to become endless sources of irritation. Moreover, all kinds of student behaviors are perceived by the professors as intended to reshape the courses to become less demanding, while many behaviors of the professors begin to be perceived as intended to "teach the students a lesson they'll remember." The spiral is thus fueled by communicational attributions.

Reaching such a stage in his course (in which I was one of the students who avoided reading), one of my professors came in one day and announced that he really wanted to teach us *his* theory, that the readings consisted of alternative views which challenged his, and that by not reading the material we in effect made the teaching far easier for him. For a while we were puzzled (at that point we disliked him and his theory sufficiently to dislike making his life that much easier). Then it gradually dawned on us that the best way to fight that professor was by challenging his views, which of course could not be done by ignorant, nonreading students. It became a class status symbol to come well prepared to class and to argue with the professor. Whoever failed to read was perceived as an outsider, not a pleasant status to have.

Looking back now on that event, I see it as having the following features:

(1) Professor and students enter an escalating dispute, the termination of which usually depends on one side or the other side giving up.
(2) Students and professor expect each other to be mutually non-supportive, thus creating reactive loops.
(3) Mutual attributions of an intent to change are given to the other party's behaviors, thus turning even neutral acts into perceived messages that escalate the spiral further.
(4) Rather than continue to use more of the same solution, the professor reframes the situation, thus causing a total change in the spiral.
(5) By his act of reframing, the professor shows how one can step out of a situation and employ a fulcrum schema ("Reading can be defined in more than one way") and how one can then employ a specific lever schema ("You do me a great favor by *not* reading challenging material").

Even if no training is involved here, there is an act of *modeling*. We, the students, have learned something from it. If we had encountered more models of this kind, we might have learned that once you learn the meta-rules of communicational reciprocity, it becomes increasingly more difficult for you to follow them blindly. An educational experience, brought about by models that communicate how to control spiral interdependencies, provides metacognitions that guide subsequent interactions. This, I think, is the essence of the reciprocal relationship between communication and education at its best.

CONCLUSION

This book is based on the overall assumption that events and behaviors, including processes of communication and educational outcomes, are reciprocally related to each other. The present chapter attempts to provide an overview of the cyclical nature of various modes of reciprocity.

On one hand we find *closed loops:* People make certain attributions to events and to the behavior of others only to see what they believed in from the outset (perceptual loops); they even shape the others' behavior in line with initial expectations (reactive loops). But on the other hand we find cycles that do not repeat themselves as closed loops do. Rather, they are *escalating loops.* For example, people enter vicious circles of increasing entrenchment, or they learn something new that allows them to communicate better and subsequently learn additional new things.

Typical of escalating loops is the increased magnitude, strength, or intensity of the factors involved. Beliefs become stronger, punishments become harsher, involvement increases. In addition, the factors involved become increasingly more interdependent (akin to closed systems); they allow increasingly less influence to outside forces (including initial intentions) and thus become more functionally autonomous.

Such escalating loops can be more vicious or more virtuous, and education easily becomes trapped in them. First, educational solutions often come to magnify the problems they are designed to solve. Second, many educational acts are perceived as change-intended messages which generate responses either of reactance or acceptance. In either case, they often come to intensify a loop's escalation.

But not all educational acts escalate loops. Some also break the spiral movement of a loop. When, then, does an act (say, punishment) break a loop (reduce rule violations) and when does it amplify it (increase violations)? The attribution of an intent to change seems to be one important factor here. Such attributions can arouse reactance which leads to entrenchment and spiteful behavior, and thus stronger interdependence between action and counteraction develops. To the extent that messages arouse reactance, they can propel or escalate loops.

However, education is not only the "beneficiary" or "victim" of communications that escalate loops. Education also affects communication and could prepare students to step out of or even avoid vicious loops. This requires that students learn to use fulcrum schemata (metacognitions) as vantage points from which they can then examine or foresee loops of which they are part. They can then use lever schemata to break the loops. For example, they can reframe an issue, avoid using a "solution" that sustains a "problem," or avoid trying to change others.

All these are changes of the second order that one can learn to use if one acquires the necessary fulcrum schemata. Thus, students learn that behaviors become interdependent, that their actions are not just responses but also stimuli, and that much may depend on the others' attribution of intent (not on real intents). Teaching youngsters to use fulcrum schemata is an ongoing communicational act which yields desirable educational outcomes, and these in turn serve as a basis for new patterns of communication and a new experience of education at its best.

NOTE

1. I can imagine that some readers might accuse me of "trying too hard" to change their views and conceptions, thereby arousing in them reactance. They may thus accuse me of "blindly" entering into a spiral in which I do not use the very fulcrum schemata I write about. By so doing, they might claim, I exemplify the difficulties described here.

References

ADAR, L. (1978) "Do we need the term 'culturally disadvantaged'?" Iunim Bechinuch 2 (Hebrew).

ALLPORT, G. W. (1966) "Traits revisited." American Psychologist 21: 1-10.

ALSCHULER, A. et al. (1977) "Social literacy: a discipline game without losers." Phi Delta Kappan 58: 606-609.

AMIR, Y. (1969) "Contact hypothesis in ethnic relations." Psychological Bulletin 71: 319-342.

ANDERSON, R. C., R. E. REYNOLDS, D. L. SCHALLERT, and E. T. GOETZ (1977) "Frameworks for comprehending discourse." American Educational Research Journal 14: 367-381.

ARONSON, E., J. TURNER, and J. M. CARLSMITH (1963) "Communicator credibility and communication discrepancy." Journal of Abnormal and Social Psychology 67: 31-36.

ASCH, S. E. (1955) "Opinions and social pressure." Scientific American 193: 31-35.

ASTIN, A. W. (1977) Four Critical Years: Effects of College on Beliefs, Attitudes, and Knowledge. San Francisco: Jossey-Bass.

ATKIN, C. K. (1978) "Broadcast news programming and the child audience." Journal of Broadcasting 22: 47-61.

——— B. GREENBERG, F. KORZENNY, and S. McDERMOTT (1979) "Selective exposure to televised violence." Journal of Broadcasting 23: 5-13.

AUSUBEL, D. P. (1978) "In defense of advance organizers: a reply to the critics." Review of Educational Research 48: 251-257.

——— (1968) Educational Psychology: A Cognitive View. New York: Holt, Rinehart & Winston.

BABAD, E. Y. (1979) "Personality correlates of susceptibility to biasing information." Journal of Personality and Social Psychology 37: 195-202.

BADDLEY, A. D. (1978) "The trouble with levels: a reexamination of Craik and Lockart's framework for memory research." Psychological Review 85: 139-152.

BALL, S., and G. A. BOGATZ (1970) The First Year of 'Sesame Street': An Evaluation. Princeton, NJ: Educational Testing Service.

BANDURA, A. (1979) "Self-efficacy: an integrative construct." Presented at the meeting of the Western Psychological Association, San Diego, April.

——— (1978) "The self system in reciprocal determinism." American Psychologist 33: 344-358.

––– (1977a) Social Learning Theory. Englewood Cliffs, NJ: Prentice-Hall.

––– (1977b) "Self-efficacy: toward a unifying theory of behavioral change." Psychological Review 84: 191-215.

BARKER, R. G. and Associates (1978) Habitats, Environments, and Human Behavior. Studies in Ecological Psychology and Eco-Behavioral Science from the Midwest Psychological Field Station, 1947-1972. San Francisco: Jossey-Bass.

BARLUND, D. C. (1975) Public and Private Self in Japan and the United States. Tokyo: The Simul Press.

BARNETT, M., K. A. MATTHEWS, and C. B. CORBIN (1979) "The effects of competitive and cooperative instructional sets on children's generosity." Personality and Social Psychology Bulletin 5: 91-94.

BAR-TAL, D. (1980) "Causal perceptions and behaviors of pupils and teachers: attributional analysis." Israeli Journal of Psychology and Counseling in Education (September): 3-19.

––– (1978) "Attributional analysis of achievement-related behavior." Review of Educational Research 48: 259-271.

––– (1976) Prosocial Behavior: Theory and Research. New York: Halsted.

––– and L. SAXE [eds.] (1978) Social Psychology of Education: Theory and Research. New York: Halsted.

BARTLETT, F. C. (1932) Remembering. Cambridge, England: Cambridge University Press.

BATES, J. A. (1979) "Extrinsic reward and intrinsic motivation: a review with implications for the classroom." Review of Educational Research 49: 557-576.

BAUMEISTER, R. F., J. COOPER, and B. A. SKIB (1979) "Inferior performance as a selective response to expectancy: taking a dive to make a point." Journal of Personality and Social Psychology 37: 424-432.

BEM, D. J. (1979) "Assessing persons and situations with the template matching technique." In New Directions 2: 1-15.

––– and A. ALLEN (1974) "On predicting some of the people some of the time: the search for cross-situational consistencies in behavior." Psychological Review 81: 506-520.

BERLO, D. K. (1977) "Communication as process: review and commentary," in B. D. Roben (ed.) Communication year, Book 1. New Brunswick, NJ: Transaction-International Communication Association.

BERLYNE, D. E. (1965) Structure and Direction in Thinking. New York: John Wiley.

BORLAND, B. L., and J. P. RUDOLPH (1975) "Relative effects of low socioeconomic status, parental smoking and poor scholastic performance on smoking among high school students." Social Science Medicine 9: 27-30.

BOTVIN, G. J., A. ENG, and C. L. WILLIAMS (1980) "Preventing the onset of cigarette smoking through life skills training." Preventive Medicine 9: 135-143.

BOWERS, K. S. (1973) "Situationism in psychology: an analysis and a critique." Psychological Review 80: 307-336.

BRAUCHT, G. N. (1970) "Immediate effects of self confrontation on the self-concept." Journal of Counseling and Clinical Psychology 35: 95-101.

BRAUN, C. (1976) "Teacher expectation: sociopsychological dynamics." Review of Educational Research 46: 185-213.

BREHM, J. W. (1966) A Theory of Psychological Reactance. New York: Academic Press.

BRIGHAM, J. C. and GIESBRECHT, L. W. (1976) "All in the family racial attitudes." Journal of Communication, 26: 69-74.

BRONFENBRENNER, U. (1977) "Toward an experimental ecology of human development." American Psychologist 32: 513-531.

BROPHY, J. E. (1979) "Teacher behavior and its effects." Journal of Educational Psychology 71: 733-750.

—— and T. L. GOOD (1974) Teacher-Student Relationships: Causes and Consequences. New York: Holt, Rinehart & Winston.

BROWN, A. L., J. C. CAMPIONE, and J. D. DAY (1981) "Learning to learn: on training students to learn from texts." Educational Researcher 10: 14-21.

BRUNER, J. S. (1964) "The course of cognitive growth." American Psychologist 19: 1-15.

BRYANT, J., R. A. CARVETH, and D. BROWN (1981) "Television viewing and anxiety: an experimental examination." Journal of Communication 31: 106-119.

BUTKOWSKY, I. S. and D. M. WILLOWS (1980) "Cognitive motivational characteristics of children varying in reading ability: evidence for learned helplessness in poor readers." Journal of Educational Psychology 72: 408-422.

CALDER, B. J., C. A. INSKO, and B. YANDELL (1974) "The relation of cognitive and memorial processes to persuasion in a stimulated jury trial." Journal of Applied Social Psychology 4: 62-93.

CALFEE, R., and P. DRUM (1978) "Learning to read: theory, research, and practice." Curriculum Inquiry 8: 183-249.

CAMPBELL, D. E. (1979) "Interior office design and visitor response." Applied Psychology 64: 648-653.

CANTOR, N. and W. MISCHEL (1977) "Traits as prototypes: effects on recognition memory." Journal of Personality and Social Psychology 35: 38-48.

CANTRIL, H. (1947) The Invasion from Mars. Princeton: Princeton University Press.

CARON, A. H. (1979) "First time exposure to television: effects on Inuit children's cultural images." Communication Research 6: 135-154.

CARPENTER, P. A. (1974) "On the comprehension, storage and retrieval of comparative sentences." Journal of Verbal Learning and Verbal Behavior 13: 401-411.

CHAFFEE, S. H., M. JACKSON-BEECK, J. DURALL, and D. WILSON (1977) "Mass communication in political socialization," in S. A. Renshon (ed.) Handbook of Political Socialization: Theory and Research. New York: Free Press.

CHAIKEN, A. L., E. SIGLER, and V. J. DERLEGA (1974) "Nonverbal mediators of teacher expectancy effects." Journal of Personality and Social Psychology 30: 144-149.

CICOUREL, A. and J. I. KITSUSE (1963) Educational Decision-Makers. Indianapolis: Bobbs-Merrill.

CLARK, R. E. (1980) "Do students enjoy the instructional method from which they learn the least? Antagonism between enjoyment and achievement in ATI studies." Presented at the Annual Convention of the American Educational Research Association in Boston.

COHEN, A. and G. SALOMON (1979) "Children's literate television viewing: surprises and possible explanations." Journal of Communication 29: 156-163.

COLLINS, W. A. (1979) "Children's comprehension of television," in E. Wartella (ed.) Children Communicating: Media and Development of Thought, Speech, Understanding. Beverly Hills: Sage.

────── (1975) "The developing child as viewer." Journal of Communication 25: 35-44.

────── and S. A. ZIMMERMANN (1975) "Convergent and divergent social cues: effects of televised aggression on children." Journal of Communicational Research 2: 331-346.

COMSTOCK, G. and others (1978) Television and Human Behavior. Santa Monica, CA: Rand Corporation.

COOPER, H. M. (1979) "Pygmalion grows up: a model for teacher expectation communication and performance influence." Review of Educational Research 49: 389-410.

CORDER-BOLZ, C. R. and S. O'BRYANT (1978) "Teachers vs. program." Journal of Communication 28: 97-103.

CRAIK, F.I.M. and R. S. LOCKHART (1972) "Levels of processing: a framework for memory research." Journal of Verbal Learning and Verbal Behavior 11: 671-684.

CRAIK, F.I.M. and E. TULVING (1975) "Depth of processing and retention of words in episodic memory." Journal of Experimental Psychology, General 104: 268-294.

CRONBACH, L. J. (1957) "The two disciplines of scientific psychology." American Psychologist 12: 671-684.

────── and R. E. SNOW (1977) Aptitudes and Instructional Methods. New York: Irvington.

CRONKHITE, G. and J. R. LISKA (1980) "The judgment of communicant acceptability," in M. E. Roloff and G. R. Miller (eds.) Persuasion: New Directions in Theory and Research. Beverly Hills: Sage.

DANCE, F.E.X. (1970) "The 'concept' of communication." Journal of Communication 20: 201-210.

────── and C. E. LARSON (1976) The Functions of Human Communication. A Theoretical Approach. New York: Holt, Rinehart & Winston.

DANZIGER, K. (1976) Interpersonal Communication. New York: Pergamon Press.

DAVIS, D. and W. T. PERKOWITZ (1979) "Consequences of responsiveness in dyadic interaction: effects of probability of response and proportion of content-related responses on interpersonal attraction." Journal of Personality and Social Psychology 37: 534-550.

DE CECCO, J. and A. RICHARDS (1974) Growing Pains: Uses of School Conflict. New York: Aberdeen.

DEFLEUR, M. and S. BALL-ROKEACH (1975) Theories of Mass-Communication (3rd ed.). New York: McKay.

DEREGOWSKI, J. B. (1968) "Difficulties in pictorial depth perception in Africa." British Journal of Psychology 59: 195-204.

DEWEY, J. (1930) "Conduct and experience," in C. Murchison (ed.) Psychologies of 1930. Worcester, MA: Clark University Press.

DIMMITT, N. M. (1970) "A study of training and photographic feedback methods for promoting accurate teacher perception of student attending behavior." Ph.D. dissertation, Stanford University.

DOMINO, G. (1974) "Aptitude by treatment interaction effects in college instruction." Presented to American Psychological Association.

DONOHUE, G. A., P. J. TICHENOR, and C. N. OLIEN (1975) "Mass-media and a knowledge gap: a hypothesis reconsidered." Communication Research 2: 3-23.

DOOB, A. N. and G. E. MacDONALD (1979) "Television viewing and fear of victimization: is the relationship causal?" Journal of Personality and Social Psychology 37: 170-179.

DORR, A., S. B. GRAVES, and E. PHELPS (1980) "Television literacy for young children." Journal of Communication 30: 71-83.

DOWNS, R. M. and D. STEA (1973) Image and Environment. Chicago: Aldine.

DUELL, O. K. (1974) "Effect of type of objective, level of test questions, and the judged importance of tested materials upon posttest performance." Journal of Educational Psychology 66: 225-232.

DUKE, D. L. (1978) "Looking at the school as a rule-governed organization." Journal of Research and Development in Education 11: 116-126.

———— and C. PERRY (1978) "Can alternative schools succeed where Benjamin Spock, Spiro Agnew and B. F. Skinner have failed?" Adolescence 13: 375-392.

DUNKIN, M. J. and B. J. BIDDLE (1974) The Study of Teaching. New York: Holt, Rinehart & Winston.

DUVAL, S. and R. A. WICKLUND (1973) "Effects of objective self-awareness on attribution of causality." Journal of Experimental Social Psychology 9: 17-31.

DYKMAN, B. M. and M. T. REIS (1979) "Personality correlates of classroom seating position." Journal of Educational Psychology 71: 346-354.

EAGLY, A. H., W. WOOD, and S. CHAIKIN (1978) "Causal inferences about communicators and their effect on opinion change." Journal of Personality and Social Psychology 36: 424-435.

EDELMAN, M. (1977) Political Language: Words That Succeed and Policies That Fail. New York: Academic Press.

EDGAR, P. (1977) Children and Screen Violence. St. Lucia, Australia: University of Queensland Press.

EDSON, L. (1973) "Schools attacking the smoking problem." American Education 9: 10-14.

ENDLER, N. S. and D. MAGNUSSON (1976) Interactional Psychology and Personality. Washington, DC: Hemisphere.

EPSTEIN, S. (1979) "The stability of behavior: 1. On predicting most of the people much of the time." Journal of Personality and Social Psychology 37: 1097-1126.

EVANS, R. I., A. H. HENDERSON, P. C. HILL, and B. E. RAINES (1979) "Current psychological, social and educational programs in control and prevention of smoking: a critical methodological review." Atherosclerosis Review 6: 203-245.

FANCHER, R. E. (1966) "Explicit personality theories and accuracy in person perception." Journal of Personality 34: 252-261.

FELDMAN, R. S. and T. PROHASKA (1979) "The student as pygmalion: effect of student expectation on the teacher." Journal of Educational Psychology 71: 485-493.

FENIGSTEIN, A. (1979) "Aggression as a cause for viewing media violence." Journal of Personality and Social Psychology 37: 2307-2317.

FIEDLER, F. E., E. H. POTTER, M. M. ZAIS and W. A. KNOWLTON, Jr. (1979) "Organizational stress and the use and misuse of managerial intelligence and experience." Applied Psychology 64: 635-647.

FISHBEIN, M. and I. AJZEN (1975) Belief, Attitude, Intention and Behavior. Reading, MA: Addison-Wesley.

FISHER, R. J. (1976) "A discussion project on high school adolescents' perceptions of the relationship between students and teachers." Adolescence 41: 87-95.

FLAVELL, J. H. (1979) "Metacognition and cognitive monitoring: a new area of cognitive-developmental inquiry." American Psychologist 34: 906-911.

——— (1978) "Metacognitive development," in J. M. Scandura and C. J. Brainerd (eds.) Structural/Process Theories of Complex Human Behavior. The Netherlands: Sijthoff and Noordhoff.

FROMKIN, H. L. (1973) The Psychology of Uniqueness: Avoidance of Similarity and Seeking of Differentness. Paper 438, Institute for Research in the Behavioral, Economic and Management Science, Purdue University.

FURU, T. (1971) The Function of Television for Children and Adolescents. Tokyo: Sophia University.

GALLOWAY, C. (1972) Analysis of Theories and Research in Nonverbal Communication. Washington, DC: ERIC Clearinghouse on Teacher Education (ED. 059 988).

GARBARINO, J. (1975) "The impact of anticipated rewards on cross-age tutoring." Journal of Personality and Social Psychology 32: 421-428.

GARDNER, H. (1977) "Senses, symbols, operations: an organization of artistry," in D. Perkins and B. Leondar (eds.) The Arts and Cognition. Baltimore: Johns Hopkins University Press.

——— (1972) "Style sensitivity in children." Human Development 15: 325-338.

——— V. HOWARD and D. PERKINS (1974) "Symbol systems: a philosophical, psychological and educational investigation," in D. R. Olson (ed.) Media and Symbols: The Forms of Expression, Communication and Education, 73rd Yearbook of the National Society for the Study of Education. Chicago: University of Chicago Press.

GERBNER, G. and L. GROSS (1976) "Living with television: the violence profile." Journal of Communication 26: 173-179.

GETZELS, J. (1974) "Images of the classroom and visions of the learner." School Review 82: 527-540.

GIBBS, J. C. (1979) "The meaning of ecologically oriented inquiry in contemporary psychology." American Psychologist 34: 127-140.

GLASS, D. C. and J. E. SINGER (1972) Urban Stress. New York: Academic Press.

GLIDEWELL, J. C. (1980) "Professional support systems: the teaching profession." Prepared for the International Colloquium on School Psychology, Israel.

GOMBRICH, E. H. (1974) "The visual image," in D. R. Olson (ed.) Media and Symbols: The Forms of Expression, Communication and Education, 73rd yearbook of the National Society for the Study of Education. Chicago: University of Chicago Press.

——— (1960) Art and Illusion. New York: Bollinger Foundation.

GOOD, T. L. and J. E. BROPHY (1974) "Changing teacher and student behavior: an empirical investigation." Journal of Educational Psychology 66: 390-405.

GOODMAN, N. (1978) Ways of Worldmaking. Indianapolis: Hackett.

——— (1968) The Languages of Art. Indianapolis: Hackett.

——— and B. REEVES (1976) "Children and the perceived reality of television." Journal of Social Issues 32: 86-97.

GREENBERG, B. S. (1972) "Children's reactions to TV blacks." Journalism Quarterly 49, 1: 5-14.

―――― and B. REEVES (1976) "Children and the perceived reality of television." Journal of Social Issues 32: 86-97.

GREENFIELD, P. (1972) "Oral or written language: the consequences for cognitive development in Africa, the United States and England." Language and Speech 15: 169-178.

HAGEN, J. and G. HALE (1973) "The development of attention in children," in A. Ack (ed.) Minnesota Symposia on Child Psychology (Vol. 7). Minneapolis: University of Minnesota Press.

HALEY, J. (1977) "Toward a theory of pathological systems," in P. W. Weakland (eds.) The Interactional View. New York: Norton.

HARGREAVES, D. H., S. K. HESTER, and F. J. MEILOR (1975) Deviance in Classrooms. London: Routledge & Kegan Paul.

HART, R. J. (1978) "Crime and punishment in the army." Journal of Personality and Social Psychology 36: 1456-1471.

HARTHMANN, P. and C. HUSBAND (1974) Racism and the Mass Media. Totowa, NJ: Rowman and Littlefield.

HARTUP, W. H. (1979) "Two social worlds: family relations and peer relations," in M. Rutter (ed.) Foundations of Psychiatry. London: Heineman.

HARVEY, J. H., K. L. YARKIN, J. M. LIGHTNER, and J. P. TOWN (1980) "Unsolicited interpretation and recall of interpersonal events." Journal of Personality and Social Psychology 38: 551-568.

HERTZ-LAZAROWITZ, R., D. FEITELSON, W. H. HARTUP, and S. ZAHAVI (1978) "Social interaction and social organization in Israeli five to seven-year-olds." Haifa University. (unpublished)

HILL, D. (1971) "Peer group conformity in adolescent smoking and its relationship to affiliation and autonomy needs." Australian Journal of Psychology 23: 189-199.

HIMMELWEIT, H. T. (1977) "Yesterday's and tomorrow's television research on children," in D. Lerner, and L. M. Nelson (eds.) Communication Research—a Half-Century Appraisal. Hawaii: University Press of Hawaii.

HODGKINSON, H. L. (1967) Education Interaction and Social Change. Englewood Cliffs, NJ: Prentice-Hall.

HORNIK, R. C. (1978) "Television access and the slowing of cognitive growth." American Educational Research Journal 15: 1-16.

―――― (1974) "Mass media use and the 'revolution of rising frustrations': a reconsideration of the theory." Paper of the East-West Communication Institute, No. 11.

―――― M. GONZALEZ and J. GOULD (1980) "Susceptibility to media effects." Presented at the ICA Convention, Acalpulco, Mexico.

HOVLAND, C., T. L. JANIS and H. H. KELLEY (1953) Communication and Persuasion. New Haven: Yale University Press.

HOWARD, N. (1971) Paradoxes of Rationality: Theory of Metagames and Political Behavior. Cambridge: MIT Press.

HOY, W. K. (1969) "Pupil control ideology and organization socialization: a further examination of the influence on the beginning teacher." School Review 77: 257-265.

HUNT, D. E. (1971) Matching Models in Education. The Coordination of Teaching Methods with Student Characteristics. Toronto, Canada: Ontario Institute for Studies in Education.

HUSTON-STEIN, A. and J. C. WRIGHT (1977) "Modeling the medium: effects of formal properties of children's television programs." Presented at the Biennial Meeting of the Society for Research in Child Development, New Orleans.

HYDE, T. W. and S. J. JENKINS (1969) "The differential effects of incidental tasks on the organization of recall of a list of highly associated words." Journal of Experimental Psychology 82: 472-481.

ICKES, W. and R. D. BARNES (1978) "Boys and girls together—and alienated: on enacting stereotyped sex roles in mixed-sex dyads." Journal of Personality and Social Psychology 36: 669-683.

INSKO, C. A. (1967) Theories of Attitude Change. New York: Appleton-Century-Crofts.

JACKSON, D. D. (1977) "The myth of normality," in P. Watzlawick and J. H. Weakland (eds.) The Interactional View. New York: Norton.

JANIS, I. R. (1972) Victims of Groupthink. Boston: Houghton Mifflin.

JONES, E. E. and V. A. HARRIS (1967) "The attribution of attitudes." Journal of Experimental Social Psychology 3: 1-24.

JONES, E. E., and R. E. NISBETT (1972) "The actor and the observer: divergent perceptions of the causes of behavior," in E. E. Jones et al. (eds.) Attribution: Perceiving the Causes of Behavior. Morristown, NJ: General Learning Press.

JONES, R. A. (1977) Self-Fulfilling Prophecies. Hillsdale, NJ: Erlbaum.

JONES, T. E. (1969) "The relations between bureaucracy and the pupil control ideology of secondary schools and teachers." Ph.D. dissertation, Oklahoma State University.

KAHLE, L. R. [Ed.] (1979) New Directions for Methodology of Behavioral Science, No. 2. San Francisco: Jossey-Bass.

KAHNEMAN, D. and A. TVERSKY (1973) "On the psychology of prediction." Psychological Review 80: 237-251.

KANE, J. M. and R. C. ANDERSON (1978) "Depth of processing and interference effects in the learning and remembering of sentences." Journal of Educational Psychology 70: 626-635.

KATZ, E., J. G. BLUMLER, and U. GUREVITCH (1974) "Utilization of mass communication by the individual," in J. G. Blumler and E. Katz (eds.) The Uses of Mass Communications. Beverly Hills: Sage.

KELLEY, G.A.A. (1970) "A brief introduction to personal construct theory," in D. Banister (ed.) Perspectives in Personal Construct Theory. New York: Academic Press.

KELLEY, H. H. and A. J. STAHELSKI (1970) "Social interaction basis of cooperator's and competitor's beliefs about others." Journal of Personality and Social Psychology 16: 66-91.

KENDZIERSKI, D. (1980) "Self-schemata and scripts: the recall of self-referent and scriptal information." Personality and Social Psychology Bulletin 6: 13-22.

KINTSCH, W. (1977) Memory and Cognition. New York: John Wiley.

KIPNIS, D. (1976) The Powerholders. Chicago: University of Chicago Press.

——— P. J. CASTELL, M. GERGEN, and D. MAUCH (1976) "Metamorphic effects of power." Journal of Applied Psychology 61: 127-135.

KNUDSON, R. M., A. A. SOMMERS, and S. L. GOLDING (1980) "Interpersonal perception and mode of resolution in marital conflict." Journal of Personality and Social Psychology 38: 751-763.

KOSSLYN, S. and J. POMERANTZ (1977) "Imagery, propositions, and the form of internal representations." Cognitive Psychology 9: 52-76.

KOUNIN, J. S., P. E. GUMP, and J. J. RYAN (1961) "Explorations in classroom management." Journal of Teacher Education 12: 235-246.

KRUGLANSKI, A. W. (1980) "Lay epistemo-logic–process and contents: another look at attribution theory." Psychological Review 87: 70-87.

——— (1975) "The endogeneous-exogeneous partition in attribution theory." Psychological Review 82: 387-406.

——— and Y. JAFFE (1981) "Lay epistemology: a theory for cognitive therapy," in L. Y. Abramson (ed.) An Attributional Perspective in Clinical Psychology. New York: Guilford Press.

KRUGMAN, H. E. (1976) "Long-range social implications of the new developments in television technology." Presented at the American Association of Public Opinion Research, Asheville, N.C.

KRULL, R. and W. HUSSON (1979) "Children's attention: the case of TV viewing," in E. Wartella (ed.) Children Communication: Media and Development of Thought, Speech, Understanding. Beverly Hills: Sage.

KUHN, T. S. (1970) "Logic of discovery or psychology of research?" pp. 1-23 in I. Lakatos and A. Musgrave (eds.) Criticism and the Growth of Knowledge. Cambridge: Cambridge University Press.

LaBERGE, D. and S. J. SAMUELS (1974) "Toward a theory of automatic information processing in reading." Cognitive Psychology 6: 293-323.

LANCY, D. F. (1978) "The classroom as phenomenon," in D. Bar-Tal and L. Saxe (eds.) Social Psychology of Education. New York: John Wiley.

LANGER, E. J. and A. BENEVENTO (1978) "Self-induced dependence." Journal of Personality and Social Psychology 36: 886-893.

LANGER, E. J. and L. E. IMBER (1979) "When practice makes imperfect: debilitating effects of overlearning." Journal of Personality and Social Psychology 37: 2014-2024.

LANGER, E. J., A. BLANK, and B. CHANOWITZ (1978) "The mindlessness of ostensibly thoughtful action: the role of 'placebic' information in interpersonal interaction." Journal of Personality and Social Psychology 36: 635-642.

LEIFER, A. D., N. J. GORDON, and S. B. GRAVES (1974) "Children's television: more than mere entertainment." Harvard Education Review 44: 213-245.

LEWIS, R. and N. ST. JOHN (1974) "Contributions of cross-racial friendship to minority group achievement in desegregated classrooms." Sociometry 37: 79-91.

LINGLE, J. H. and T. M. OSTROM (1979) "Retrieval selectivity in memory-based impression judgments." Journal of Personality and Social Psychology 37: 180-194.

LORCH, P. P., D. R. ANDERSON, and S. R. LEVIN (1979) "The relationship of visual attention to children's comprehension of television." Child Development 50: 722-727.

LORD, C. G. (1980) "Schemas and images as memory aids: two modes of processing social information." Journal of Personality and Social Psychology 38: 257-269.

——— L. ROSS, and M. R. LEPPER (1979) "Biased assimilation and attitude polarization: the effects of prior theories on subsequently considered evidence." Journal of Personality and Social Psychology 37: 2098-2109.

LOWENFELD, V. and W. L. BRITTAIN (1966) Creative and Mental Growth. New York: Macmillan.

LUCE, S. R. and R. D. HOGE (1978) "Relations among teacher rankings, pupil-teacher interactions, and academic achievement: a test of the teacher expectancy hypothesis." American Educational Research Journal 15: 489-500.

LURIA, A. R. (1976) Cognitive Development–Its Cultural and Social Foundations. Cambridge, MA: Harvard University Press.

MACCOBY, E. E. [ed.] (1966) The Development of Sex Differences. Stanford: Stanford University Press.

MacNAMARA, J. [ed.] (1977) Language Learning and Thought. New York: Academic Press.

MANGHAM, I. L. (1978) Interactions and Interventions in Organizations. New York: John Wiley.

MARKUS, H. (1977) "Self-schemata and processing information about the self." Journal of Personality and Social Psychology 35: 63-78.

MAYER, R. E. (1979) "Can advance organizers influence meaningful learning?" Review of Educational Research 49: 371-383.

––– (1976) "Integration of information during problem solving due to a meaningful context of learning." Memory and Cognition 4: 603-608.

––– (1975) "Information processing variables in learning to solve problems." Review of Educational Research 45: 525-541.

McARTHUR, L. and D. POST (1977) "Figural emphasis and person perception." Journal of Experimental Social Psychology 35: 63-78.

McCARTHY, E. D., T. S. LANGER, J. C. GERSTEN, J. G. EISENBERG, and L. ORZECK (1975) "Violence and behavior disorders." Journal of Communication 25: 71-85.

McGUIRE, W. J. (1973) "The yin and yang of social psychology; seven koan." Journal of Personality and Social Psychology 26: 446-456.

––– and S. PAPAGEORGIS (1963) "Effectiveness of forewarning in developing resistance to persuasion." Public Opinion Quarterly 26: 24-34.

McLUHAN, M. (1965) Understanding Media: The Extension of Man. New York: McGraw-Hill.

MEHAN, H. (1974) "Ethnomethodology and education," in D. O'Shea (ed.) Sociology of School and Schooling. Proceedings of the Second Annual Conference of the Sociology of Education Association, Washington, NIE.

MEICHENBAUM, D. H., K. S. BOWERS, and R. R. ROSS (1969) "A behavioral analysis of teacher expectancy effect." Journal of Personality and Social Psychology 13: 306-316.

MERINGOFF, L. K. (1980) "Influence of the medium on children's story apprehension." Journal of Educational Psychology 72: 240-249.

MERTON, R. K. (1957) Social Theory and Social Structure. (Rev. Ed.). New York: Free Press.

MESSARIS, P. and L. GROSS (1977) "Interpretations of a photographic narrative by viewers in four age groups." Studies in Anthropology of Visual Communication 4: 99-111.

MEYER, J. W. and B. ROWAN (1978) "The structure of educational organizations," in M. W. Meyer et al. (eds.) Environments and Organizations. San Francisco: Jossey-Bass.

MEYER, J. W., W. R. SCOTT, S. COLE, and J. K. INTILI (1978) "Instructional dissensus and institutional consensus in schools," in M. W. Meyer et al. (eds.) Environments and Organizations. San Francisco: Jossey-Bass.

MIALARET, G. (1966) The Psychology of the Use of Audio-Visual Aids in Primary Education. London: Harrap.

MILGRAM, S. (1974) Obedience to Authority. New York: Harper & Row.

MILLER, G. A., E. GALANTER, and K. H. PRIBRAM (1960) Plans and the Structure of Behavior. New York: Holt, Rinehart & Winston.

MILLER, G. R. (1966) "On defining communication: another stab." Journal of Communication 16: 88-98.

——— and M. STEINBERG (1975) Between People: A New Analysis of Interpersonal Communication. Chicago: Science Research Associates.

MILLER, R. L., P. BRICKMAN, and D. BOLEN (1975) "Attribution versus persuasion as a means for modifying behavior." Journal of Personality and Social Psychology 31: 430-441.

MINOR, M. W. (1970) "Experimenter-expectancy effect as a function of evaluation apprehension." Journal of Personality and Social Psychology 15: 326-332.

MISCHEL, W. (1979) "On the interface of cognition and personality." American Psychologist 34: 740-754.

——— (1977) "On the future of personality measurement." American Psychologist 32: 246-254.

——— (1968) Personality and Assessment. New York: John Wiley.

MITA, T. H., M. DERMER, and J. KNIGHT (1977) "Reversed facial images and the mere-exposure hypothesis." Journal of Personality and Social Psychology 35: 597-601.

MONSON, T. C. and M. SNYDER (1977) "Actors, observers, and the attribution process: toward a reconceptualization." Journal of Experimental Social Psychology 13: 89-115.

MOOS, R. H. (1979) Evaluating Educational Environments. San Francisco: Jossey-Bass.

——— and B. S. MOOS (1978) "Classroom social climate and student absences and grades." Journal of Educational Psychology 70: 263-269.

MORELAND, R. L. and R. B. ZAJONC (1979) "Exposure effects may not depend on stimulus recognition." Journal of Personality and Social Psychology 37: 1085-1089.

——— (1977) "Is stimulus recognition a necessary condition for the occurrence of exposure effects?" Journal of Personality and Social Psychology 35: 191-199.

MORGAN, M. (1980) "Television viewing and reading· does more equal better?" Journal of Communication (Winter): 159-165.

——— and L. GROSS (1980) "Television viewing, IQ and academic achievement." Journal of Broadcasting 24: 117-133.

MORTENSEN, C. D. (1972) Communication: The Study of Human Interaction. New York: McGraw-Hill.

MYRICK, R. and B. S. MARX (1968) An Exploratory Study of the Relationship between High School Building Design and Student Learning. Washington, DC: Bureau of Research, Office of Education, U.S. Department of Health, Education and Welfare.

NEISSER, U. (1976) Cognition and Reality, San Francisco: Freeman.

NEWMAN, I. M. (1970) "Peer pressure hypothesis for adolescent cigarette smoking." School Health Review 1: 15-18.

NIELSEN, G. (1962) Studies in Self-Confrontation. Viewing a Sound Motion Picture of Self and Another Person in a Stressful Dyadic Interaction. Copenhagen: Monksgaard.

NISBETT, R. and L. ROSS (1980) Human Inference: Strategies and Shortcomings of Social Judgment. Englewood Cliffs, NJ: Prentice-Hall.

NISBETT, R. E., C. CAPUTO, P. LEGANT, and J. MARALEK (1973) "Behavior as seen by the actor and as seen by the observer." Journal of Personality and Social Psychology 27: 154-164.

NUTTIN, J. R. (1977) "A conceptual frame of personality world interaction: a relational theory," in D. Magnusson and N. S. Endler (eds.) Personality at the Crossroads: Current Issues in Interactional Psychology. Hillsdale, NJ: Erlbaum.

OLSON, D. R. (1978) "Three cognitive functions of symbols." Presented at the Terman Memorial Conference, Stanford University, Stanford, CA.

——— (1977) "Oral and written language and the cognitive processes of children." Journal of Communication 27: 10-26.

——— and J. S. BRUNER (1974) "Learning through experience and learning through media," in D. R. Olson (ed.) Media and Symbols, the Forms of Expression, Communication and Education. Chicago: University of Chicago Press.

OLWEUS, D. (1977) "A critical analysis of the 'modern' interactionist position," in D. Magnusson and N. S. Endler (eds.) Personality at the Crossroads. Hillsdale, NJ: Erlbaum.

PACKARD, V. (1957) The Hidden Persuaders. New York: McKay.

PAIVIO, A. (1978) "Dual coding: theoretical issues and empirical evidence," in J. M. Scandura and C. J. Brainerd (eds.) Structural/Process Models of Complex Human Behavior. Leiden, The Netherlands: Nordhoff.

PALAZZOLI, M. S., G. CHECHIN, G. PRATA, and L. BOSCOLO (1978) Paradox and Counterparadox. New York: Aronson.

PALMER, A. B. (1970) "Some variables contributing to the onset of cigarette smoking among junior high school students." Social Science Medicine 4: 359-366.

PERKINS, D. and B. LEONDAR [eds.] (1977) The Arts and Cognition. Baltimore: Johns Hopkins University Press.

PERLOFF, R. M. and T. C. BROCK (1980) "And thinking makes it so: cognitive responses to persuasion," in M. E. Roloff and G. R. Miller (eds.) Persuasion: New Directions in Theory and Research. Beverly Hills: Sage.

PETERSON, D. R. (1979) "Assessing interpersonal relationships in natural settings." New Directions 2: 33-54.

PETTY, R. E. (1977) "A cognitive response analysis of the temporal persistence of attitude changes induced by persuasive communications." Ph.D. dissertation, Ohio State University. (unpublished)

——— and J. T. CACIOPPO (1977) "Forewarning, cognitive responding, and resistance to persuasion." Journal of Personality and Social Psychology 35: 645-655.

PICHERT, J. W. and R. C. ANDERSON (1977) "Taking different perspectives on a story." Journal of Educational Psychology 69: 309-315.

PIPPERT, R. (1969) A Study of Creativity and Faith. Manitoba Department of Youth and Education Monograph, No. 4.

PITTMAN, T. S. and M. L. PITTMAN (1980) "Deprivation of control and the attribution process." Journal of Personality and Social Psychology 39: 377-389.

PRASAD, V. K., T. R. RAO and A. A. SHEIKH (1978) "Mothers vs. commercials." Journal of Communication, 28: 91-96.

PRESSLEY, M. (1977) "Imagery and children's learning: putting the picture in developmental perspective." Review of Educational Research 47: 585-622.

RAFALIDES, M. and W. K. HOY (1971) "Student sense of alienation and pupil control orientation of high schools." High School Journal 55: 102.

RAPPAPORT, M. M. and M. RAPPAPORT (1975) "The other half of the expectancy equation: Pygmalion." Journal of Educational Psychology 67: 531-536.

RAUSH, H. L. (1979) "Epistemology, metaphysics, and person-situation methodology: conclusions." New Directions 2: 93-106.

RIST, C. (1970) "Student social class and teacher expectations: the self-fulfilling prophecy in ghetto education." Harvard Educational Review 40: 411-451.

ROBERTS, D. (1979) Testimony before the Federal Trade Commissions Rulemaking on Children and TV Advertising. San Francisco.

––– and C. M. BACHEN (forthcoming) "Mass communication effects." Annual Review of Psychology, 32.

ROBERTS, D. and N. MACCOBY (1973) "Information processing and persuasion: counterarguing behavior," in P. Clarke (ed.) New Models for Communication Research. Beverly Hills: Sage.

ROGERS, E. M. and R. AGARWALA-ROGERS (1976) Communication in Organizations. New York: Free Press.

ROGERS, T. B., N. A. KUIPER, and W. S. KIRKER (1977) "Self-reference and the encoding of personal information." Journal of Personality and Social Psychology 35: 677-688.

ROKEACH, M. (1975) "Long-term value change initiated by computer feedback." Journal of Personality and Social Psychology 32: 467-476.

ROLOFF, M. E. (1976) "Communication strategies, relationships, and relational change," in G. R. Miller (ed.) Perspectives on Interpersonal Communication. Beverly Hills: Sage.

––– and G. R. MILLER (1980) Persuasion: New Directions in Theory and Research. Beverly Hills: Sage.

ROSCH, E. and C. B. MERVIS (1975) "Family resemblances: studies in the internal structure of categories." Cognitive Psychology 7: 573-605.

ROSENBLATT, P. C. and M. R. CUNNINGHAM (1976) "Television watching and family tensions." Journal of Marriage and the Family 38: 105-111.

ROSENHAN, D. L. (1973) "On being sane in insane places." Science 179: 250-258.

ROSENTHAL, R. (1973) "The pygmalion effect lives." Psychology Today 56-63.

––– and D. B. RUBIN (1978) "Interpersonal expectancy effects: the first 345 studies." Behavioral and Brain Sciences 3: 377-415.

ROSS, L. (1977) "The intuitive psychologist and his shortcomings: distortions in the attribution process," in L. Berkowitz (ed.) Advances in Experimental Social Psychology, Vol. 10. New York: Academic Press.

––– T. M. AMABILE, and J. L. STEINMETZ (1977) "Social roles, social control, and biases in social perception processes." Journal of Personality and Social Psychology 35: 485-494.

ROSS, L., M. R. LEPPER, and M. HUBBARD (1975) "Perseverance in self-perception and social perception: biased attributional processes in the debriefing paradigm." Journal of Personality and Social Psychology 32: 880-892.

ROSS, L., M. R. LEPPER, F. STRACK, and J. L. STEINMETZ (1976) "The effects of real and hypothetical explanation upon future expectations." Stanford University. (unpublished)

ROTHBART, M. K. and E. E. MACCOBY (1966) "Parents' differential reactions to sons and daughters." Journal of Personality and Social Psychology 4: 237-243.

ROUPAS, T. G. (1977) "Information and pictorial representation," in D. Perkins and B. Leondar (eds.) The Arts and Cognition. Baltimore: Johns Hopkins University Press.

RUBOVITZ, P. C. and M. L. MAEHR (1973) "Pygmalion black and white." Journal of Personality and Social Psychology 25: 210-218.

――― (1971) "Pygmalion analyzed: toward an explanation of the Rosenthal-Jacobson findings." Journal of Personality and Social Psychology 19: 197-203.

SAEGERT, S., W. SWAP, and R. B. ZAJONC (1972) "Exposure, context, and interpersonal attraction." Journal of Personality and Social Psychology 25: 234-242.

SAFER, M. A. (1980) "Attributing evil to the subject, not to the situation: student reaction to Milgram's film on obedience." Personality and Social Psychology Bulletin 6: 205-209.

SALANCIK, G. R. (1975) "Notes on loose coupling: linking intentions to actions." University of Illinois, Urbana, Champaign. (unpublished)

SALOMON, G. (1979) Interaction of Media, Cognition and Learning. San Francisco: Jossey-Bass.

――― (1977) "Effects of encouraging Israeli mothers to coobserve 'Sesame Street' with their five-year-olds." Child Development 48: 1146-1151.

――― (1976) "Cognitive skill learning across cultures." Journal of Communication 26: 138-145.

――― (1974) "Internalization of filmic schematic operations in interaction with learner's aptitudes." Journal of Educational Psychology 66: 499-511.

――― (1971) "Heuristic models for the generation of aptitude-treatment interaction hypotheses." Review of Educational Research 42: 327-343.

――― (1968) "Cross-cultural differences in map reading." Presented at the Annual Meeting of the American Educational Research Association, Chicago.

――― and A. A. COHEN (1977) "Television formats, mastery of mental skills, and the acquisition of knowledge." Journal of Educational Psychology 69: 612-619.

SALOMON, G. and F. G. McDONALD (1970) "Pretest and posttest reactions to self-viewing one's teaching performance on videotape." Journal of Educational Psychology 61: 280-286.

SALOMON, G. and J. SIEBER (1970) "Relevant subjective response uncertainty as a function of stimulus-task interaction." American Educational Research Journal 7: 337-349.

SALOMON, G., D. KING, and S. YUEN (1980) School of Governance and its Sociological Correlates: Summary of Secondary Analysis. Research report, Institute for

Research on Educational Finance and Governance, Stanford, CA: Stanford University.

SAMUELS, S. J. (1970) "Effects of pictures in learning to read, comprehension and attitudes." Review of Educational Research 40: 397-407.

SARASON, S. B. (1971) The Culture of the School and the Problem of Change. Boston: Allyn and Bacon.

SARNACKI, R. E. (1979) "An examination of test-wiseness in the cognitive test domain." Review of Educational Research 49: 252-279.

SCHLECHTY, P. C. (1976) Teaching and Social Behavior. Boston: Allyn & Bacon.

SCHMUCK, R. A. (1978) "Applications of social psychology to classroom life," in D. Bar-Tal, and L. Saxe (eds.) Social Psychology of Education. Washington, DC: Hemisphere.

——— (1971) "Influence of the peer group," in G. Lesser (ed.) Psychology and Educational Practice. Glenview, IL: Scott, Foresman.

——— and E. VAN EGMOND (1965) "Sex differences in the relationship of interpersonal perceptions to academic performance." Psychology in the School 2: 32-40.

SCHNEIDER, W. and R. U. SHIFFRIN (1977) "Controlled and automatic human information processing: I. Detection, search, and attention." Psychological Review 84: 1-68.

SCRIBNER, S. and M. COLE (1978) "Literacy without schooling: testing for intellectual effects." Harvard Educational Review 48: 448-461.

SEAVER, W. B. (1973) "Effects of naturally induced teacher expectancies." Journal of Personality and Social Psychology 28: 333-342.

SHANNON, C. and W. WEAVER (1949) The Mathematical Theory of Communication. Urbana: University of Illinois Press.

SHEPARD, R. N. (1978) "The mental image." American Psychologist 33: 125-137.

SHOHAM-SALOMON, V. (1981) "The ways in which differences between the medical and psycho-social paradigms are reflected in therapists' perceptions of labeled schizophrenics." Ph.D. dissertation, Tel Aviv University, Israel.

SIEBER, J. E., and J. T. LANZETTA (1964) "Conflict and conceptual structure as determinants of decision-making behavior." Journal of Personality 32: 622-642.

SILBERMAN, C. H. (1970) Crisis in the Classroom. New York: Random House.

SINCLAIR DE ZWART, H. (1967) Acquisition du language et development de la pensee: Sous-systemes linguistiques et operation concretes. Paris: Dunod.

SINGER, J. L. (1980) "The powers and limitations of television," in P. H. Tennenbaum (ed.) The Entertainment Functions of Television. Hillsdale, NJ: Erlbaum.

SLAMECKA, M. J. and P. GRAF (1978) "The generation effect: delineation of a phenomenon." Journal of Experimental Psychology: Human Learning and Memory 4: 592-604.

SNOW, R. E. (1977) "Research on aptitudes: a progress report," in L. Shulman (ed.) Review of Research in Education, Vol. 4. Hasca, IL: Peacock.

——— and G. SALOMON (1968) "Aptitudes and instructional media." AV Communication Review 16: 341-358.

SNYDER, M. (forthcoming) "Seek, as ye shall find: testing hypotheses about other people," in T. Higgins, C. P. Herman, and M. P. Zanna (eds.) Social Cognition:

The Ontario Symposium on Personality and Social Psychology. Hillsdale, NJ: Erlbaum.

SOMMER, R. (1965) "Further studies of small group ecology." Sociometry 28: 337-348.

——— (1959) "Studies in personal space." Sociometry 22: 247-260.

SOTLAND, E. and L. K. CANON (1972) Social Psychology: A Cognitive Approach. Philadelphia: W. B. Saunders.

STEWART, L., and N. LIVSON (1966) "Smoking and rebelliousness: a longitudinal study." Journal of Consulting Clinical Psychology 30: 225-229.

STROLLER, F. M. (1967) "Group psychotherapy on television: an innovation with hospitalized patients." American Psychologist 23: 158-163.

STULAC, J. (1975) "The self-fulfilling prophecy: modifying the effects of an unidimensional perception of academic competence in task-oriented groups." Ph.D. dissertation, Stanford University.

SURLIN, S. H. and E. D. TATE (1976) " 'All in the Family': is Archie funny?" Journal of Communication 26: 61-68.

TAYLOR, S. E. and S. T. FISKE (1975) "Point of view and perceptions of causality." Journal of Personality and Social Psychology 32: 439-445.

TAYLOR, S. E., J. CROCKER, S. T. FISKE, M. SPRINZEN, and J. D. WINDLER (1979) "The generalizability of salience effects." Journal of Personality and Social Psychology 37: 357-368.

TENNANTS, F. S., S. C. WEAVER, and C. E. LEWIS (1973) "Outcomes of drug education." Pediatrics 52: 246-253.

THOMAS, J. W. (1980) "Agency and achievement: Self-management and self-regard." Review of Educational Research 50: 213-240.

TICHENOR, P. J., G. A. DONAHUE, C. N. OLIEN (1970) "Mass media and differential growth in knowledge." Public Opinion Quarterly 34: 158-170.

TJOSVOLD, D. (1978) "Alternative organizations for schools and classrooms," in D. Bar-Tal, and L. Saxe (eds.) Social Psychology of Education, Theory and Research. New York: Halsted Press.

——— and T. KASTELIC (1976) "Effects of student motivation and the principal's values on teacher directiveness." Journal of Education 68: 768-774.

TUCKER, D. H. and P. M. ROWE (1979) "Relationship between expectancy, causal attributions, and final hiring decisions in the employment interview." Journal of Applied Psychology 64: 27-34.

TVERSKY, A. (1977) "Features of similarity." Psychological Review 84: 327-352.

TYACK, D. B. (1974) The One Best System. Cambridge, MA: Harvard University Press.

VIDMAR, N. and M. ROKEACH (1974) "Archie Bunker's bigotry: a study in selective perception and exposure." Journal of Communication 24: 36-48.

VON BERTALANFFY, L. (1965) "On the definition of the symbol," in J. R. Royce (ed.) Psychology and the Symbol. New York: Random House.

WACKMAN, D., E. WARTELLA, and S. WARD (1979) "Children information processing of television advertising." University of Minnesota. (unpublished)

WALSTER, E. and L. FESTINGER (1962) "The effectiveness of 'overhead' persuasive communications." Journal of Abnormal and Social Psychology 65: 395-402.

WALTERS, J. K. and V. A. STONE (1971) "Television and family communication." Journal of Broadcasting 15: 409-414.

WALZ, G. R. and J. A. JOHNSTON (1963) "Counselors look at themselves on videotape." Journal of Counseling Psychology 10: 232-236.

WARD, S. and D. B. WACKMAN (1973) "Children's information processing of television advertising," in P. Clarke (ed.) Annual Review of Communication Research, Vol. 2. Beverly Hills: Sage.

WATZLAWICK, P. (1978) The Language of Change. New York: Basic Books.

——— (1977) How Real is Real? New York: Vintage Books.

——— J. H. BEAVIN, and D. D. JACKSON (1967) Pragmatic of Human Communication. New York: Norton.

WATZLAWICK, P., J. WEAKLAND, and R. FISCH (1974) Change: Principles of Problem Formulation and Problem Resolution. New York: Norton.

WEBB, N. M. (1980) "A process outcome analysis of learning in group and individual settings." Educational Psychology 15: 69-83.

WEICK, E. W. (1976) "Educational organizations as loosely coupled systems." Administrative Science Quarterly 21: 1-19.

WEICK, K. E. (1980) "Loosely coupled systems: relaxed meanings and thick interpretations." Presented at the Annual Meeting of the AERA, Boston.

——— (1979) The Social Psychology of Organizing. Reading, MA: Addison-Wesley.

WEINER, B. (1979) "A theory of motivation for some classroom experiences." Journal of Educational Psychology 71: 3-25.

WENDNER, P. H. (1968) "Vicious and virtuous circles: the role of deviation-amplifying feedback in the origin and perpetuation of behavior." Psychiatry 31: 309-324.

WICKER, A. W. (1979) "Ecological psychology: some recent and prospective developments." American Psychologist 34: 755-765.

WILHOIT, G. C. and H. DE BOCK (1976) " 'All in the Family' in Holland." Journal of Communication 26: 75-84.

WILLIAMS, F., J. L. WHITEHEAD, and L. MILLER (1972) "Relations between language attitudes and teacher expectancy." American Educational Research Journal 9: 263-277.

WILLIS, B. J. (1970) "The influence of teacher expectation on teachers' classroom interaction with selected children." (Ph.D. dissertation, George Peabody College, 1969). Dissertation Abstracts International 30: 5072A (University Microfilms 70-07647).

WILLOWER, D. J. (1975) "Some comments on inquiries on school and pupil control." Teachers College Record 77: 219-230.

WILSON, G. T. (1980) "Toward specifying the 'nonspecific' factors in behavior therapy," in M. J. Mahoney (ed.) Psychotherapy Processes. New York: Plenum.

WINN, M. (1977) The Plug-In Drug. New York: Viking Press.

WINNER, E., A. K. ROSENSTIEL, and H. GARDNER (1976) "The development of metaphoric understanding." Developmental Psychology 12: 289-297.

WORTMAN, C. B., and J. W. BREHM (1975) "Responses to uncontrollable outcomes: an integration of reactance theory and the learned helplessness model," in L. Berkowitz (ed.) Advances in Experimental Social Psychology (Vol. 8). New York: Academic Press.

WRIGHT, J. C. and A. HUSTON-STEIN (1979) "The influences of formal features in children's television on attention and social behavior." Presented at invited symposium: Television and Children: The Medium is Unique in its Form, Not its

Content. Biennial Meeting, Society for Research in Child Development, San Francisco.

WRIGHT, J. C. and A. G. VLIESTRA (1975) "The development of selective attention: from perceptual exploration to logical search," in H. W. Reese (ed.) Advances in Child Development and Behavior, Vol. 10. New York: Academic Press.

WRIGHT, J. C., B. A. WATKINS, and A. HUSTON-STEIN (forthcoming) "Active vs. passive television viewing: a model of the development of television information processing by children." Monographs of the World Federation of Mental Health.

ZAJONC, R. B. (1980) "Feeling and thinking: preferences need no inferences." American Psychologist 35: 151-175.

ZIGLER, E. and E. C. BUTTERFIELD (1968) "Motivational aspects of changes in IQ test performance of culturally deprived nursery school children." Child Development 39: 1-14.

ZILLMANN, D. (1980) "The anatomy of suspense," in P. H. Tennenbaum (ed.) The Entertainment Functions of Television. Hillsdale, NJ: Erlbaum.

Author Index

Adar, L., 114-115, 212
Agarwala-Rogers, R., 56
Ajzen, I., 42
Allen, A., 104
Alschuler, A., 164
Amabile, T. M., 103
Amir, Y., 119
Anderson, D. R., 80
Anderson, R. C., 60, 63, 64, 71, 78, 96, 97, 129, 130
Aronson, E., 63
Astin, A. W., 117, 180
Atkin, C. K., 82, 91
Ausubel, D. P., 97, 98

Babad, E. Y., 105-106, 109, 115
Bachen, C. M., 86
Baddley, A. D., 130
Ball, S., 141
Ball-Rokeach, S., 38
Bandura, A., 16, 24, 25, 28, 35, 108, 135, 144, 108, 135, 136, 142, 144, 190, 213
Bar-Tal, D., 104, 115, 185, 228
Barker, R. G., 170
Barlund, D. C., 49
Barnes, R. D., 103, 111
Barnett, M., 186
Bartlett, F. C., 60
Bates, J. A., 101
Baumeister, R. F., 114, 193, 212
Beavin, J. H., 16, 46, 114, 150, 158
Bem, D. J., 104, 184-185
Benevento, A., 103-104, 108, 115, 212

Berlo, D. K., 16, 49
Berlyne, D. E., 631
Biddle, B. J., 180
Blank, A., 132-133
Blumler, J. G., 127
Bogatz, G. A., 141
Bolen, D., 108, 193, 227
Borland, B. L., 30 ·
Bowers, K. S., 15, 16, 23, 27, 32, 55, 56, 61, 119
Braucht, G. N., 235
Braun, C., 27, 109
Brehm, J. W., 44, 45, 65, 164, 224, 226
Brickman, P., 108, 193, 227
Brigham, J. C., 79, 122
Brittain, W. L., 101
Brock, T. C., 56
Bronfenbrenner, U., 15, 22, 28, 29
Brophy, J. E., 109, 152
Brown, A. L., 235
Brown, D., 77
Bruner, J. S., 82, 200
Bryant, J., 77
Butkowsky, I. S., 147, 166
Butterfield, E. C., 190

Cacioppo, J. T., 64, 65
Calder, B. J., 55
Calfee, R., 83
Campbell, D. E., 19
Campione, J. C., 235
Canon, L. K., 60
Cantor, N., 103
Cantril, H., 87

Subject Index

Advanced organizers, 97-99; transfer of learning and, 98

AIME (amount of invested mental effort). See mental effort

All in the Family, 78-79, 212

Aptitude treatment interaction (ATI), 16, 19-22; changes over time, 27, 183; school structure and, 20-22; second order change as, 68

Assimilation and accommodation, 61f; causes for weak schemata accommodation, 63-67; consensual schemata of, 119; media in, 81f; school learning and, 96f

Attribution, basic error of, 71, 98-99, 103, 173, 176, 186, 195; of causes as related to mental effort investment, 145; of communicational intent, 41-42; as function of schemata, 69f; of meaning, 47, 158; nature of, 41; of the nature of communication, 38f; of symbolic meaning, 47-48. See also attribution of communicational intent

Attribution of communicational intent, to advertisements, 86; as amplifier of loops, 220, 224-227; and behavior outcomes, 43; in communication, 10, 40f; and the communication of expectations, 106-107; to changes of dispositions, 188-189, 192-193; to convey or inform, 44-45, 66, 85-86, 107-108, 117, 120, 148, 224-226; in educational systems, 117-119; to

entertain us, 66, 85-86; and freedom, 42; to interactional changes, 194f; kinds of, 44-46, 52; nature of, 41-42; to persuade, change or control, 43-45, 66, 85-86, 107-108, 117, 120, 148, 194, 223-226, 236, 238-239; and reactance, 44, 46, 148, 224; reverse direction of feedback, 224; and self-serving motives, 43, 107, 225-226; and self-sustaining prophecies, 118, 193

Bias, in attributing causes, 187; in epistemic processes, 70, 72, 121; in interpretation and inference, 9, 58, 121, 214-215, 228; in responses, 58, 71-72, 121; due to "trivial but highly salient" information, 160

Bureaucratic harassment, 118

Change, "change of change" 229; and the cultivation of alternatives, 102; failure in anti-smoking campaigns, 30-31; failure in misbehavior management, 30, 189f, 222; first and second order, 67-68, 74, 212, 222, 229-231, 238; and learning, 102; theory of, 221-223

Circularity, as assimilation, 62; breaking out of, 229, 231-238; communication, part of, 213; in discipline, 164-165; in educational systems, 112, 227; and escalating loops, 218f,

ABOUT THE AUTHOR

GAVRIEL SALOMON is currently Professor in the School of Education and Department of Communication at the Hebrew University in Jerusalem. He has published many journal articles in the United States, Holland, and Israel, and is the author of *Interaction of Media Cognition and Learning* (Jossey-Bass, 1979), which won the 1981 award of the Association for Educational Communication and Technology. Dr. Salomon was a field psychologist for the Israeli Army, Marsh Professor at the University of Michigan, Adjunct Professor at the University of Southern California, and a Senior Research Associate at Stanford University. His current research interests include "Don't confuse me with facts" and children and television.